CHILDREN
OF THE
RISING

CHILDREN OF THE RISING

The untold story of the young lives
lost during Easter 1916

JOE DUFFY

HACHETTE
BOOKS
IRELAND

First published in 2015 by Hachette Books Ireland

A CIP catalogue record for this title is available from the British Library.

ISBN 978 1 47361 705 6

Interior design and typeset by redrattledesign.com
Printed and bound in Germany by Mohn media

Front cover and spine image © Central Press/Getty Images; Back cover © RTÉ Stills Library;
Front flap reproduced from Spitalfields Nippers by Horace Warner;
Back flap courtesy *Evening Herald*/National Library of Ireland.

Hachette Books Ireland's policy is to use papers that are natural, renewable and recyclable
and made from wood grown in sustainable forests. The logging and manufacturing processes
are expected to conform to the environmental regulations of the country of origin.

Hachette Books Ireland
8 Castlecourt Centre
Castleknock
Dublin 15, Ireland

A division of Hachette UK Ltd
Carmelite House, Victoria Embankment,
London EC4Y 0DZ

www.hachette.ie

In memory of Peter Mooney

1949–2015

Youth worker, educator, colleague, friend

The Forty Children Aged Sixteen and Under Who Died in the Easter Rising

Bridget Allen (16), 27 Arran Quay

Christopher Andrews (14),
8 Stephens Place, Mount Street

Mary Anne Brunswick (15),
57 Lower Wellington Street

Christina Caffrey (2),
27b Corporation Buildings

Christopher Cathcart (10),
28 Charlemont Street

Charles Darcy (15), Murphy's
Cottages, Gloucester Street

Moses Doyle (9), 7 Whitefriar Street

Patrick Fetherston (12), 1 Long
Lane, Dorset Street

Sean Francis Foster (2),
18 Manor Place, Stoneybatter

James Fox (16), 3 Altinure
Terrace, Cabra Park

William Fox (13), 6 Holy Cross
Cottages, Clonliffe Road

Neville Fryday (16), Dundrum,
County Tipperary

James Gibney (5), 16 Henrietta Place

Sean Healy (14), 188 Phibsborough Road

Christopher Hickey (16),
168 North King Street

Patrick Ivers (14), 15 Cumberland
Street North

Charles Kavanagh (15), 4 North King Street

James Kelly (15), 205 Phibsborough Road

Mary Kelly (12), 128 Townsend Street

Patrick Kelly (12), 24 Buckingham Buildings

John Kirwan (15), 3 Lower Erne Place

Eugene Lynch (8), 4 Vincent Street, Inchicore

Bridget McKane (15), 10 Henry Place

John Henery McNamara (12), 45 York Street

William Mullen (9), 8 Moore Place

Joseph Murray (14), 2 St Augustine Street

William O'Neill (16), 93 Church Street

'Male' O'Toole (14), Adelaide Hospital

Mary Redmond (16), 4 St Mary's Abbey

Patrick Ryan (13), 2 Sitric Place

George Percy Sainsbury (9),
54 South Circular Road

Walter Scott (8), 16 Irvine Crescent, East Wall

Bridget Stewart (11), 3 Pembroke Cottages

William Lionel Sweny, (14), 1 Lincoln Place

Margaret 'Madge' Veale (13),
103 Haddington Road

Philip Walsh (11), 10 Hackett's Court

Eleanor Warbrook (15), 7 Fumbally Lane

Christopher Whelan (15),
30 North Great George's Street

Boy unidentified

Infant unidentified

'In no city in these islands with which I am acquainted have the children such freedom, I might say such possession, of the streets as Dublin.'
Evidence of John Cooke, Honorary Treasurer,
National Society for the Prevention of Cruelty to Children,
to the Dublin Housing Inquiry, 1913

'It was the beginning of a new world and a different age.
My childhood of happy illusion was over.'
Wilmot Irwin, *The Years of Revolution*, 1916–24

The Easter egg painted by Joe Duffy for the Jack and Jill Children's Foundation, containing the names of children who died during the 1916 Rising.

Contents

The 1916 Rising: Day by Day   xi

Prologue   1

1. As I Strolled Out One Easter Morning   15

2. A Tale of Two Cities   43

3. 'The Sole Gorge of Their Lives'   67

4. A World at War   91

5. 'We Suffer in Their Coming and Their Going'   115

6. 'Oh, Please Don't Kill Father'   133

7. Bloody Friday   155

8. The Child Workers   181

9. 'The Reply Is in the Negative'   201

Epilogue   231

Endnotes   239

Select Bibliography   246

Index   251

Acknowledgements   260

Permissions Acknowledgements 264

General Post Office, 17 May 1916. The flag staff on the upper left corner was the one on which the tricolour was flown during the Rising, while the flag of the Provisional Government was flown from the main flag staff.

The 1916 Rising: Day by Day

A guide to events each day including a list of all deaths

Monday, 24 April

NUMBERS SHOT AND FATALLY WOUNDED:

–CHILDREN: 9 (CHRISTOPHER CATHCART, CHARLES DARCY, MOSES DOYLE, PATRICK FETHERSTON, SEAN FRANCIS FOSTER, NEVILLE FRYDAY [DIED THE FOLLOWING SUNDAY], JOHN KIRWAN, 'MALE' O'TOOLE, ELEANOR WARBROOK)

–CIVILIANS: 6

–REBELS: 11

–MILITARY: 28

–POLICE: 3

A warm, sunny bank holiday – it has rained for thirteen of the previous fourteen days. There's a sense of curiosity and unease, even giddiness, around Sackville Street (O'Connell Street) – rumours of rebellion have been rife but are quelled somewhat by the countermanding order by Eoin MacNeill. But Dubliners still think there's a chance of an uprising. There's a whiff of uncertainty and excitement in the city-centre air.

Monday, 24 April

- Attack on the Magazine Fort in the Phoenix Park, George Playfair (twenty-three) is killed.
- Barricades are set up in Church Street. British lancers coming from North Wall to Islandbridge Barracks are engaged by Rebels.
- Attack on the Four Courts under the command of Ned Daly.
- Confusion reigns. Rebels turn out in reduced numbers (1,400). Families enjoy glorious sunshine – as they gather to watch the spectacle at the GPO.
- First shots of the Rising are fired at Dublin Castle at noon – Dublin Metropolitan Police (DMP) policeman James O'Brien is shot dead. The castle gates are locked.
- At Beggars Bush, members of the auxiliary army, Georgius Rex, are attacked and some are killed as they return from a drill in the Dublin Mountains.
- A band of Volunteers marches from Liberty Hall, up Abbey Street, past Wynn's Hotel and takes a sharp right into Sackville Street to bemused looks and some jeering from onlookers. (Such a march in itself was not unusual but many carried assorted weapons, including ropes and sledgehammers – this looked serious.)
- The GPO is charged. 'A woman from the slums – a shawlie, so called because of the black shawl wrapped tightly around her – cried out "Glory be to God would you look at them smashing all the lovely windows."'[1]
- The passengers on the open upper decks of the trams look down in bemusement from the terminus at Nelson's Pillar. Between 1 p.m. and 2 p.m. shots are fired from the GPO on British troops coming from Parnell Square onto Sackville Street.
- A number of Rebels are despatched from the GPO to set up barricades at Abbey Street. Reels of newsprint are commandeered from *The Irish Times* and the *Freeman's Journal*, a tram is overturned, a bicycle shop is broken into for material

for the makeshift barricade – this leads to the first public looting as a young lad makes off with one of the pushbikes that has been commandeered by the Rebels. Other civilians take the lead and looting begins in earnest.

• Rebels are sent out on a commandeering mission to procure food, provisions, blankets and mattresses for the siege – they effectively break in to shops and steal the necessary items.

• The DMP is withdrawn following the shooting dead of three of their number.

• By 3 p.m., twenty-seven looters have been arrested.

• Noblett's and Lemons sweet shops are among the first shops to be looted. The cry goes out: 'They're raiding Nobletts.' The famous shop is quickly stripped of its stock, the crowd at one stage nearly developing into a dangerous stampede.

• Next to be looted are Dunns hat shop, Frewen and Ryans hosiery and the Cable Shoe Company.

• The crowd has been growing all afternoon in Sackville Street. A group of priests, in the absence of the DMP, link arms across the street trying to calm people – but quickly give up!

• Lancers arrive at the top of Sackville Street. Moving down towards Nelson's Pillar, they are fired on from the GPO.[2] A number of lancers and their horses are shot and killed.

• The Rebels, watching from the GPO, are dumbstruck by the mayhem caused by the looting – is this what they were willing to sacrifice their lives for?

• 3.30 p.m. Troops coming from Bull Island training camp to the city centre are fired on at Annesley Bridge and the North Strand.

• The British attack the South Dublin Union but Rebels, led by Éamonn Ceannt, hold out in the nurses' home.

• Late afternoon, looting continues around Sackville Street – British troops charge down the thoroughfare. At St Stephen's

Monday, 24 April/Tuesday, 25 April

Green the Irish Citizen Army begin digging trenches as the military take the 'commanding heights' of the Shelbourne Hotel. There's confusion in Portobello – Rebels retreat from Davy's public house at Portobello Bridge.

- Having met with fierce local resistance from the residents of Fumbally Lane, the Rebels abandon the strategically high buildings there.
- 9.30 p.m. The first fire has started in Sackville Street in the looted Cable Shoe Company.
- Looting continues until after midnight.
- A light drizzle starts.
- There's rainfall at night.

Tuesday, 25 April

Numbers shot and fatally wounded:
- Children: 5 (Christina Caffrey, James Fox, William Fox, James Kelly, Sean Healy)
- Civilians: 16
- Rebels: 8
- Military: 7
- Police: 0

Another day of confusion, if less so than Monday. Barricades are set up by the Rebels across the city centre – in North Earl Street, Talbot Street and Townsend Street – to add to the makeshift barriers in Church Street and Mount Street.

- The GPO Rebel garrison is strengthened by the arrival of other Volunteers, as they wait in vain for word from other parts of the country that the Rising has spread.
- *The Irish Times* is the only newspaper to be published – but

the Rebels are disappointed that there is very little mention of the insurrection.

- Rebel leaders James Connolly and Pádraig Pearse are now worried about what to do with the looters.
- 'A sultry, lowering day and dusk skies fat with rain.'[3]
- Machine-gun fire from the Shelbourne Hotel forces the Irish Citizen Army garrison to retreat from St Stephen's Green to the College of Surgeons. British reinforcements with artillery arrive – troops from The Curragh and Belfast via Kingsbridge (Heuston) and Amiens Street stations respectively. British strategy is to throw a cordon around the Rebel positions and then strike.
- Up to 7,000 British troops are now in the centre of Dublin.
- Martial law is proclaimed in the city and county.
- The Rebels broadcast in Morse code the declaration of an Irish Republic from the Wireless School of Telegraphy in Sackville Street: 'Irish republic declared in Dublin today. Irish troops have captured the city and are in full possession. Enemy cannot move in the city. The whole country rising.'
- Fighting around Annesley Bridge, but the Rebels are beaten back.
- Pearse issues a 'Manifesto to the Citizens of Dublin' via handbills that are printed and distributed: 'The country is rising in answer to Dublin's call and the final achievement of Ireland's freedom is now, with God's help, only a matter of days.'
- In the meantime, more spectators, including some from the outer suburbs, arrive in the city centre as word of the rebellion spreads.
- Looting restarts just after noon – pubs are now among the businesses targeted, which leads to an increased frenzy among many of the looters.
- Lawrence's toy and photography shop is targeted – the children let off looted fireworks in Sackville Street.

• Pearse issues a message to the people of Dublin urging them to assist the rebellion. He adds: 'Such looting as has already occurred has been done by hangers-on of the British Army. Ireland must keep her new honour unsmirched.'[4]

• British sniping takes place from the roof and windows of Trinity College towards the GPO.

• Battle commences at Amiens Street railway station as Rebels attempt to halt the advance of arriving British reinforcements.

• 5 p.m. 'H and N have just come in having seen Dr Wheeler (now Major Wheeler), surgeon to the forces in Ireland. He told them that so far we have had about 500 casualties, two thirds of them civilians, shot in the street.'[5]

• In the GPO, the garrison awaits the British attack. Would they attack under cover of darkness, as the rebellion entered its third day?

• Two British infantry brigades land at Kingstown (Dún Laoghaire).

Evening rainfall stops at 11 p.m.

Wednesday, 26 April

NUMBERS SHOT AND FATALLY WOUNDED:
 –CHILDREN: 4 (PATRICK RYAN, LIONEL SWENY, MADGE VEALE [DIED THE FOLLOWING SUNDAY], PHILIP WALSH)
 –CIVILIANS: 26
 –REBELS: 13
 –MILITARY: 30
 –POLICE: 2

Wednesday, 26 April

A clash between the Dublin Fusiliers and insurgents leads to the erection of barricades on the north side of the city – access to Glasnevin Cemetery from the North Circular Road is blocked, as are Cross Guns Bridge, Whitworth Road and Finglas Road.

• 8 a.m. British gunboat the *Helga* targets Liberty Hall, reducing the empty building to a shell. This signals the beginning of a massive intensification of the British attack on the Rebels.

• Fires take hold and spread across the city centre. Fighting intensifies.

• The Irish Citizen Army flag is hoisted over Clerys and the Imperial Hotel. The triumphant symbolism of this – the Irish Citizen Army was formed after the 1913 Lockout and the Imperial Hotel is owned by employers' leader William Martin Murphy – cannot be underestimated.

• There is persistent machine-gun fire on the GPO, while heavy gun shelling of the building from the D'Olier Street/ College Street junction intensifies just after 2 p.m.

• Rebels break into the Metropole Hotel beside the GPO.

• The Four Courts garrison holds out under heavy attack from Parkgate Street.

• Troops marching from Kingstown towards the city centre are halted at Mount Street Bridge. The bloodiest engagement of the Rising rages – two British battalions are held down by thirteen Rebels. The Battle of Mount Street Bridge results in 234 British casualties, half their total for Easter week. At the end of the fierce fighting, the military gain control.

• Sean Heuston's post in the Mendicity Institute is retaken by the British. Clanwilliam House is burned down.

• Martial law is proclaimed throughout Ireland. Food is becoming scare, many are looking for bread.

• While shops, public buildings and banks are closed, public houses are allowed to open from 2 p.m. until 5 p.m.!

- A gun battle around Grafton Street ends in the afternoon – and then looters descend on Knowles fruit shop.
- The military seize the Guinness brewery, while the Rebels occupy another brewery in the neighbourhood.
- *The Irish Times* is once again published.
- There's heavy and unrelenting artillery and gunfire from Sackville Street and College Green on the GPO. There is also fire from Trinity College – where there are 4,000 troops stationed – and the Tara Street fire station tower.
- Heavy fighting at the South Dublin Union.
- The Lord Lieutenant issues statement: 10,000 troops have arrived, Liberty Hall has been destroyed.

Thursday, 27 April

> NUMBERS SHOT AND FATALLY WOUNDED:
> –CHILDREN: 5 (BRIDGET ALLEN, CHRISTOPHER ANDREWS, CHARLES KAVANAGH, MARY REDMOND, GEORGE PERCY SAINSBURY)
> –CIVILIANS: 27
> –REBELS: 7
> –MILITARY: 15
> –POLICE: 0

'By Thursday something approaching a food famine was imminent.'[6]

- The British believe they have retaken control of the city.
- The stench of rotting dead horses on Sackville Street is now overwhelming. Dublin is awash with rumours, including that there is a submarine in the Liffey and animals are escaping from the zoo!

- A cordon has been thrown around the city – between the canals, west to Kingsbridge station and east to the Custom House – with north and south side Rebels separated.
- The main British objective is the retaking of the GPO. There's heavy fighting on North King Street. The shelling of Sackville Street intensifies – the Imperial Hotel/Clerys building collapses.
- James Connolly is wounded in the shoulder outside the GPO and is later hit by a ricochet in the ankle.
- There's an intense battle to retake the South Dublin Union.
- The city is in flames. There's fierce fighting in the Four Courts.
- There are no wages, no separation allowances are being paid, people are starving, there is nothing to buy, the shops are closed. The military commandeer shops and warehouses and open them. The St Vincent de Paul is used to distribute tickets for emergency food rations.
- The *Helga* gunboat continues shelling. Food is scarce, typhoid is threatened.
- The north Dublin suburbs have been cut off since the previous day, people in Phibsborough are kept behind a cordon and now food shortages are widespread.
- Shops are besieged and the flour mills at Cross Guns Bridge are targeted. Men and women of all classes are seen carrying away parcels of flour, potatoes, bread and everything in the way of foodstuff.
- 'During the first half of Easter week one might see bread carts and milk carts standing in the road with a crowd of hungry urchins and mothers all round them waving pennies and sixpences at the miserable drivers. I once saw no less than eight bread carts and three milk carts at the same time in one street barely 150 yards long. After the barricades had been put up however the

poor could no longer do this and excellent photographs were afforded of crowds of poor people behind barricades waving jugs and money at the soldiers who had commandeered the carts and were serving the sufferers across the excellent counter of sandbags and kitchen tables and sofas.'[7]

Friday, 28 April

NUMBERS SHOT AND FATALLY WOUNDED:
 −CHILDREN: 11 (MARY ANNE BRUNSWICK,
   PATRICK IVERS, PATRICK KELLY, EUGENE
   LYNCH, BRIDGET McKANE, JOHN HENERY
   McNAMARA, WILLIAM MULLEN, JOSEPH
   MURRAY, WALTER SCOTT [DIED ON 5 JULY],
   BRIDGET STEWART, CHRISTOPHER WHELAN)
 −CIVILIANS: 32
 −REBELS: 7
 −MILITARY: 8
 −POLICE: 8

The sun is shining, streets are lively. There is no bread, milk, news. Families are fleeing from fires.

• There are now over 20,000 British troops in Dublin (rumours put the figure at 60,000!). General Sir John Maxwell arrives in the city to take charge of the army.

• In Ashbourne, County Meath, Volunteers under the command of Thomas Ashe defeat a larger force of the Royal Irish Constabulary.

• 8 p.m. The Metropole Hotel and the GPO are evacuated as the Rebels retreat to Moore Street where they set up new headquarters.

• Maxwell issues his own proclamation: 'The most vigorous

measures will be taken by me to stop the loss of life and damage to property which certain misguided persons are causing in their armed resistance to the law. If necessary I shall not hesitate to destroy any buildings within any area occupied by the rebels and I warn all persons within the area specified below and now surrounded by HM troops forthwith to leave such area.'

• There's sniping in and around Camden Street.

• Sackville Street is smouldering, buildings are collapsing, there's the smell of clothes burning.

• Pádraig Pearse, James Connolly, Joseph Plunkett, Tom Clarke, Sean McDermott and, among others, Michael Collins and Seán Lemass make their way to a cottage on Henry Place off Moore Street.

• The North King Street massacre begins; fifteen civilians including Christopher Hickey (on Saturday morning) are killed by the military.

Saturday, 29 April

Numbers shot and fatally wounded:

   –Children: 2 (Christopher Hickey, William O'Neill)

   –Civilians: 43

   –Rebels: 12

   –Military: 21

   –Police: 0

Another warm, sunny morning. There is still no milk or bread available to the hungry people.

• Rebel leaders are concentrated around Moore Street, Henry Place and Moore Lane. Women – including Margaret McKane, whose daughter Bridget had been accidentally killed by the Rebels the night before – cook food for over 200 retreating Rebels.

• 12 noon: Pearse sees a publican, Robert Dillon, killed by British soldiers and his family shot down and decides on a ceasefire.

• 12.45 p.m. Nurse Elizabeth O'Farrell leaves 16 Moore Street and approaches the military with a message of surrender from the Rebels.

• 3.30 p.m. Pearse leaves 16 Moore Street and surrenders.

• Ned Daly, Rebel commander in the Four Courts, surrenders, and marches with his men to the surrender point at the Gresham Hotel on Sackville Street.

• By 7.30 p.m., calm is almost completely restored. The sound of a rifle shot is now only heard at long intervals.

Sunday, 30 April

NUMBERS SHOT AND FATALLY WOUNDED:

–CHILDREN: 1 (MARY KELLY)

–NO FIGURES AVAILABLE FOR OTHER CASUALTIES ON THIS DAY

Rebels at Boland's Mills, Jacob's, the South Dublin Union and Marrowbone Lane surrender.

• Prisoners are marched to Richmond Barracks having been held overnight in the grounds of the Rotunda Hospital.

• Neville Fryday and Madge Veale die today from their wounds.

Subsequent Events

- 2 May: James Gibney dies.
- Two dead children remain unidentified to this day. Their deaths were registered on 4 May.
- 3–12 May: Fifteen Rebel leaders are executed.
- 5 July: Walter Scott dies from wounds received on Friday, 28 April.

DAILY SKETCH

½D

FRIDAY, SEPTEMBER 5, 1913.

Telephones—Editorial and Publishing: 6676 Holborn.
Advertisements: 2972 Holborn.

LONDON'S BEST PICTURE PAPER.

LONDON: 46-47, Shoe-lane, E.C.
MANCHESTER: Withy-grove.

DUBLIN A CITY OF HOMELESS PEOPLE AND GRIEF-STRICKEN PARENTS.

Hanna Dignam and her "home."

Jr. Paul

A Capuchin friar prays with the bereaved and gives absolution.

Old Mary Dunne, now homeless.

Searching among the debris for imprisoned victims buried underneath tons of masonry.

Thomas Devlin with his wife and child, and Bessie Smith (inset), a cripple whom he saved.

There was nothing left of the house but the walls—and a few ornaments.

When the two tenement houses in Church-street, Dublin, collapsed scenes of anguish and of horror were witnessed. Many of the victims were crushed almost beyond recognition, and mothers were wild with grief when their little ones were dug out of the piles of stone and mortar in which they had been engulfed. Priests tried to console the bereaved, who lost both friends and homes, and comfort the dying. Even strong men joined with them when they offered up prayers for the repose of the souls of the humble victims.

Printed and Published by E. HULTON and CO., LIMITED, London and Manchester.—FRIDAY, SEPTEMBER 5, 1913.

Details of the collapse of two tenement houses on Church Street published in London's Daily Sketch *newspaper, 5 September 1913.*

Prologue

When my grandmother, Agnes Carroll, was aged ten and growing up in Dublin's inner city, two neighbouring tenement houses collapsed into Church Street behind Dublin's Four Courts, killing three adults and four children. Three years later, Church Street was the scene of the first death of a child in the Easter Rising, when two-year-old Sean Foster, who was being wheeled in his pram with his younger brother Ted, was shot in a gun battle between the Rebels and the British Army. It was the first of nine deaths that day of children aged sixteen and under as a result of the Rising, and of five that week in the locality. On that Easter Monday, as Agnes Carroll witnessed the death and mayhem outside her home when the Rebels took on the might of the British Army, one of her two older brothers lay dead near Arras in France.

Twenty-three-year-old Christopher 'Kit' Carroll had been killed in the trenches eight days previously; his body was never

THE DAILY MIRROR, Tuesday, May 2, 1916.

DUBLIN REBELS SENT OVER TO ENGLAND—OFFICIAL

The Daily Mirror

CERTIFIED CIRCULATION LARGER THAN THAT OF ANY OTHER DAILY PICTURE PAPER

No. 3,907. Registered at the G.P.O. as a Newspaper. TUESDAY, MAY 2, 1916 One Halfpenny.

THE BATTLE OF SACKVILLE STREET: FIRST PHOTOGRAPHS FROM THE SCENE OF THE FIGHTING IN DUBLIN.

Sackville-street as seen from O'Connell Bridge. The material damage has been heavy, and the city's most noble thoroughfare is more or less in ruins.

Civilian has to show his passport.

Tradesmen's carts, motor cars and baskets used to make a street barricade.

From his column, which dominates the whole of Sackville-street, Nelson looks down upon a heap of smouldering debris and reeking stones, which are still red with the blood of soldier, rebel and peaceful civilian alike. Dublin indeed has been sadly battered, and the rebellion, brief as its course has been, has resulted in a large number of casualties. It appears now, however, to be practically over, and it was officially reported yesterday that all the commanders in the capital itself had surrendered.

Front page of the Daily Mirror, *2 May 1916, noting that 'the city's most noble thoroughfare is more or less in ruins'.*

2

returned to Ireland. Christopher, along with his brother Tom, were just two of the 146,000 Irish men who were fighting in France; nearly a third of whom were killed. Four days after Kit Carroll died, and four days before the Rising began, the 16th (Irish) Division of the British Army lost 550 men in a single gas attack in Hulch, Belgium.

In Easter week of 1916, Dublin was full of newly widowed and distressed women, now totally dependent on British Army pensions and 'separation allowances' for survival. The world was in turmoil: countless thousands were dying in horrendous conditions on the western front as the war raged into its third calendar year.

It is likely that more children died violently in Dublin during Easter week 1916 than anywhere else on God's earth, making it the most dangerous place in the world for young people to be that historic week. Forty children aged sixteen and under died as a result of the Rising, which broke out at noon on Easter Monday. All bar one died by gunfire but, for the vast majority, we do not know whose bullets killed them. Indeed, given the chaos of that fateful week and the time that has passed since, it is sometimes difficult to glean accurate information on what actually happened. Consequently, there are occasional discrepancies between the official documentation relating to the Rising and information provided to me by the relatives of those killed.

For nearly a hundred years, the deaths of these children have been forgotten. In many cases, they weren't even recorded: the victims were simply included in the estimated total of around 300 civilians killed in the Rising, with seventy-seven Rebels, 116 British soldiers and twenty others in forces' uniform. In truth, the civilians were the forgotten casualties of the Rising and, within that group, the children were erased.

Between the two canals to the north and south, and bordered east and west by the Customs House and Kingsbridge (now Heuston) station, Dublin city centre was dangerous for children that week – but it was also tremendously exciting. When James Connolly stood opposite the GPO on Easter Monday and bellowed 'Charge!' to his motley crew of Rebels, as the Angelus bell struck in the nearby Pro-Cathedral, he unleashed a revolution – and the greatest excitement Dublin had seen in centuries.

Thirteen-year-old Charles Dalton, who lived in St Columba's Road in Drumcondra, a few miles from O'Connell Street, remembered playing outside his home when he heard that the Volunteers had seized the GPO and other buildings in O'Connell Street – and that they had erected barricades across the streets: 'The news of the Rising came as a great surprise to me and I was most anxious to go into town and find out what was happening. When we sat down to dinner, my father told us that a party of lancers had ridden down Sackville Street and that they had been fired on by Volunteers. A few of the soldiers and horses were killed.'

Like every other child of his age, he was excited. His father saw this and told him that on no account was he to go into town, and then instructed Charles's mother to 'lay in provisions and buy two hundredweight of flour'![1]

The Dublin of this story was very different in size, population, poverty and density from the capital city we know today, but the main geographical features haven't changed. It is just over three miles from the North Circular Road to its counterpart on the south side, and a similar distance from where the Royal

Summerhill (Gardiner Street), rear view, c. 1913.

and Grand canals enter the Liffey around Barrow Street to the Phoenix Park, but the nine square miles of the teeming second city of the British Empire was where the Easter Rising – the seminal event in our national history – effectively started and finished.

In 1903, the year of my grandmother's birth, Dublin had the second highest child mortality rate in the British Isles. By 1916, more than 5,000 of the Georgian houses that stood in the city centre had been turned into tenements, with many families squeezed into individual rooms. How anyone could call such conditions 'home' is beyond me. A single toilet was located outside, usually beside a single water tap: those were the only sanitary facilities for up to a hundred men, women and children.

Interior of a Newmarket tenement, c. 1913.

Unsurprisingly, Dublin was riddled with typhoid, dysentery and tuberculosis. Its housing conditions were the worst in the British Isles. As the nineteenth century had drawn to a close, Dublin's economic strength had been decreasing. Belfast had outstripped it as the ninth port in the United Kingdom, Dublin having slipped to twelfth. The First World War brought a brief economic resurgence to the city, through supplying the war effort.

The tenements were a product of the influx of country people to Dublin after the Famine of 1845–52. With the 1800 Act of Union, many of the gentry had moved to London, leaving their opulent mansions empty. Eventually, those houses were subdivided between many families, something for which they had not been designed. Between 1841 and 1911, the population of Dublin increased by more than 50 per cent, from 265,316 to 404,492, with the majority of the people living in the city (304,802) and 99,690 in the suburbs.[2] Of the 304,802 living between the two canals (among which were some 62,365 families), about 26,000 families lived in tenements. A government report in 1914 estimated that nearly 120,000 people – half of Dublin's working-class population – lived in 5,322 tenement houses in and around the city centre.[3]

In the 1911 Census, the population of the city was 83 per cent Catholic and 17 per cent Protestant. By any measure – class, religion, education, prospects, jobs, health or nutrition – Dublin was a deeply divided city. As we will see, enormous wealth existed beside immense poverty.

In 1914, for every thousand babies born in Dublin, 142 never saw their second birthday; in London, it was 103. The two Dublin workhouses, the North and South Dublin Unions – where, respectively, the Dublin Institute of Technology in Grangegorman and St James's Hospital are now located – sheltered at least 6,500 'paupers'.

Tenement dwellers in Dublin, c. early 1900s. According to the 1911 Census, housing conditions in Dublin were the worst in the United Kingdom. Tenements were common in the great Georgian houses of the inner city where overcrowding, disease and malnourishment were common.

Church Street following the collapse of tenements, c. 1913.

My granny loved living in Church Street. She had been born in the top back room of number 89, and later gave birth to eight children there – one of whom, sadly, was killed accidentally on the street. In 1916, the street's main landmarks were the imposing Kings Inns, Patrick Monks' bakery on the corner of North King Street, and the nearby wholesale markets, supplying fruit, vegetables and fish to the capital's retailers.

In 1911, there were 1,420 bakers in the city – there were more bakers than teachers, nurses, soldiers, policemen and butchers!

One report of the time states that 'A large proportion of Dubliners are at present living on tea and bread. Bread now costs 1s [one shilling] where before the war it cost 5 and a half pence [less than half]. Tea, which cost 1s 6d, costs 2s 4d (an increase of 60%) – there are many families in Dublin where 25–30 loaves are used each week and there are a certain number where the figure is as high as 40. Houses where there are two workers and eight young children consume this amount without waste when they have no other food.'[4] Coal was simply too expensive for most people: it cost fifty-five shillings a ton.

Living in one of the hundreds of tenements that dominated Church Street, Henrietta Street or one of the area's other narrow thoroughfares guaranteed that you were in the heart of the city's action, morning, noon and night. And tenement life was central to the fate that befell many, but not all, of the forty children who died violently during Easter week 1916 in Dublin city centre.

A tenement's lobby, hall and stairs were public areas, swarming with noisy children and young people, running, shoving, shouting, kissing, courting. The women took turns washing down the landings and stairs – but still the stench of

Chancery Lane (Bride Street), c. 1913.

Rear of dwelling in Faddle's Alley, off Dowker's Lane, c. 1913.

cramped human existence dominated. The front door, if there was one, would be closed only at night, and seldom locked, though tenants were always wary of 'lobby watchers' – down-and-outs, who would sleep in the hallway.

Imagine living in a tenement: extended families were cramped into one room, which meant that, whether you liked it or not, you spent most of your childhood outside your 'home'. Mischievous children streamed around this lively part of the city, no more so than at Easter time, when better weather arrived – and Easter 1916 was gloriously sunny. Many were barefoot as they careered around the warren of streets, alleys, laneways and shortcuts that wove through the city centre.

The awful tenements were the target of an acerbic onslaught by Bernard Shaw, the playwright, himself born in Synge Street, when he declared after the Rising: 'Why didn't the artillery knock down half Dublin whilst it had the chance? Think of the unsanitary areas, the slums, the glorious chance of making a clean sweep of them! Only 179 houses, and probably at least nine of them quite decent ones. I'd have laid at least 17,900 of them flat and made a decent town of it.'[5]

So this is where this story begins: in the heart of Dublin in 1916. For me, it started as a quest to find out more about the short lives of the children who were killed in the battle for a new Ireland. It was only when I was halfway through unearthing details about them that I realised why I had become so engrossed in this project: they had all died within a couple of miles of where my parents were born and reared, from where my father was born in Church Street on the north side of the city centre to where my mother lived in York Street off St Stephen's Green. When my parents married, they continued to live in the city centre, in Mountjoy Square, where I was born in 1956, before moving out to Ballyfermot when I was two. When I look at the map of where those children died in 1916, I feel a profound connection with them.

In a bizarre twist of fate, my own three children, triplets, will come of age on Easter Monday, 28 March 2016 – the weekend that the Irish Republic marks the centenary of the Easter Rising. Born a century earlier, who knows what their fate would have been. All we know is that children in the Dublin of a hundred

Poor children of Dublin collecting firewood from the ruined buildings damaged in the Easter Rising.

years ago had the run of the city centre. As one observer put it, 'In no city in these islands with which I am acquainted have the children such freedom, I might say such possession, of the streets as Dublin.'[6]

All of those forgotten children were from the heart of the city, my city. That was why their young lives ended so tragically during the rebellion. Those children were not only lost to their families but also to the Irish people. The six days of the Rising resulted in a massive civilian death toll, including those forty children. As Pearse wrote in the first line of the surrender command signed on Saturday, 29 April, at 3.45 p.m.: 'In order to prevent the further slaughter of the civilian population …'

Such was the confusion of that week that it is only today that we know the detail and extent of child deaths. In each chapter, I have tried to tell each child's life story in as much as it can be known, linking them in varying ways, such as by location, class, family circumstances, occupation or cause of death.

A view of Upper Sackville Street (now Upper O'Connell Street), showing the damage sustained by buildings during the Easter Rising. Two children are in the foreground and a policeman is in the background. Note the cobblestones on the street.

1. As I Strolled Out One Easter Morning

WITHIN 24 HOURS OF THE RISING STARTING, 14 CHILDREN WERE KILLED. THESE ARE THE STORIES OF SEAN FOSTER, PATRICK IVERS, CHRISTOPHER CATHCART, WILLIAM FOX AND MOSES DOYLE.

It is astonishing this early in the spring the weather
should be so beautiful.
From *The Insurrection in Dublin*, James Stephens

. . . the older ones, thinking of the children, would be getting ready
for a trip to Portmarnock's velvet strand or Malahide's silver one; and
those who weren't would be poring over the names of horses booked to
run at Fairyhouse on Easter Monday.
From *Drums Under the Windows*, Sean O'Casey

It had been over a decade since Easter had fallen so late. The previous year, Easter Sunday had been three weeks earlier. The latest date Easter can fall is 25 April and, in 1916, it took place on 23 April, as close to summer weather as the Church calendar allows. With a population of more than 300,000 living between the two canals, and almost 50 per cent aged under twenty-five, Dublin city centre was a busy, lively place at the best and worst of times.[1] More than a third of the population – 102,731 – was aged sixteen and under, the age range for this book.[2]

It was the end of Lent, deep into spring, with the merry month of May only seven days away and Bank holiday Monday, 24 April, was sunny. Little wonder that so many took advantage of it and headed out on to Dublin's streets early in the day to enjoy the perfect Easter weather.

For two-year-old Sean Foster, ten-year-old Christopher Cathcart, fifteen-year-old newsboy Patrick Ivers, thirteen-year-old William Fox and nine-year-old Moses Doyle, the weather was a magnet. By the time the sun went down, though, on the grey brick and declamatory bronze of Dublin on that historic Easter week, each one would have become an innocent victim of the rebellion that ultimately secured Irish freedom.

The first child to die in the Rising, Sean (John) Frances Foster, shot in his pram on Church Street on Easter Monday, 1916.

Katie Foster pushed her pram through the door of her neatly kept terraced home in Stoneybatter, her two sons placed end to end. Seventeen-month-old Terence lay snugly under the canopy, while Sean, two months short of his third birthday, sat proudly at his mother's end, opposite the baby, surveying all before him. Katie was going to take a leisurely half-hour walk to the Father Mathew Hall in nearby Church Street – she had long been a member of the Choral Society there and, among other things, helped

16

out with the many activities that took place in the busy venue. Easter Monday each year saw the start of the annual Father Mathew Feis, and Katie was on her way to help with the running of the competition. It had been founded in 1909 by the Capuchin Friars in Church Street to foster Irish culture, dancing, drama and art, and had grown in popularity. That morning, seventy young competitors were assembling for the solo reel event.

Sean Foster's mother, Katie, pictured in London, 1960.

Katie, née O'Neill, was from a family of tailoresses, born and reared in Stoneybatter, a settled warren of red-brick 'artisan dwellings' populated by tradesmen and their families, behind Dublin's Four Courts. It was an ordered part of the city, with one family per house – unusual in the Dublin city centre of 1916. Katie had married a Guinness employee, John Foster, on 16 March 1912, and they had moved into 18 Manor Place. One of their prized wedding gifts was the mantelpiece clock they had received from their friends in the Father Mathew Choral Society.

John was originally from Ballymore Eustace and the couple had met while he was in lodgings in Norseman Place, near her family home in Sitric Place. John had started work in the cooperage department at Guinness in 1905 and, like 800 others in the brewery, was a member of the British Army Reserve. He

John Foster, father of the first casualty of the Rising, with his brother Patrick, taken on John's wedding day, 16 March 1912. John died on 9 May 1915 on the Western Front. His name is on the Ploegsteert Memorial to the Missing in Belgium. It stands in the Royal Berkshire Cemetery extension and is dedicated to those who died and are without a grave.

had been called up on 5 August 1914 for duty in the Great War, and sent to France two weeks later. Guinness workers who enlisted had half their wages sent to their spouse, so Katie received nineteen shillings a week from his employment, and the soldiers' wives allowance of £1 3s 9d, double the average weekly wage of a Dublin labourer at the time. John was guaranteed his job in the brewery after the war ended, provided, of course, he came back safe and sound.

After less than three months on the battlefield, in October 1914, he was sent home. Two reasons have been put forward as to why Private John Foster returned so soon: the first suggests he was on leave to await the birth of his son, Terence, another that he was injured, having been wounded in the retreat from Mons. Two months later, he had recovered but had been arrested for being absent without leave and confined to barracks. When Terence was born, Katie sent her youngest brother, Joseph, to the barracks to tell her husband the good news – but John never saw his youngest son as he was sent back to the trenches that night.[3]

By Christmas 1914, John Foster was back fighting on the Western Front.[4] Within months, he was missing. In May 1915, his distraught wife placed an advert in the *Evening Herald* seeking information about him.

Private John Foster (6903) D Company 1st battalion Royal Irish Rifles, wounded in action October 1914, returned to the firing line and was reported missing May 9th 1915. His wife would be glad of any news of him through the editor, *Evening Herald*.[5]

Shortly afterwards, Katie discovered that her young husband was one of the 103 Guinness workers killed during the Great War.

On that Easter Sunday 1916, Katie continued on her way in the glorious sunshine through the busy streets, past the imperious red-brick St Lawrence's Hospital on North Brunswick Street and turned into Church Street. The aroma of freshly baked bread, wafting from Monks' bakery, coupled with the roasting barley in the Jameson distillery in Bow Lane, where her father, also Terence, worked, were the dominant smells that morning, but they were soon replaced by the whiff of cordite and sulphur.

Sean, her eldest child, with long blond hair, was sitting up in the pram. He was nearly three and, no doubt,

Atkinson's Shop, 45 Church Street, Dublin, c. 1914.

THE BOY WHO NEVER DIED IN THE RISING

One of the more remarkable discoveries during the search for the names and stories of the children killed in the Easter Rising revolves around fourteen-year-old Gerald Playfair.

Until 2013, it was believed by many that this boy was in fact the first casualty of the Rising, callously shot in the back by Rebels taking the Magazine Fort in the Phoenix Park – where his father was the soldier in charge – at noon on Easter Monday.

Indeed not a year has passed since 1916 without this atrocity being quoted as a reminder of the 'callousness' and 'blood lust' of the Rebels.

When the 'egg' I painted with the names of the children who were killed appeared on *The Late Late Show* in March 2013, I was contacted by a number of people that night, informing me that I had left out one child – Gerald Playfair.

Indeed even the most highly regarded history books on the Rising repeated this mistake up to 2014. In his seminal work on the Rising, *The Easter Rebellion*, Max Caulfield described the first victim as 'a boy – who was barely seventeen years of age'.

In fact, this is the only mention of a child being killed in the Rising in Caulfield's 300-page volume – something that is not unusual among works on the subject.

But, gradually, in the course of researching this project, a different story has unfolded, and demonstrated once again the great complexity and confusion of everything that happened during that fateful week in April 1916.

It was in fact Gerald Playfair's older brother George, twenty-three, who was shot and killed – he is buried in St Mary's Hospital in the Phoenix Park, a few miles from where he lived and died.

Furthermore, the man who shot him, Volunteer Gary Holohan, was the same age as his victim, but his own testimony of the event – in which he stated that he believed the person he had shot was 'about seventeen' – helped create the myth that 'Gerald' Playfair was the young boy killed.

Gerald Playfair – the boy who didn't die in the Rising – emigrated to Canada and married in 1923, but died in 1934. He was thirty-three years of age.

the object of many admiring glances from passers-by as he and his younger brother were wheeled towards the city centre. Shortly after midday, at the busy junction of North King Street and Church Street, Katie noticed a group of men in slouch hats behind a makeshift barricade. Her surprise hardened into shock when she spotted her brother, Joseph O'Neill, with a group of Rebel Volunteers behind the barricade. Terry O'Neill, Joseph's son, reports that Katie, the eldest in the family, bantered with her brother about 'playing soldiers, telling him to get home – "You're only fooling around."'[6]

At that moment, a party of British Army Lancers on horseback was escorting a convoy of five lorry-loads of ammunition from the Dublin docks along the north quays to the Magazine Fort munitions depot in the Phoenix Park. The Volunteers, under Peadar Clancy, could not believe their luck and fired on the unsuspecting convoy as it passed Church Street Bridge. The Rising had started.

Katie Foster was unaware of what was about to unfold but her brother knew. Joseph shouted to his sister, 'Go home! This is serious.'

Katie raced with the pram towards the shelter of Father Mathew Hall a few hundred yards away. At that moment, a group

No. (1)	Date and Place of Death (2)	Name and Surname (3)	Sex (4)	Condition (5)	Age last Birthday (6)	Rank, Profession, or Occupation (7)	Certified Cause of Death and Duration of Illness (8)	Signature, Qualification and Residence of Informant (9)	When Registered (10)	Signature of Registrar (11)
287	1916 Twenty fourth April in Church St.	John Francis Foster of 18 Manor Place	M.	Bachelor	2 Years	Son of a labourer	Shot through head at level 9 Years No. med att.	Catherine Foster Mother. Present at death, 18 Manor Plc,	Second May 1916	MS Walsh oof Registrar

Sean Foster's death certificate, 2 May 1916.

11–13 North Cumberland Street Upper, rear of houses on Gardiner Street in the background, c. 1913.

of lancers broke from their escort duties and charged up Church Street towards the Rebel barricades. Savage fighting broke out. Katie was caught in the crossfire. As she fled into Father Mathew Hall, her brother heard her cry out, 'They've killed my baby!'

Christine Pepper, a competitor in the Father Mathew Feis reel event, subsequently revealed what happened next: 'I had just taken my place on the stage and the accompanist was preparing to play the opening bars of the reel when the heartrending cry of a woman echoed through the hall. The doors burst open and the woman, covered in the baby's blood, ran up the hall shouting, "They have shot my baby."'[7]

The children were shepherded away, and the feis was abandoned. Two-year-old Sean Foster became the first of forty children to die in the Easter Rising. A single bullet had hit him under the left ear, killing him instantly. Katie was never in any doubt that the bullet had come from the revolver of one of her brother's Volunteer comrades. The Reverend George O'Neill comforted Katie, took the dead child from the pram and ran towards nearby St Lawrence's Hospital. Joseph later said, 'I watched from behind the barricades as my nephew's head bobbed lifelessly on the priest's shoulder.'

Sean was officially pronounced dead at the hospital he had been wheeled past less than ten minutes previously.

In 1883, when twenty-year-old Kate Connell and her family were evicted from their farm in Waynestown, near Dunboyne in County Meath, Kate sought refuge with her aunt in North King Street in the heart of Dublin. Unlike many migrants to the city, she did not continue the journey onwards to England or America because she met Michael Ivers, a quay labourer from Limerick, and married him.

Kate Ivers was thirty-six when she had her first child in 1899, also called Kate. At that time, they were living in 40 Kelly's Row, near the Blessington Basin, less than half a mile from the top of Sackville Street. Two years later, Kate gave birth to Patrick. Like so many others on Easter Monday 1916, the Ivers family made the short walk from where they were now living in Cumberland Street North, just behind the Gresham Hotel, to Sackville Street to get the tram to Howth for the day. The innocence and gaiety of that bright bank-holiday morning can be glimpsed in this record by one of the Rebels:

Easter Monday morning was a glorious spring day such as seldom comes to our island. A warm bright sun shone from a cloudless sky over a gay city scene. The streets were crowded to capacity. Thousands of people seemed to have come up for the Fairyhouse races and most of them, like a great number of citizens, were promenading the streets, obviously enjoying the glorious weather and savouring city life at its happiest and most peaceful moment. Children swarmed everywhere, racing and screaming at their unrestrained play. Occasionally Volunteers in uniform, passing here and there, were greeted with cheery curiosity. British soldiers were to be met in every street, swagger canes under arms, ogling the girls.[8]

The Ivers family was oblivious to the occupation of the GPO by the Rebels until soldiers on horseback appeared at the top of Sackville Street from the Parnell Square direction. The Lancers, in full battle mode, charged down the street and were promptly fired on from inside the GPO. It was just after 2 p.m. Men, women and children scattered, scurried and ran in all directions as the fighting, which had started two hours previously in other parts of the city centre, arrived in the main street with a bang.

Panic and confusion broke out. Michael and Kate Ivers grabbed their children and headed back through the side streets to their nearby home. Their son, Patrick, was now fifteen and a newsboy; he knew his way around the city-centre streets. As the family hurried back to their tenement room in nearby North Cumberland Street, others who had heard the commotion were heading in the opposite direction. Mayhem meant opportunity.

Waste ground, ruined houses, stables etc., North Cumberland Street, c. 1913.

Christopher Cathcart lived in one room in 28 Charlemont Street with his father Patrick, a coach-builder, his mother Julia, and eight siblings; two had died at birth.

Anyone leaving Dublin city centre on Easter Monday morning was literally heading away from trouble, but that was not to be the case for ten-year-old Christopher Cathcart who, with a group of his pals, was crossing the canal beside his home to the leafy southside suburb of Rathmines.

A great adventure awaited the children of 28 Charlemont Street as Easter Monday dawned. Twenty-seven people from four families were packed into the small four-roomed house beside the Grand Canal.[9] Little wonder that, for children, the best place, regardless of weather, was outside on the street, and today the weather was obliging. Also, as most tenement dwellers

Jacob's biscuit factory, Dublin, at the time of the Easter Rising.

knew, public space was better than private squalor. The children of the four families – the Burtons, Whelans, Cathcarts and Condrons – all knew each other well: they had shared the same house for more than five years.[10] When they walked over the canal that spring morning, they were in playful spirits as they passed Portobello Army Barracks towards Palmerston Park.

The sequence of events that led to Christy's death began in St Stephen's Green just after midday when Volunteers under the leadership of Thomas MacDonagh marched to nearby Bishop Street and stormed the Jacob's biscuit factory, which was operating on a skeleton staff because of the bank holiday. While MacDonagh was not regarded as a great military strategist, the biscuit factory, with its commanding towers, ideal for observing Portobello Barracks and Dublin Castle, was a prime military target. A giant triangular, red-brick building surrounded by a maze of small streets, the factory would be impregnable once captured. It employed more than 3,000 workers in the middle of Dublin's industrial area and its products, from cream crackers to custard creams, were a treat for many a Dubliner, young and old.

Nearby Portobello Bridge was also a key strategic target for the Rebels as it was the main artery for the British troops from the Portobello Barracks to get into the city centre to reinforce the soldiers who were under attack.

Thomas MacDonagh despatched a squad of Volunteers to try to hold Portobello Bridge. Shortly after noon, ten Rebels took over Davy's, a very large public house that dominated the corner of the canal and Charlemont Street, overlooking the vital bridge. A passing British soldier was fired on from the pub and immediately ran to Portobello Barracks for support. It was the beginning of a fierce gun battle.

Strong reinforcements from the barracks took up positions with machine-guns on the other side of the bridge. Amid the confusion, the few Dublin Metropolitan Policemen left on the streets had great difficulty keeping civilians out of harm's way.

In her diary of the Easter Rising, Lady Eileen Chance of Merrion Square, wrote on Tuesday, 25 April: 'We hear that yesterday the firing at Portobello Bridge was awful. Sinn Féiners in Davy's public house firing on the people and soldiers. The Royal Irish Rifles fired on them from the grounds of the barracks.'[11]

Newsboy Patrick Ivers was a few years older than Christy Cathcart and, like most children of his age, was very streetwise.

The mantra to children in cramped, overcrowded tenement rooms was 'Could you not go out and play?' Living in the heart of the city, young Patrick Ivers was well used to the rough and tumble of street life and Cumberland Street North was the venue for a very busy street market, selling second-hand clothes, furniture and bric-a-brac – it still is today. Patrick's father, Michael, issued strict instructions that Patrick was not to venture outside when the rebellion was in full flow – but how could that diktat be enforced in a crowded tenement room? After all, who would run for the 'messages', the bread, milk and whatever scraps of meat and vegetables were needed daily? A child, fleet of foot, streetwise and small, would have more luck in the search for food than a gangly adult target.

With six families – twenty-eight people – living at 15 Cumberland Street, it was little wonder that Michael Ivers' edict did not last the full week. By Friday, Patrick was out playing football in the back yard of a tenement in 9 Gloucester Street (now Sean McDermott Street) when he was shot – nobody knows by whom.

Soon after midday on Easter Monday, as the Rising spread on the other side of the city, Christopher Cathcart's mother, Julia, frantically sent word to her children to return home immediately – nearby Portobello Bridge had become a battleground. If Christopher had stayed and played near his home, instead of crossing the canal to Rathmines and Ranelagh, he would almost certainly not have become the second of the eight children to die on Easter Monday.

The children from 28 Charlemont Street tried to get home, amid the confusion, gunfire, excitement and chaos, but ten-year-old Christopher – according to his family and Essie Coady, one of the friends who was with him – panicked and got lost in the maelstrom.[12] He was hit by a bullet near Portobello Bridge as Rebels inside Davy's pub fought a savage battle with British troops. His family maintains that his mother retrieved his body that night, and it was laid out in his grandfather's house in nearby Pleasant Street in a coffin hastily made by his father.

Other reports state that he was taken with injured soldiers, police and a civilian to the fully equipped military hospital in the nearby barracks, run by Major Charles Augustus John Albert Black RAMC, who had been honorary surgeon to the Viceroy of India and had served with the South Africa Force during the Boer War.[13] Christopher's death certificate states the cause as: 'Probably haemorrhage from gun-shot wound.'

The writers James Stephens tells of some of the activity at Portobello Bridge on the Monday: 'The police had disappeared from the street – at that hour I did not see one policeman, nor did I see one for many days, and men said that several of them had been shot earlier in the morning; that an officer had been shot on Portobello bridge, that many soldiers had been killed and that a good many civilians were dead also.'[14]

Patrick Ivers was killed four days after Christopher Cathcart on the afternoon of Friday, 28 April but he was buried before him in Glasnevin Cemetery. Patrick's frantic family heard about the shooting and set out to find him. His father first approached Fitzgibbon Street police station while Kate, his elder sister, and his mother searched the hospitals. Kate found him at the Mater

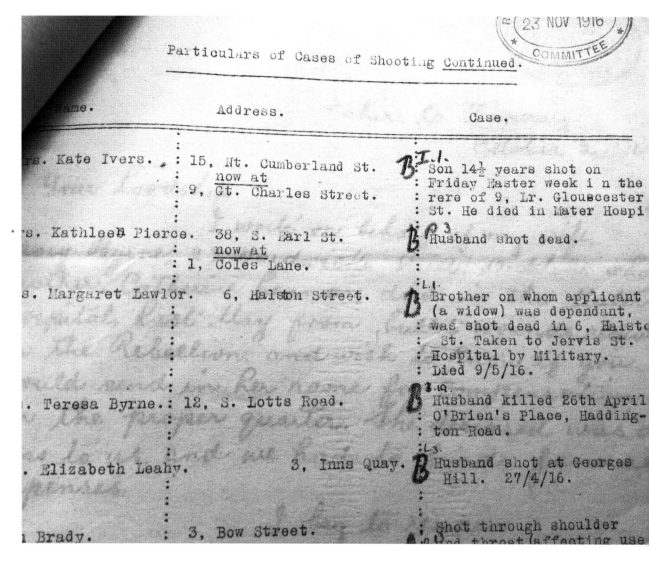

Report of the Rebellion Committee listing the 'particulars of cases of shooting', lists Patrick Ivers as shot 'in the rere [sic] of 9 Lr. Gloucester Street'.

Hospital on nearby Eccles Street and sent a message to their mother but, by the time she arrived, Patrick had died. The nun looking after Patrick remarked to Kate Ivers, 'You were a long-called-for mother.' Although Kate was just fifty-three when Patrick was killed, she was referred to in the documentation relating to his death as an 'old woman'.[15]

Two other boys, James Jessop and John Doyle, both aged seventeen, died at the Mater Hospital too.

Joseph Jessop, a Protestant originally from Queen's County (Laois), was a bootmaker. He married Mary, a Catholic, who was originally from Kilkenny, in 1890. The family of seven lived in Stafford Street in north Dublin with seven other families – a total of thirty-seven inhabitants.

By 1916, the Jessops had moved to 3 Upper Gloucester Street – Joseph was now working as a grocer's porter. Two days into the Rising, a few hundred yards from the GPO, Joseph's son, James, was shot and killed on the footpath near the Pro-Cathedral two weeks after his seventeenth birthday, opposite number 33 Marlborough Street.[16] John Doyle, a waiter from Summerhill, also died of gunshot wounds in St Aloysius' ward – his death certificate states he was sixteen but he was in fact seventeen.

In 2014, a family contacted me to tell me about an uncle, John O'Connor. Although his death certificate gave his age as seventeen, the family believes he was sixteen when he was shot as he returned from a confraternity meeting in St Laurence O'Toole's church in Sheriff Street. They were told that John, of nearby Emerald Street, was caught in crossfire and shot in the head by a sniper. His death certificate states that he died 'from gunshot wounds to the head, brain, lacerated, meningitis certified'. John died in Mercers Hospital.

The Mater Hospital's casualty unit was one of the busiest in Dublin that week – many of the young people, including Patrick Ivers, were taken to St Aloysius' ward. Mater records show that Patrick Ivers, Sean Healy and James Kelly, children who died in

John O'Connor shot on his way home from Sodality in St Laurence O'Toole Church, Sheriff Street. His family believe he was 16, though his death certificate states 17.

the Rising, lay side by side in the same ward.[17]

The Pro-Cathedral was a dangerous place to be during the Rising. On Tuesday, thirteen-year-old William Fox, from Clonliffe Road, was shot and killed there. Monsignor Michael Curran, secretary to the Archbishop of Dublin, later recorded, 'Many people had taken refuge in the Pro-Cathedral. People entering or leaving were shot at by the military.'[18]

William Fox was removed to Jervis Street Hospital and was eventually included in the list of fatalities published in the *Evening Herald* a week after the Rising.[19] In the 1911 Census, William was

No. (1)	Date and Place of Death (2)	Name and Surname (3)	Sex (4)	Condition (5)	Age last Birthday (6)	Rank, Profession, or Occupation (7)	Certified Cause of Death and Duration of Illness (8)	Signature, Qualification and Residence of Informant (9)	When Registered (10)	Signature of Registrar (11)
396	1916 Eighth May Mercers Hospital	John O'Connor 1 Emerald St	M	Bachelor	14 Years	Messenger	Gun Shot Wound Head Brain Lacerated Meningitis Certified	J Prendiville Inmate Mercers Hospital	Ninth May 1916	Geo McOne Registrar

(Superintendent Registrar's District *South Dublin* Registrar's District *No 3 South City*. 19 16. DEATHS Registered in the District of *No 3 South City* in the Union of *South Dublin* in the County of *City of Dublin*)

John O'Connor's death certificate, 9 May 1916.

the youngest of five children of Edward Fox, a printer, and his wife, Alice; they lived with three other families at 21 Richmond Cottages, in Summerhill. The arithmetic was simple in the Dublin of those days: three rooms, three families, fifteen people.

We do not know what William was doing near Marlborough Street on the day he was shot but he was a good distance from home. Maybe, like so many others, he had come into the city to enjoy the good weather and see the excitement or perhaps, as we shall see later, to look for the spoils of chaos and insurrection, as this typical newspaper account of the time describes: 'One looter filled a rug with stolen goods … in Marlborough Street in the sight of the passers-by … some women looted even under the heaviest rifle fire, and many were shot and injured.'[20]

Two death certificates were issued, eight weeks apart, for young William Fox. One tells us he was a schoolboy, the other a hairdresser's apprentice, who lived at 6 Holycross Cottages, Clonliffe Road. The certificates agree on his name, age, address and the date of his death, but not on either the place at which he died or the cause of his death: the earlier certificate tells us he died at the Pro-Cathedral, Marlborough Street, from 'shock', while the second says he died in Jervis Street Hospital from 'gunshot wounds in body and abdomen – no med. attendant'.

The second, more detailed death certificate was obviously issued in anticipation of a compensation claim – the parents of a child who was working could expect some small award – which William's mother subsequently received, but there is no further correspondence on the file. We must presume that, like the majority of applications, she received a small amount.

William Fox is buried in a communal grave in the St Paul's section of Glasnevin Cemetery.[21]

Recommendation made by the Committee at their
Meeting of 13th February, 1917.

Class of case –   Dependent of deceased,

Name of deceased – IVERS, PATRICK.   (aged 14½ years).

Ascertained average
weekly earnings of deceased – 10/- to 14/-

Compensation claimed –   £100.

There was no misconduct or default in this case.

Solicitor for Applicant – Messrs. Wm. Smyth & Son,
                            29 Lr. Gardiner St.,
                            DUBLIN.

Dependent –   ————

**Applicant – Father. Deceased contributed to the support
                of the family.**

Recommendation made by the Rebellion Committee with regard to Patrick Iver's mother's case for compensation. Mrs Ivers, a widow, was granted the sum of £50 sterling, half her claim.

Patrick Ivers, who was killed near the Jessops' home on Gloucester Street, was buried the following Wednesday, 3 May, also in a communal grave in the St Paul's section of Glasnevin Cemetery, near to William Fox and James Jessop and James's younger brother, Joseph, who died of gastroenteritis that same week. The Ivers family claimed compensation of a hundred pounds, stating that Patrick earned between ten and fourteen shillings a week as a newsboy and contributed to the support of the family.

In response, a representative of the British government's Rebellion (Victims) Committee – set up by the British government to award compensation and help the wounded of the Rising and the relatives of the 'innocent civilians' who died – wrote of Patrick's parents: 'I beg to state that I made careful inquiries and learned that Michael Ivers is a hardworking labouring man who never takes drink to excess and his wife is a respectable old woman who keeps her home clean and tidy and in my opinion the approved award could safely be made to them without the intervention of the trustee.'

They were awarded fifty pounds.[22]

Michael Ivers died, aged fifty-four, less than two years after Patrick. His family maintains that his death was hastened by the shooting of his son in 1916.[23] Kate Ivers was seventy-five when she died on 18 August 1938, twenty-two years after her son was killed in the Easter Rising.

Like so many other families in Dublin of the 1900s, the sudden death of their son Christopher was just one of many tragedies that befell the Cathcarts. They had lost an eighteen-month-old child, Patrick, to 'the croup' – one of the many contagious illnesses that killed young Dubliners – a number of years previously. Christopher was buried on 3 May in Glasnevin Cemetery, nine days after his death; his family claims that the British Army callously delayed the burial.

Three years later, in September 1919, Christopher's brother Patrick – named after his dead sibling – who had been playing with him on the day he was killed, drowned in the Grand Canal, when he became 'caught in the canal locks'. In December

1921, the boys' father, also Patrick, died suddenly from a brain haemorrhage, aged fifty-one.

To this day, there are conflicting reports of who shot two-year-old Sean Francis Foster. The area was teeming with military – another large contingent of British soldiers was making its way up the quays through Stoneybatter that morning on their way to Grangegorman Military Cemetery to bury one of their comrades killed in the Great War, but they missed the action. One of the Volunteer leaders, Piaras Béaslaí, later wrote: 'A second Lancer galloped up Church Street and was shot down after he killed a child.'[24]

However, the other child in the pram, Terence, known to his family as Ted, subsequently told a different version of events. On the fiftieth anniversary of the Rising and his brother's death, he related the events as told to him by his mother. He said there were two Volunteers in the foyer of the Father Mathew Hall: when they opened fire on passing lancers, his baby brother was hit by a bullet from a revolver.[25]

With Ted's father missing – presumed dead – in the Great War, it was left to Katie Foster's

The war records for Sean Foster's father John show:[26]
'Foster, John, service no. 6903, Rifleman, Royal Irish Rifles, 1st Battalion.

Killed in action, Aubers Ridge, France, 9 May 1915. Born Dowdenstown, Ballymore Eustace, Co. Kildare, 1882.

Husband of Kate Foster (née O'Neill), 18 Manor Place, Dublin.

Grave or memorial reference panel 9, Ploegsteert Memorial, Belgium.
Supplementary information: Enlisted Dublin. His son Sean, aged two years ten months, was killed by a stray bullet in Dublin on Easter Monday 24 April 1916.'

The Last General Absolution of the Munsters at Rue du Bois *by Fortuninio Matania.*
Fr Francis Gleeson from Tipperary gave absolution on the evening before the Battle of
Aubers Ridge in May 1915.

own father, also Terence, to arrange the funeral for his grandson.
Three days later, at six o'clock on Thursday morning – the smoke
from the Rising hanging over the city – he placed Sean's small
coffin on a hired handcart and pushed it from the hospital to
Constitution Hill, then two miles uphill to Glasnevin Cemetery.
By this point, the main artery into the city from Finglas and
Ashbourne was a flashpoint, and the army had set up a roadblock
on the route into Phibsborough. Terence O'Neill was forced to
stop: the troops would have searched the coffin for ammunition.

Sean Francis Foster was laid to rest at seven o'clock – his
Irish name recorded as 'John' – in the family grave in the main
Glasnevin Cemetery, with his distraught grandfather the only
mourner in attendance. He was the first victim of the Easter
Rising to be buried. His father had been killed almost exactly
a year earlier, among the 32,000 British soldiers killed in the

disastrous battle of Aubers Ridge by Fortuninio Matania on 9 May 1915, immortalised in Ireland by the famous painting of Irish chaplain Fr Francis Gleeson on horseback blessing the troops on the eve of battle.

After her husband's death, Katie Foster's soldiers' wives' allowance was reduced to eighteen shillings and sixpence per week, but when she told the authorities her baby son had been killed in the Rising, the allowance was cut again to fifteen shillings because she had one less mouth to feed. *The Freeman's Journal* of 9 May 1917 described this as the 'depths of meanness', and it was raised in the House of Commons during the debate on the Rising in May 1917. Nothing changed.

Katie's application to the Rebellion (Victims) Committee for a hundred and fifty pounds yielded an award of twenty-five pounds, slashed to ten by the red fountain pen of the ever-parsimonious assistant under-secretary, John Taylor.

Forty-eight years after Sean was buried, the remains of his widowed mother, eighty-two-year-old Katie Foster, were laid to rest with him in Glasnevin, the locket photograph she had carried all her life of her dead

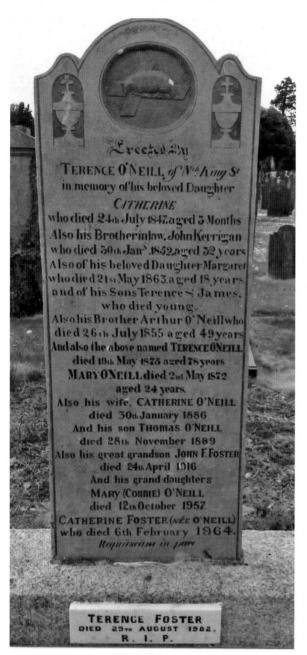

Foster gravestone: 'His great grandson John F. Foster died 24 April 1916'.

husband and baby still her treasured possession. She died in February 1964, two years before the Irish state would commemorate the fiftieth anniversary of the Easter Rising. Her family insists that Katie Foster was deeply affected by the double tragedy, blaming the British Army for killing her husband and the Rebels for killing her child. Her only surviving child lived with her until the day she died.

Sean Foster was the second youngest child to die in the Rising: at thirty-four months, the boy shot in his pram was six months older than Christina Caffrey, who was to die in her mother's arms twenty-four hours later.

Ship Street Little, which leads to the back gate of Dublin Castle, was where Moses Doyle was shot and killed on Easter Monday in 1916. Despite its location behind the seat of power – in fact the living quarters of the large contingent of British troops in Dublin Castle bordered it – Ship Street Little and its

One half of a locket including a detail from the studio portrait of Katie Foster's son Sean.

A year after Sean's death, Katie placed another notice in the *Evening Herald*, this time with a short poem:[27]

Foster – first anniversary. In fond and loving memory of John Francis (Shawn), the darling eldest child of Katie and the late John Foster, 18 Manor Place, who was accidentally shot in the Rising, Easter Monday, April 24th, 1916 aged 3 years.

His little face and gentle form,
Are pleasant to recall,
He had a little smile for each,
And was dearly loved by all,
We little thought his time so short,
In this world to remain,
Nor thought that when from home he went,
He'd ne'er return again.

People gathered outside buildings on Upper Sackville Street damaged during the Easter Rising. The business premises in shot include, from left to right: Thwaite's mineral water manufacturers at number 57, the Edinburgh Hotel (56), the Edinburgh Life Assurance Company (55), Mercredy, Percy and Co (54), The ABC Guide (53) and the Carlton Cinema (52) (partly cut out of frame).

continuation, Ship Street Great, were often photographed as an example of the horrendous living conditions for Dublin's poor in the early twentieth century. Forty-seven families, comprising 214 people, lived in the seventeen houses of Ship Street Little. Ship Street Great had twenty-four houses, with ninety-eight families and a population of 447!

On Easter Monday, the area was busy as British Army

reinforcements rushed through Ship Street Little to the back of Dublin Castle, which was being attacked from the front gate in Parliament Street – there were many reports of sniper fire at the back of the castle. Nine-year-old Moses lived around the corner in Whitefriar Street, famous for its Carmelite church, which contains the remains of St Valentine. In 1916, Whitefriar Street was a teeming mass of tenements, shops and stalls, one of the busiest thoroughfares in central Dublin.

In the 1911 Census, Moses Doyle, then four years old and the youngest of four, was living with his father, Patrick, a general labourer, his mother, Mary, and siblings, Mary, Henry and Bridget, in 50A New Street, near Merchant's Quay. According to the census, three families, comprising twelve people, were living in the two-roomed house. Patrick and Mary Doyle were from Wicklow, and their two older children, Mary and Henry, were born there; Bridget and Moses are both recorded in the 1911 Census as having been born in Dublin. Moses is buried in a communal grave in the St Paul's section of Glasnevin Cemetery, where the Register reveals that he was 'killed by gunfire' in Ship Street Little on 24 April 1916 and buried ten days later on 4 May.[28]

The compensation claim made by his mother states, 'Applicant's eldest son was shot dead during the rebellion.'[29]

From noon on Easter Monday, the various Rebel garrisons had successfully taken the GPO, the Jacob's biscuit factory in Bishop Street, Boland's Mills, the Mendicity Institute, the South Dublin Union and the College of Surgeons in St Stephen's Green. Nine hours later, as dusk settled on a city in shock, nine children had been fatally wounded, one to die later. One child killed for each hour.

A group of children posing for a photograph, c. 1913.

2. A Tale of Two Cities

They lived in different worlds in the centre of Dublin, but John Kirwan, William Lionel Sweny, Christopher Andrews and Madge Veale were united in death in Easter week.

The dust and mire in which the people lived and died were being sprinkled everywhere through the gallant, aristocratic streets; it drifted on to the crimson or blue gold-braided tunics of the officer; on to the sleek morning coat and glossy top-hat of the merchant and professional man; on to the sober black gown and grey-curled wig of the barrister and judge; on to the rich rochet of immaculate surplice and cocky biretta; on to the burnished silk and lacquer-like satin frocks and delicate petticoats of dame and damsel.
From *Drums Under the Window*, Sean O'Casey

They were born within a few hundred yards of each other, at the start of an exciting new century in the heart of Dublin city centre – but while their lives could not have been more different, their brutal deaths during the Rising united them for ever.

John Kirwan, aged fifteen, was the youngest son of a stoker in the Dublin Gas Company and Christopher Andrews, aged fourteen, the oldest surviving child of a labourer in the same firm. William Lionel Sweny, fourteen, was the youngest son of a pharmacist immortalised in James Joyce's *Ulysses*, and Margaret 'Madge' Veale, thirteen, was the daughter of a wealthy self-made seed merchant.

They were all born within a short distance of Merrion Square in the centre of Georgian Dublin. The four children lived close to each other – but they inhabited two completely different worlds. Lionel Sweny, John Kirwan and Christopher Andrews probably passed each other every day on Westland Row, as Lionel walked to St Mark's Protestant School in Brunswick Street (now Pearse Street) while John and Christopher made their way to Westland Row School (St Andrew's) beside their tenement homes in Cumberland Street South and Stephens Place, off Mount Street. Westland Row was an elegant street in the late nineteenth and early twentieth centuries, with a bustling railway station, a magnificent Catholic church, the busy St Andrew's school and imposing Georgian houses, including the birthplace of Oscar Wilde. A pleasant thoroughfare, it belied the squalor and poverty that lay directly behind it.

The following notice appeared in the births column of *The Irish Times* on 25 January 1902: 'Sweny: January 23, 1902, at 1 Lincoln Place, to the wife of Frederick William, of a son.' William Lionel Sweny was born into the well-off family, who lived in the imposing house at the top of Westland Row above the pharmacy that bore his family name, as the shop still does to this day.

John and Annie Kirwan had married in 1895, both aged twenty. Annie gave birth to thirteen children, of whom twelve survived: Dan, Paddy, James, Leo, Nick, Tommy, John, May, Maggie, Sadie, Annie and Lily. Lily, the youngest, was born three weeks before the Rising. John Kirwan junior had been born

Ruined stable in a lane at the rear of 20 South Cumberland Street, c. 1913. The loft is tenanted, the lower part is used as a stable. John Kirwan was born at 8 South Cumberland Street.

at 8 Cumberland Street South, a tenement house immediately behind Westland Row. It was much the same as every other house in the terrace, one of twenty-six from which more than 600 emerged every single morning. Thirty-two people lived at number 8, and by the time three of their older children had left home, the Kirwans had two rooms. At number 20, up the row from the Kirwans, ten families, fifty-eight people, shared the single tap and toilet outside the back door.

Christopher Andrews was born in 1902 at 3 Grattan Court, off Mount Street, in a five-roomed tenement that housed nine families; the new baby brought to thirty-seven the number of tenants living there. By 1911, after nineteen years of

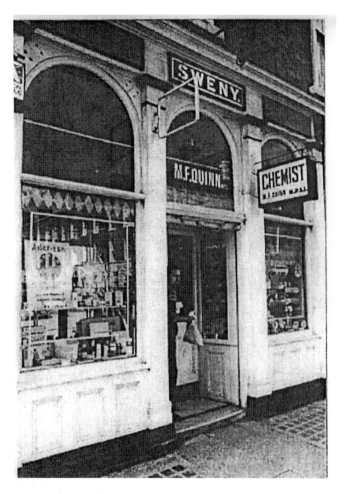

Sweny's shop.

marriage, Maria and Patrick Andrews had eight children, four of whom died, leaving Esther, fifteen, Christopher, nine, Patrick, six, and Maria, two, still alive. By 1916, the family had moved around the corner to another tenement, a five-roomed house at 8 Stephens Place, between Upper and Lower Mount Street, in which five families lived, twenty-five people in all.[1]

Things were much better around the corner in Sweny's chemist, which would have been the first port of call if any of the Kirwans was unwell; a visit to the doctor was unaffordable. 1 Lincoln Place was a 'first-class house with 6 rooms and 24 windows to the front'.[2] It was so big that the Swenys could take in boarders and accommodate servants.

Frederick Lionel Sweny was a qualified pharmacist; he married twice and fathered sixteen children – and had seen child tragedy long before Lionel was born in 1902. In 1884, Frederick married Sophia Mary Johnson but, between 1891 and 1892, they lost three of their children – Eveleen Ruby, Ethel Sophia and Walther Theodore – to a flu epidemic. Chronic infant mortality was not only a feature of working-class life in Dublin. A report relating to one part of inner-city Dublin in the late nineteenth century recorded the shocking reality that sixty-two out of every hundred children born were dead before they reached their tenth birthday.[3] Frederick's wife, Sophia, died in 1895 – also, according to the family, from influenza.[4] In 1897, he married Sara Jane Owens and, by 1901, they had three young children of their own, as well as four children from his first marriage; they also had a servant, Maria Doyle, from Kilkenny.

Frederick William Sweny in the dickie bow (middle row right), sitting beside his wife, Sarah Jane Owens, taken with his extended family, c.1910. Lionel might be one of the boys in the front row.

It was called the 'Mosque of the Baths' in *Ulysses*, and Leopold Bloom also called to Sweny's to consult Frederick in such detail that it is still possible to recreate the scene Bloom describes: 'He waited at the counter, inhaling the keen reek of drugs, the dusty dry smell of sponges and loofahs. Lots of time taken up by telling your aches and pains.'

Sweny's waxy lemon soap, mentioned in *Ulysses*, is still sold in the shop today.[5]

F.W. Sweny's had opened its doors as a dispensing pharmacy in 1853 – the building and the name of the business remain to this day. It is located between the birthplace of Oscar Wilde and what was to become one of the most exotic buildings in Dublin, the Turkish Baths, complete with minarets, half-moon apertures, elaborate fretwork and a tall, variegated brick shaft rising eighty-five feet off the ground.

By the time of the 1911 Census, the older Sweny boys, George, Charles and Alfred, were attending Ranelagh School in Athlone, modelled on English public schools, leaving the two daughters, Edith and Lillie Caroline, with Lionel and his new-born brother, Cecil Desmond, at 1 Lincoln Place. At that time, along with the six members of the Sweny family, they could have up to five boarders, including vaudeville performers from the nearby Theatre Royal – such as the 'Klabs' from St Louis and the actor George Albert Laundy. The Swenys were one of the first families in the city to have a telephone – Dublin 1199.

Meanwhile, the impoverished Kirwan family had moved again, just a few hundred yards to number 3 Lower Erne Place – occupied by nine tenants in the 1911 Census – off Great Brunswick Street (later Pearse Street). After the Rising, the family decamped to nearby 28 Sandwith Place, whose multi-occupancy houses boasted 312 people, in sixty-two families, living under the shadow of the railway line. Like so many in tenement Dublin, the Kirwans moved often.

If you rented a few tenement rooms, moving wasn't exactly a logistical nightmare. You might hear of a bigger room becoming available in a better house and within hours you could gather up your few belongings – a bedstead, mattress, other bits of furniture, tea chests, pots, pans – and you would either manhandle them the few hundred yards to your new home or commandeer a passing horse and cart for the short journey. Stories are told of children returning from school in the afternoon to be redirected 'home' by neighbours as their family had moved again. There was a hierarchy among tenement rooms. All had a fireplace, for cooking, heat and light, but rooms at the front and back differed in size while two windows were a sought-after luxury. Rooms on the ground floor were sought after because they were nearer the outdoor tap and toilet!

In 1916, the four children were still living close to each other but their prospects were very different. Lionel Sweny would likely follow his three older brothers to Ranelagh School and then have a professional career; John Kirwan and Christopher Andrews were destined for manual work on the banks of the Liffey; Madge Veale, the merchant's daughter from Haddington Road, would have been expected to marry well and live the sort of comfortable life to which she had been accustomed from birth. John, now fifteen, had left Westland Row School and was earning six shillings a week as a messenger boy. His father had joined the Royal Navy and was away fighting in the Great War, like so many other Irishmen, and never far from danger. Christopher, at fourteen, was working at the Hammond Lane Foundry in Dublin's docks, earning twelve shillings a week.[6]

49

The lives of these four young people were catastrophically interrupted when, in the words of James Stephens, 'our city burst into a kind of spontaneous war' on Easter Monday at noon. Within forty-eight hours, all three boys had disappeared and Madge Veale was lying wounded in the hospital beside her home. One child's body was lost for more than a month; another has never been found. That day the nearest outbreak of trouble to the Kirwan, Andrews, Sweny and Veale households took place at Boland's Mills, near Mount Street Bridge, which was under the command of Eamon de Valera. Sean O'Keeffe, quartermaster of the 3rd Battalion of the Irish Volunteers, operated in the Lower Erne Street area.

The Rebels had gathered at 144 Pearse Street on Easter Sunday and paraded for four hours until they were dismissed and told to await further instructions. O'Keeffe remained on guard there throughout the night, but as it became clear early on Easter Monday morning that the Rising would go ahead, O'Keeffe managed to get home to Marino for an hour to 'settle up some domestic affairs'. He began his 'rising' by leading a group to cut a vital telephone cable at the junction of Lombard Street and Pearse Street.

As this was happening, nearby Westland Row railway station was being taken over by the Rebels: it was a vital artery from the port of Kingstown to the city centre – and the landing port for British reinforcements when they inevitably arrived.

De Valera had taken Boland's Mills, and the area around it was being sandbagged and secured. O'Keeffe was detailed to take charge of a party that would keep a 'portion of Pearse Street between the junction of Sandwith Street and Erne Street clear while the stores were being removed from Headquarters'.[7]

Within hours of the pell-mell that the Rising generated on

Easter Monday, young John Kirwan, with his pals in the bright sunshine and excitement, was seen 'enjoying himself with others in Sackville Street playing with a toy elephant'.[8] The street was thronged with 'spectators' soaking up the excitement: 'There was a great lot of people about from the entrance into O'Connell Street, near Parnell Street, and onwards mainly on the footpaths. I actually saw two boys with cricket bats and balls playing in the middle of the road, before reaching Nelson's Pillar where I saw two dead horses lying in the road, on the left-hand side of the pillar, and an immense lot of blood all over that part of the road.'[9]

John Kirwan's family tell me that he was sent up to Sackville Street to buy the toy elephant for his three-week-old baby sister Lily, who had been born on 4 April. Like all the children of the tenements, he was an outdoor boy, who loved playing football and was well used to the city centre. He headed for Elvery's Elephant House, a sports goods store on the corner of Abbey Street and Sackville Street, fifty yards from the GPO. The family says that Elvery's, whose emblem was an elephant, sold toy elephants, and there was a large one in the store that children could play on.[10]

Margaret by Sarah Henrietta Purser, c. 1915. In this painting, Purser depicts her distant cousin with her prize toy elephant, a popular toy at the time. John Kirwan is described on the day of his death as holding one bought as a present for his baby sister, Lily.

'The cricket bat that died for Ireland.' The bat that was in Elvery's shop window, the very shop that John Kirwan was either in or near when he was shot.

John was never seen alive again. The family believe he was shot in or near the sports shop. One of the best-known artefacts from 1916 is the 'cricket bat that died for Ireland', which was in the Elvery's window and still has a British .303 bullet lodged in it'.[11] John's family believe he took refuge in the sports shop from the shooting – but, unlike the cricket bat, he could not survive a bullet.

Meanwhile, on Monday afternoon, as the British Lancers prepared to charge down Sackville Street towards the GPO, another battle was erupting around Mount Street Bridge, again only a short distance from the Kirwan, Andrews, Sweny and Veale homes.

Madge Veale's family agree on one thing: that the thirteen-year-old was shot at her home, 103 Haddington Road, when she was mistaken for a combatant as she was wearing a khaki-green jumper. According to her brother, Joseph, she was 'peeping out through the window curtains of an upstairs room at the back of 103 Haddington Road and was shot by a spray of bullets from a Gatling-type gun – a total of ten bullets were counted'.[12] His sister was carried on a mattress, which they had put on a ladder, to the nearby Royal City Hospital in Baggot Street.

Family accounts differ slightly as to the actual day that Maggie Veale was shot. But it is pretty clear at this stage that it was Wednesday, 26 April, and that she was shot by British troops, who were the only ones in the area using a Gatling gun.

Another version of the tragedy comes from Aine O'Rahilly – a member of Cumann na mBan and sister of The O'Rahilly, one of the Rebel leaders who was killed in the Rising – who mentioned the child in her witness statement to the Bureau of Military History in 1950. The O'Rahillys lived in nearby Northumberland Road and arms had often been stored in their home. On Easter Monday, Aine O'Rahilly saw a group of 'Georgius Rex', the army reserve, returning from a route march:

> The poor old things were carrying their rifles but we did not then know they had no ammunition for them. The Volunteers held their fire until the GRs were in front of 25. Suddenly a volley rang out. Several of them fell, but I only remember one not getting up. Some of them took shelter behind the trees. They then turned down the laneway to get to Beggars Bush Barracks.

At the end of her statement, she added:

> A little girl called Veale aged about 12 or 13 years to whom I used to teach Irish was killed during Easter week by a soldier, who aimed at her as she stood at her window in Haddington Road, looking out through binoculars. After the fighting was over I noticed an ambulance taking another dead body from the corner house in Haddington Road. I think it had been buried in the garden for some days.[13]

Madge Veale was the youngest and ninth child of John Veale, an accountant, and Mary Johanna Kelly. The children born directly before her, Annie Teresa (1900) and Francis Patrick (1895), had both died before she arrived in 1903, so when she was born her nearest sibling was seven years older and two of her brothers were over thirty. That gives us a glimpse into how treasured the child would have been in her middle-class, Catholic family during the years leading up to the tragedy in 1916.

Haddington Road, a leafy stretch running parallel to the Royal Canal, is a street of fine gentrified red-brick Victorian houses – two storeys over a basement – close to the city centre. In the 111 houses on this road, there were 127 families – mostly owner-occupiers – with a total of 572 people, an average of around five per spacious house. It was a far cry from the tenements less than a mile away. Just over 80 per cent of the residents were Catholic, with 116 Protestants.

Its location, near Beggars Bush Barracks and beside the main artery from the ferry port of Kingstown – Northumberland Road and Mount Street Bridge – ensured that, from the moment Eamon de Valera's company arrived at Boland's Mills shortly after twelve thirty on Easter Monday, it was destined to be a key flashpoint of the Rising. De Valera's company hardly fired a shot: the devastating attack on the British troops was led by a small group of Rebels closer to Mount Street Bridge.

At eleven o'clock on Easter Monday morning, sixteen Volunteers, led by twenty-eight-year-old carpenter Lieutenant Michael Malone and Section Commander James Grace – an expert marksman – headed to Mount Street Bridge and took three key positions, including two houses, a school and a parochial hall.

However, the botched mobilisation on Sunday following

John and Mary Johanna Veale, whose daughter Madge was shot dead in the bedroom of her house on Haddington Road.

the countermanding order by Eoin MacNeill meant that de Valera's company's plans were curtailed: the farthest southern engagement by the Rebels was around Haddington Road, not, as planned, the takeover of Kingstown. As is often the way in war, time and chance led to an unplanned and bloody engagement.

The Dublin Battalion Associated Volunteer Corps – the British Army reservists whom Aine O'Rahilly had seen – were wearing civilian clothes with the military armband 'GR', Georgius Rex.

They had been drilling in Ticknock in the Dublin Mountains and were marching back in formation to Beggars Bush Barracks, which was effectively a continuation of Haddington Road. At that stage, sixteen Volunteers had three outposts, including the corner of Haddington Road and Northumberland Road.

The Rebels spotted the reservists and opened fire. Five were killed – not one, as Aine O'Rahilly had thought. We can only imagine the fighting that broke out after this ambush.

Three civilian residents of Haddington Road, as well as Madge Veale, were killed during the Rising. Thomas Cowley and George Synott, of number ninety-three, and Abalone Scherzinger, a German clockmaker, of number ninety-five, lost their lives on the street. Indeed, the area around Haddington Road, Northumberland Road and Mount Street was the scene of some of the heaviest fighting and highest death toll during Easter week. The area around Mount Street Bridge accounted for the most casualties: three Volunteers died, as did twenty civilians, and of 234 British casualties, twenty-eight were killed, the remainder wounded.[14] The Volunteers at Mount Street, led by Michael Malone and James Grace, were the most lethal group of Rebels operating anywhere in the city that week.

The British Army subsequently admitted killing civilians in this area. In a statement to the Bureau of Military History, Dubliner Captain E. Gerrard, who was home on leave from the Dardanelles in 1916, recalled: 'One of the sentries in Beggars Bush Barracks about Tuesday evening said to me, "I beg your pardon, sir, I have just shot two girls." I said, "What on earth did you do that for?" He said, "I thought they were rebels. I was told they were dressed in all classes of attire." At a range of about two hundred yards I saw two girls – about twenty years old, lying dead.'[15]

A poignant letter to Madge's brother Willie from his sister-in-law Teresa tells of the turmoil that engulfed the area for the week. On 5 May, she wrote, 'No doubt you have learned through some source by now of the death of your beloved sister Madge and it is to tell you how sorry we all . . . are for you and all your people, that I now write this letter.' She concluded the long missive, 'I am sure Willie you all know how deeply we feel for you in this trouble especially as you are away from home, but as your Mother was saying last night she is now a little Saint in Heaven.'

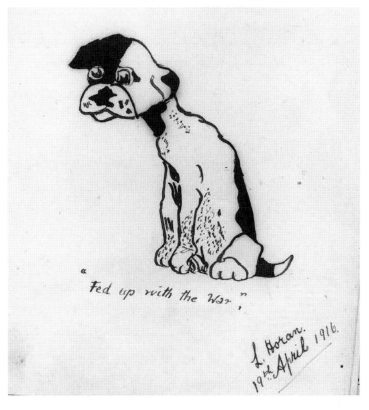

'Fed up with the war' by L. Horan, 19 April 1916. A sketch from the autograph book given to Madge Veale at Christmas 1915. Madge, who would be dead four months later, asked friends and neighbours to write in it for her.

Madge Veale died in one of the most intense and bloody episodes of the Rising, the battle of Mount Street Bridge. It was there that Lionel Sweny, the chemist's son, and Christopher Andrews, working at Hammond Lane Foundry, were also to meet their deaths.

On the last day, Saturday, 29 April – the day Pearse surrendered – a death notice appeared in *The Irish Times*: 'Sweny – April 26th, at Lower Mount Street as a result of a gunshot wound, William Lionel, son of F. Sweny, 1 Lincoln Place, age 13 years.' At that point a bereft Frederick Sweny and his large family knew the child was dead but could not locate his body. They never would. Lionel Sweny and Christopher Andrews were killed on the same day in the same place: Mount Street.

The battle of Mount Street Bridge was at its height on the afternoon of Wednesday, 26 April. L.G. Redmond, coincidentally a nephew of Irish nationalist leader John Redmond, worked as a volunteer stretcher bearer in the area and described what happened that day, and the subsequent scene in nearby Sir Patrick Dun's Hospital:

> I arrived on the scene a few minutes after the start of the engagement, but already one could see the poor fellows writhing in agony in the roadway, where the advanced line had been sniped by the terrible leaden bullets of the Sinn Féiners.
>
> The smell of roasting flesh was still around the blazing buildings at 10 o'clock, when we brought in the last of the dead – some of them mere boys of thirteen – and laid them out in dread rows like a Raemakers cartoon. One lad of twelve whom I carried in afterwards I interrogated as to why he was out in such an exposed position. He wanted to give poor Tommy [British soldier] a drink and got sniped as he was preparing to get down to the water of the canal.[16]

The next day Redmond returned to the hospital.

The small boy who had been sniped while trying to get the soldiers a drink lay stiff now and my mind went back to the scene of the night before as I made a little space of a couple of yards in the corner of the crowded ward, with everyone lying on the floor, while the good priest anointed him just before he died.[17]

The child he referred to was either Lionel Sweny or Christopher Andrews.

The front page of the *Saturday Evening Herald* on 20 May was dominated – as it had been every day since the Rising – by stories about the casualties of the conflict. There were nine photographs of six civilians and one soldier killed and two others injured during the Rising the previous month.

The photo of John Kirwan reproduced above shows a healthy young boy in a jacket and a white-ribbon bow-tie, possibly his confirmation photograph. When he didn't return home at teatime, his family became alarmed. His father

In the Evening Herald *on 20 May 1916 was a single-column piece, with information clearly supplied by John Kirwan's mother.*

was a strict disciplinarian, who used his leather belt to keep his boys in check, so it was unusual for any of them to go missing without permission – but, of course, their father was away at war.

Annie Kirwan must have received a response to her plea in the *Evening Herald* for news of her missing child, John: on 1 June she registered his death.[18] In a subsequent compensation claim, she stated that his father was 'away on active service with the navy'.[19] While John's death was well known to his relatives, who

THIS BOY IS LOST

John Kirwan who is 15, whose mother lives in 3 Lower Erne Place, has been missing since Monday, April 24th.

At about two on that day he left his home and later that afternoon was seen enjoying himself with others in Sackville Street on the back of . . . a toy elephant. This was the last sighting of him. He was very fair in complexion, of delicate appearance. He . . . has a marked scar over the right eye . . . and a grey overcoat and grey cap . . . khaki-coloured knickers and . . . [last word is unclear].'

BURIALS AT DEAN'S GRANGE CEMETERY.

Forty-six interments have taken place at Dean's Grange Cemetery of the bodies of military, civilians, and insurgents who were killed during the rebellion. Fourteen bodies were not identified, two or three were those of insurgents, and the remainder civilians.

The following military officers and men were buried at Dean's Grange:—

Captain F. C. Dietricksen, Captain P. H. Browning, Second Lieutenant M. B. Brown, Privates J. Blissett, A. Farnsworth, and Daniel Byrne, all of the Sherwood Foresters; Privates Ellis and Maxwell, of the Scots Guards; Private A. Ellis, 5th Royal Dublin Fusiliers; and Charles Sandes, of the 6th South Staffordshire Regt.

The civilians identified were:—Wm. O'Flaherty, Pembroke road, Ballsbridge; Joseph Byrne, no address; Joseph Clarke, no address; James Delahunt, no address; Edward Muldowney, no address; James J. Carroll, Municipal place, Kingstown; Jeremiah Hogan, Summerhill, Kingstown; John Doyle, Ringsend; Richard Waters, Recess, Monkstown; Thomas Hickey, North King street, Dublin, and his son, Christopher Hickey; William Gregg, Irishtown; Mary Kelly, aged 12 years, Townsend street, Dublin; Johannah Kearns, Dublin; A. Cunningham, Pigeon House road, Dublin; Bridget Stewart, aged 11 years, 3 Pembroke place, Ballsbridge; W. H. Sweeney, aged 13 years, Wentworth place, Dublin.

The following identified insurgents were also buried at Dean's Grange:—John Flynn, aged 63 years, Dodder View; John Costelloe, Athlone; Wm. Carrick, and John Kealy, Ballyboden.

Burials at Dean's Grange Cemetery, The Irish Times, 12 May 1916.

contacted me, they were unaware that his father had enlisted.[20]

John's death certificate deepens the mystery about where his body disappeared to on Easter Monday. It states that John Kirwan of 3 Erne Place died on 21 April 1916 'on way to Jervis Street hospital'. It adds that he had a 'bullet wound in thorax – no med. attention'.

Relatives of Lionel Sweny agree that his large family, led by his bereft father, searched frantically for the missing child. They believed he was dead but not where his body had been taken. In *The Irish Times* of Friday, 12 May, it was reported that 'There were 46 interments at Deans Grange Cemetery of military, civilians and insurgents killed during the rebellion. Civilians identified and buried at Deans Grange include W.H. Sweny, aged 13, of Wentworth Place, Dublin.'[21] W.H. Sweny was, in fact, Lionel, but the paper printed the incorrect initials, address and age. Family members Ken Cooke and Norma Furlong tell me that, while initial family lore mentions O'Connell Street as the location of Lionel's death, most believe that he was killed at nearby Mount Street while giving water to an injured soldier.

A granddaughter of Lionel's sister writes:

According to my grandmother, Lilian Caroline Sweny, her brother lost his life, shot by the IRA while giving a dying British soldier a drink of water on O'Connell Bridge. Her parents went to collect this body from a mass grave to take him home for burial. The accuracy of this I have no reason to disbelieve, the content never wavered and she remembered the time vividly.[22]

In those few days, searching for information was a risky business, as you travelled from hospital to hospital, all of which were inside the battle zone and curfew area. The first mention of where Lionel Sweny might have been buried came in that *Irish Times* report of

DUBLIN, SATURDAY, MAY 27, 1916. PRICE

TRAGEDIES OF THE REBELLION

PETER FAHY, aged 23, killed while in his own residence, during the rebellion, on April 25, 1916. His wife resides at 18 Usher's Island, Dublin.

MARTIN O'LEARY, 13 Dorset road, killed on April 27 while on his way home from work. Deceased was an employe of Guinness's. He had three sons and a son-in-law with the colours. His second son, George, was killed in action in the beginning of the present war.

CHRISTOPHER ANDREWS, 14 years, who was killed on Mount street Bridge on Wednesday, April 26. He resided at 8 Stephen's place, Lower Mount street.

Christopher Andrews (far right) featured in 'Tragedies of the Rebellion',
Saturday Evening Herald, *27 May 1916.*

12 May. The family are baffled by the absence of a marked grave, which added to his father Frederick's grief at the loss of his child and left him a broken man.

Meanwhile, Christopher Andrews' photograph, with two others, was published on the front page of the *Saturday Evening Herald* of 27 May, under the heading 'Tragedies of the Rebellion', a regular column: Peter Fahy, Martin O'Leary (a Guinness employee with three sons in 'the colours', one having been killed in the Great War), and Christopher Andrews, 'who was killed on Mount Street Bridge on Wednesday, 26 April. He resided at 8 Stephens Place, Lower Mount Street.' Christopher's family believed he also had 'been shot whilst in the act of giving a drink of water to a wounded soldier'.[23] He was killed by a 'bullet wound to the thorax between the neck and the diaphragm'.[24] (Sheahan's, the undertakers, arranged the funeral, and the fourteen-year-old was buried the following Sunday on 30 April at 2.30 p.m. in Glasnevin Cemetery.[25])

Christopher's mother, Maria Andrews, applied for compensation to the government's Rebellion (Victims) Committee, and because it was accepted that her son died giving water to a wounded soldier, his family received the highest single award given to any child: £150.

Frederick Sweny made his final will six weeks after his son was killed. His family tell me that his health deteriorated after the tragedy. In 1924, he died in Grangegorman Mental Asylum a few months after his wife Sara Jane had passed away. He was in his late fifties. A Sweny family headstone was erected by Frederick in Mount Jerome Cemetery naming his children who predeceased him, with one exception. There is no mention of Lionel on the headstone, or indeed on any other family headstone.

John Veale died eleven years after his daughter had been killed in the Rising. Madge was buried in the family plot in Glasnevin Cemetery on 3 May after mass in Haddington Road church.

By the time Annie Kirwan's compensation claim for the loss of her son was heard, she had moved yet again. It was just over a year later that her application to the Rebellion (Victims) Committee was processed. In a letter from the Dublin Metropolitan Police Detective Department on 5 May 1917, in reference to the Committee, it was noted:

> In the case of Mrs Anne Kirwan, who lives in 8 Lower Erne Street and is the mother of a large family, so far as I can ascertain, she is a respectable woman, but owing to her surroundings, it is, in

my opinion, desirable that her award should be administered through a trustee. Mr George Kiernan, manager of the Shamrock Works and President of the local St Vincent de Paul conference, is willing to act as same.

Annie Kirwan claimed four hundred pounds compensation for the death of her son, stating that he earned six shillings a week. In the response, it was noted that: 'Her husband is on active service in the Navy and has seven other children all younger than deceased. Deceased gave his mother all his wages.

Annie Kirwan with two of her children, Sadie and Tommy.

Compensation grant of fifty pounds sterling to deceased's mother, Mrs Anne Kirwan, of 3 Lower Erne Place, Great Brunswick Street Dublin (reported by police to be now residing at 28 Sandwith Place, Dublin).[26]

After John's death the indomitable Annie and her family moved many times, always in the area of Westland Row. She died of pneumonia in 1947 at 15f Pearse House, Pearse Street, behind Pearse railway station. She was seventy-two. She had outlived her husband by a year and it was thirty-one years since her son had been killed on Easter Monday.

The boy with the toy elephant, the girl in the green jumper, the chemist's son and the young foundry worker – John Kirwan, Madge Veale, Lionel Sweny and Christopher Andrews – began Easter week 1916 full of the joys of spring. Sadly, they died in the springtime of their lives.

A drawing from Madge Veale's autograph book, 'The Lieutenant', by M. Horan.

Knowles fruit shop was a popular target for looting during the Rising, printed in the Daily Mirror, *2 May 1916.*

3. 'The Sole Gorge of Their Lives'

LOOTING WAS WIDESPREAD BUT THE LIVES OF
PADDY FETHERSTON AND JOHN HENERY MCNAMARA
WERE SHATTERED BY THEIR INNOCENCE AND HUNGER.

Tales of looting in Dublin during the Rising are the stuff of folklore, literature and anecdote. While the unarmed Dublin Metropolitan Police (DMP) spent the first few hours of the Rising trying to control the populace, they were quickly withdrawn to barracks after three of their number were shot dead.

Most of the looting took place in the first three days of the Rising, before the fires took hold of the city centre. Contemporary reports of looting are vivid:

> The looters were mostly young lads and women . . . All along the east side of the street [Sackville] the looters were working with frenzied energy. Every now and then the shouts from the shops would be drowned by the crash of glass as another window was hammered in . . . [A] little girl of twelve or so is tottering under the weight of a huge circular office chair. A passer-by knocks

against it and is rewarded with a string of the most appalling blasphemy. A fresh-faced youth is crossing the street with an armful of boots. He is brandishing a pair of white satin shoes and shouting hysterically, 'God save Ireland.'[1]

I do not know precisely when or how the looting started. It was early evening, to the best of my recollection, and I think it was young chaps who started it, not so much in the form of looting as in a spirit of mischief. The first intimation I had was a sudden and lavish display of fireworks in the middle of O'Connell Street a short distance from our position.

It appears that a number of boys broke into Messrs Lawrence's, the toy shop. Carrying out armfuls of fireworks, they piled them up in the centre of the street and ignited them. They made a dramatic and impressive display and brought forth vociferous cheers. This, I believe, was sufficient to start wholesale looting in the centre of the city.[2]

In his memoir, the only one written by an active senior participant on the Rebel side, W.J. Brennan-Whitmore wrote wryly:

Nothing brings out the base covetousness of human nature more than a period of disorder in a city. People of normally honest social behaviour seem to break out in a rash of seizing other people's property even though the goods they steal are not of the least personal use to them.[3]

When a birth or death was imminent around Dominick Street in Dublin city centre, Annie Gaynor from nearby Long Lane was sent for. She had been born in Chapelizod in west Dublin in 1881 and had two sisters, Maggie and Esther. After their parents had died, the three girls looked after their younger brother, Joseph.

When Joseph was old enough, he joined the Hibernian Military School in the Phoenix Park, now St Mary's Hospital, for the orphaned sons of soldiers. In their twenties, his sisters could not read or write, but at twelve Joseph could do both. Maggie looked after the home at 8 New Row, Kilmainham, while Annie worked as a 'cook and domestic servant' and Esther as a 'housemaid and domestic servant.'[4] On 29 April 1901, Annie married Paddy Fetherston, a 'machine man'.

For the first ten years of their marriage, they lived

Annie and Patrick Fetherston in their later years, c. 1959.

with Paddy's widowed mother, his two brothers, Thomas and

James, and a nephew at 48.5 North Brunswick Street, a five-roomed house of which the family occupied just one room. The three brothers worked as boilermakers' assistants in the railway works at Inchicore.

By 1911 Annie had given birth to six children, but had buried two. The family had moved to another tenement at 1 Long Lane, just off Dorset Street, which was bigger, with seven rooms and twenty-four tenants. Annie was energetic, streetwise and bright, but illiterate. She quickly became the 'handywoman' around the teeming tenements of Dominick Street. If no midwife was available, she delivered babies, and would stay with the new mother for ten days; she also laid out the dead. As late as 1948, she delivered her grandson, Paddy, named after the twelve-year-old son she had lost thirty-two years earlier after he was shot in the thigh on Easter Monday afternoon.[5]

Paddy Fetherston at school. Paddy is marked (back row, fifth from the right) by his brother who wrote: 'Killed Brother Paddy.' A note on back reads 'Taken C Nicholas School, Halston Street, Dublin. Paddy in this photo about 1912'.

Patrick 'Paddy' Fetherston – described by his family as a 'robust' boy – and his pals were no different from any other tenement children of Dublin city centre in the early twentieth century. They had nothing, in many cases not even shoes, and lived by their wits on the streets. To come home with firewood or a few pieces of coal was a triumph. The second of the seven surviving children of Annie and Paddy, Patrick originally went to Halston Street School, where he was photographed in a school group in 1912, when he was about eight. The picture shows thirty-nine children, including two babies; a number of the children are barefoot. In the Dublin of those days, children were more likely to have something on their head than on their feet.

Since 1821, primary education had been free, and had been compulsory since 1892 for all those aged between six and fourteen. In reality, the basic necessities of life ensured that many left school before they were of an age to do so. When the Fetherston family moved to Long Lane, Paddy transferred to Great Denmark Street School.

According to his family, Paddy's death was never spoken about, perhaps because 'he was looting a shop at the junction of Parnell Street and Dominick Street'.[6] They accept that he was one of the many Dubliners who, upon hearing of the 'commotion' in town, dashed for the city centre to collect the spoils of war. The withdrawal of the DMP to barracks following the shooting dead of three of their members – Constable Michael Lahiff in St Stephen's Green, Constable James O'Brien in Dublin Castle and Constable William Frith in Store Street – on Easter Monday left the shops vulnerable.

Noblett's sweet shops were among the first places to be hit. One of the more famous pieces of loot was a toffee axe, used

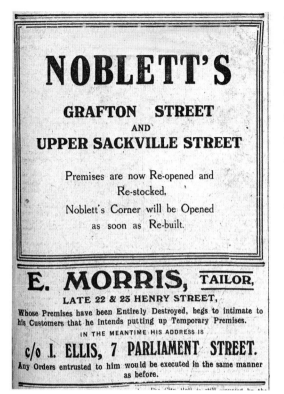

Advertisements like these for businesses destroyed during the Rising were prevalent in newspapers in the weeks that followed. Premises such as the famous sweetshop at Noblett's Corner and the tailor's E. Morris suffered extensive damage and looting, Evening Herald, *10 May 1916.*

to break up slabs of the delicacy – it was thrown at a passer-by, who eventually gave it to the National Museum. Children who could, in normal circumstances, only gaze at chocolate Easter eggs in Noblett's windows now had a slim chance of grabbing one of the leftovers on Easter Monday.

The shops attacked were mainly haberdashers, shoe shops, and sweet shops. Very many sweet shops were raided, and until the end of the rising sweet shops were the favourite mark of the looters. There is something comical in the looting of sweet shops—something almost innocent and child-like. Possibly most of the looters are children who are having the sole gorge of their lives. They have tasted sweet stuffs they had never toothed before, and will never taste again in this life, and until they die the insurrection of 1916 will have a sweet savour for them.[7]

The Dublin-born writer Sean O'Casey captures the almost carnival atmosphere that accompanied the Rising. As the 1,550 Rebels fought it out against over 20,000 British soldiers, civilians felt free to have a go at the shops.

The tinkle of breaking glass wandered down the whole street and people were pushing and pulling each other, till through broken windows all the treasures of India, Arabia, and Samarkand were open before them. [They] flung clothing all over the place; while one woman, stripped naked, was trying on camisole after camisole. All who were underdressed before were overdressed now.[8]

St John Greer Ervine, an author, playwright and manager of the Abbey Theatre, described in detail the looting as he walked around Dublin that week, but took a broader view of the mischief.

Some harsh things have been said about the looting, perhaps no harsher than ought to have been said, but I doubt whether in similar circumstances in any city in the world there would have been so little looting as there was in Dublin on those two days.

One tries to imagine what London would have been like if it had suddenly been completely abandoned for two days to the mercy of the mob. I think a Whitechapel mob would have sacked London in that time.

While I was standing in O'Connell Street,

The toffee axe looted from Noblett's sweet shop during the Rising.

73

Francis Sheehy Skeffington came up to me. He had half a dozen walking-sticks under his arm, and he said to me: 'I'm trying to form a special constabulary to prevent looting. You'll do for one,' and he offered a walking-stick to me. I looked at the stick and I looked at the looters and I said, 'No.'[9]

Most of the looting took place in and around Sackville Street and was in full flow by Monday evening. Nowhere was safe: grocers, butchers, pubs, clothing and shoe shops were hit with abandon, the looters driven by opportunity, hunger, need and sheer wonderment. Push, shove, grab, elbow, run, escape.

But the view of the Rebels towards their rampaging fellow city dwellers was of a darker hue. Sean T. O'Kelly – a future president of Ireland – was sent out from the GPO to stop the looters, but he was powerless against them. On his return, Commandant James Connolly admonished him: 'Shooting over their heads is useless. Unless a few of them are shot you won't stop them. I'll have to send someone over there who'll deal with the looters.'[10]

Thousands lived close to the main shopping area – and word quickly spread through the tenements that there was free stuff to be had. Looters complained that there were no police to stop thieves taking their looted goods; young boys were seen in silk hats mimicking Charlie Chaplin; children played with looted toy guns, uniforms and army hats and played 'Shoot the German' as the Rebels tried with real guns to shoot the British soldiers and vice versa.

Monsignor Michael Curran, the secretary to Archbishop Walsh of Dublin, noted:

As a result of my reports to His Grace on the recklessness of the people, especially of the women and children crowding the

THE MAN WHO WAS SHOT AND KILLED BY A CHILD DURING THE RISING

James Crawford Neil worked as a library assistant in the National Library of Ireland in Kildare Street in Dublin.

He was a poet, a pacifist and a Presbyterian, and was about to be married in 1916.

On Tuesday of Easter week, he was returning from the home of his fiancée in Glasthule to where he lived with his widowed mother in Fairview.

Avoiding Sackville Street by walking up Liffey Street, the family story goes that he came across children looting a sports shop and warned them that they might be shot for what they were doing. However, one of the children had an air rifle from the shop in his hand and it discharged, a pellet hitting James in the spine.

He was taken to nearby Jervis Street Hospital, in general good humour and spirits with a relatively minor injury. His condition gradually deteriorated, however, and he died on 10 May. Shortly before he died, he asked the hospital chaplain to perform the wedding ceremony to his fiancée 'Gyp' – the Abbey actress Patricia Walker, whose own family were involved in the Rising – but the priest refused as 'the bride will soon be a widow'.

streets in dangerous places, His Grace adopted my suggestion that notice should be sent to the local parish priests and to the churches of the religious, asking the Catholic people to observe this caution. With great difficulty the notice was printed and circulated. In making this suggestion to the Archbishop I had in mind the widespread looting in and about O'Connell Street.[11]

John Joly, professor of geology and mineralogy at Trinity, recorded:

It was related that looting was going on on a most disgraceful scale. Shops of all sorts were broken open and the goods freely distributed to the citizens of the Irish Republic. Men stripped off their old clothes and dressed themselves anew in the open streets, donning fashionable suits. Women selected jewels for their personal adornment, and rich and rare were the gems they wore on toil-stained fingers and grimy wrist. Watches were carried off heaped in aprons. Toys were given to the young. Fruit and champagne and other expensive luxuries were freely partaken of. The wines were in some cases retailed for a few pence a bottle. Bookshops only were immune from attack. It is related that some officers captured by the Rebels on Monday were conveyed by the enemy to a tobacconist's shop, and, with true Irish hospitality were treated to the best cigars, the owner of the shop having fled.[12]

INCIDENTS OF THE DUBLIN RISING.

Gold watches were sold for a shilling each.

Only the giant pillars of the Post Office remain.

The Metropole and Imperial Hotels are wrecked.

The Liberty Hall secretary is among the prisoners.

A sort of Press Bureau has been opened in Dublin.

Looted cigars sold at 1s per box.

An 18-pounder was used to demolish barricades on Phibsborough Bridge.

In a cavalry charge down Sackville Street, which cleared the barricades, the only losses were two horses.

It is understood that the casualties among the troops have been numerous.

It is stated that many of the Sinn Feiners who started out on the "route march" of Easter Monday had no idea that rebellion was intended that day.

It is calculated that the damage amounts to £2,000,000, and people are concerned to know whether the Government will give financial help to enable the street to resume its business when the rebellion is finished. Most of the firms have lost practically all their capital in this demolition, and will hardly be able to start again without assistance.

Report of looting during the Rising, Dundee Courier, *3 May 1916.*

Riddall's Row (Moore Street), c. 1913.

The claims by businesses after the Rising to the Property Losses (Ireland) Committee detail what was looted. O'Gormans at 15 Moore Street lost '2,000 Woodbine cigarettes, 500 Player's, 300 Gold Flake and 700 Park Drive . . . Cogans lost all its stock, valued £780. Other shops in Moore Street lost tins of Jacob's biscuits, John West salmon, Oxo cubes, fruit, pickles and jam!'[13]

It seems that young Paddy Fetherston, his brother and pals headed down Dominick Street towards Great Britain Street (now Parnell Street). Coles Lane, Henry Place, Simpsons Lane, Canes Court, Denmark Street, Moore Street, Masons Market, Anglesea Market, Horseman's Row and Riddall's

Anglesea Market (Coles Lane-Henry Street and Parnell Street), c. 1913.

Row, between Henry Street and Great Britain Street, were a warren of indoor and outdoor markets, selling second-hand clothes, hats, haberdashery, beds, furniture, boots, fruit, meat and vegetables. Everything from skinned rabbits to empty tea chests and second- or third-hand clothes was to be bargained for in this Aladdin's cave in the heart of Dublin.

And people not only traded but lived there – 343 people lived in Coles Lane, a hundred in Riddall's Row, seventy-two in Horseman's Row. The Anglesea Market may have had only seven houses – but twenty-eight people lived there. Even Simpsons Lane, with only two houses, had twenty-four inhabitants, while forty-seven people crowded into the six houses in Masons Market. Today, this whole area is covered by the ILAC Centre, but then in the small area between Moore Street (where sixty-two families comprising 338 people lived) and Great Britain Street (now gone) there were fifteen lanes, cul-de-sacs and streets, all bustling microcosms of the throbbing city. On the pavements in the narrow lanes, there was bargaining, haggling, buying and selling. It was a magnet of noise, smells and colour in an otherwise grey and drab Dublin.

Even Henry Street, a shopping thoroughfare then as now, had fourteen families living there – a total of seventy-six people – while the much smaller Henry Place boasted twenty-two families with a total of 108 people in five tenement houses!

Look at the Dublin of 1916 another way: where the ILAC Centre now stands was home to the busiest market in the city and to more than a thousand men, women and children![14]

Boys with their boxcar, c. 1910. Paddy Fetherston was playing with something similar with his friends before he died.

And it was to this Mecca that Paddy Fetherston, with his boxcar and his screaming pals, headed when the sounds of gunfire, horses charging, battle and mayhem spread from the GPO to the top of O'Connell Street. They had reached the bottom of Dominick Street, opposite Coles Lane, when Paddy was hit in the thigh by a bullet. One family member believes he was scavenging in a shop at the time. His friends immediately ran back to Long Lane to fetch Annie, his mother.

In the tenements, Monday was always washday, a tiring job done by the mother in a large metal tub before the open fire.

My mother used to do her washing and you hated Monday because everything was getting done in one room. There was a washing-board and she stood over the big vat of washing and brought the water to the boil and she had a big stick and she'd beat the clothes down, down, and they were snow white. And she'd iron them then. She had two irons. They were heavy and you'd put them into the fire. And the sweat used to be pouring off her it was so hot. On Monday she'd be in terrible bad form, she was so tired and so weary.[15]

Annie Fetherston was now thirty-five, the handywoman of Dominick Street who greeted the newborn and prepared the newly dead for the grave. Now she was about to face another death – but this time it was her own child's.

Annie dashed from Long Lane to her stricken son and immediately sprang into action. Seeing that Paddy was bleeding heavily, she bundled him into his boxcar and began to make her way towards nearby Jervis Street Hospital. But the commotion made the journey long, dangerous and arduous. By the time she got to the hospital, Paddy had already bled to death.

His death certificate states that he died from a 'bullet through thigh, shock and haemorrhage'.[16]

Annie and her husband Patrick took away their twelve-year-old son's remains on a handcart. Paddy's older brother, John – 'Jack' – aged fourteen, was a member of the Republican Boy Scouts, Na Fianna, and was acting as a runner between the GPO and the Four Courts. He was distraught at the news of his brother's death. Family say he draped a 'Republican flag' over Paddy's coffin. They believe it to have been the first time it was used during the Rising.

Na Fianna was founded by Countess Markievicz and Bulmer Hobson, a twenty-six-year-old Quaker from Belfast and a supporter of Irish nationalism. They believed that the organisation, which would encourage the outdoor adventure and exploration that Robert Baden-Powell had championed, could be built 'into a strong force to help in the liberation of Ireland'.[17] In 1916, it had around 500 members. However, a week before Easter Sunday, Bulmer Hobson opposed the Rising: '. . . no man had a right to risk the fortunes of the country in order to create for himself a niche in history.'[18]

Twelve-year-old John Henery McNamara and his family lived in a tenement in York Street. Being loyalists, they would have revelled in the visit of King George V and Queen Mary to Dublin in 1911.

John's father, Henery McNamara, gave his place of birth as Dublin, and his mother, Lucy, was from Ballycassidy, Enniskillen in County Fermanagh; their family believe they met when working in the Hamilton Hotel, Bundoran, where Henery was a waiter. John, their second oldest child, was born in Fermanagh but raised in Dublin, living close to the quality shops of the south city, and a hundred yards from every child's dream, Noblett's sweet shop at the top of Grafton Street, just down from the vaudevillian delights of the thriving Gaiety Theatre.

John McNamara and his pals might only have been able to gaze longingly into the windows of Grafton Street – but they owned the streets. They would weave their way through cyclists, horse-drawn vans and carts, trams and the few noisy delivery trucks, often with homemade boxcars made from wood and old bicycle wheels. And all around Grafton Street was heaven: Woolworths, Switzers, the Cairo Café, Weirs, Knowles, the high-class fruiterer, Martelares, the French cake shop, and the Turkish baths. The scents of coffee, pastry and fruit mingled with the perfumes worn by the wealthy to make it the most fragrant thoroughfare in a city of stench and decay.

Henery McNamara, a man who worked in hotels and liked to gamble, described himself as a casual labourer in the 1911 Census. The McNamaras were one of 267 families living in the forty-three hulking tenement houses on York Street, adjoining St Stephen's Green; 171 of the 1,052 tenants on the street were Protestant, including the McNamaras. They had settled well, and were active members of the St Peter's Church of Ireland congregation in nearby Aungier Street, becoming friendly with Catherine McSorley, the hymn writer and historian. While the conditions the McNamaras lived in were appalling, Lucy McNamara had, like so many other tenement women, made the best of the family's one room.

From the 1911 Census, this family had suffered more than most. Henery and Lucy had married in 1896, and Lucy had given birth to seven children, of whom only three were still alive in 1911.[19] The family had arrived in Dublin sometime around 1908: William, the youngest, was born in the city. The family of five lived in their one room at number 13 York Street – eight families lived in the seven rooms in the three-storey house. Lucy suffered with crippling arthritis all her life and, for many years until her death, had to use a wheelchair. The family made no bones about their support for the Crown – and their dislike of the insurrection:

Lucy McNamara.

Dublin people never wanted the insurrection. Sure it was only a short time since they had seen 'God Save the King and Queen' lit by gas on top of the Bank of Ireland to welcome the King and Queen of the Empire in great acclamation. Indeed the same applied to Edward VII when he came to the Phoenix Park races. So there was still a lot of loyalty in Dublin to the Crown.[20]

York Street was at the heart of the fighting – beside the battle in St Stephen's Green, where the Rebels dug trenches to fight the British troops in the Shelbourne Hotel, a pointless and bloody strategy. The Royal College of Surgeons was also used, and the Rebels erected barricades in York Street, much to the annoyance of many of the thousand people living there. 'Most people got their furniture back in York Street after the Rebels had finished their blockade of the road. It was a question of parting with your bits and pieces or be shot by these people.'[21]

We can only imagine the hunger that would have gripped those who lived on York Street by Friday, hemmed in all week by the constant gun battles. Attempts were made to get more bread into the city centre. Sir Simon Maddock, the secretary of Mount Jerome Cemetery, bought a 'van load of bread to distribute' but before he could he 'was chased into the cemetery – and to appease the crowd he distributed over 1,000 loaves'.[22]

While most of the looting took place around Sackville Street, Grafton Street, the city's most exclusive thoroughfare, did not escape:

On Thursday morning, the top of Grafton Street was the scene of operations. During the night of Wednesday the corner sweet shop was raided but on Thursday morning shortly after eight o'clock, as I was passing through, the work was being started methodically and in real earnest. I found afterwards however that the looters were unable to get further down the street than Knowles fruit shop. The street here makes a bend which brings it within view of Trinity College and I was told that a rifle volley definitely put an end to the industry as far as Grafton Street was concerned.[23]

John McNamara had gone to Grafton Street for food on the Friday of the Rising and, according to his family, was shot 'as he was peeling an orange ... there was a belief that he may have stolen it'.[24] His death certificate states he died from 'gunshot wound to the head, lacerated brain'.[25]

The anger of the McNamara family at the killing of John was never hidden:

> [It was] a rebellion which killed a lot of innocent people, including my uncle John, who was killed in Stephen's Green at the age of twelve and a half. There was only one person allowed to follow the hearse to the graveyard. No doubt on account of the many deaths, and to this day no one has ever apologised for the slaughter of the innocents. The leaders of the so-called rebellion and their children's children have a lot to answer for.[26]

After John's death, the loyalty of the McNamara family to the Crown was surely broken by the response they got from the Rebellion (Victims) Committee. Lucy McNamara applied for financial help after her son 'was shot while crossing Grafton Street during the rebellion'.

To the Chief Secretary,
Dear Sir,
Referring to the ten pounds received from you on the 11th May

compensation for the life and loss of my son which barely covered funeral expenses. I sincerely thank you but I do not consider it by any means sufficient. My lad would be earning now and would not be long earning that small amount as I explained in my application. I have been an invalid since his birth and his father is in bad-paying employment. I did not employ a solicitor but left it entirely to the generosity of the rebellion committee whom I expected to give me something that would help me to a little business. Trusting you will see your way to consider my call,

I remain your humble servant,

Lucy McNamara

She received no reply, or any more than the miserly ten pounds already granted.

Lucy McNamara died a few hundred yards from her home in the Adelaide Hospital, Bishop Street, on 20 July 1939. Although she relied on a wheelchair, she was still an active homemaker and helped out in her local church and at St Peter's School in Aungier Street. Her husband Henery died in 1944.

A relative said, 'They were a very poor family so I don't think there would be a headstone in Mount Jerome, and I never looked to see where John Henery might be buried.'[27]

Nowhere was safe as the population rampaged.

The act of looting in a city under fire, with buildings collapsing from incessant shelling, was a very risky undertaking. Those availing themselves of the chaos, smoke and confusion to take food, drink and clothes were also taking their lives into their own hands, as we have seen from Paddy Fetherston's killing. Research shows clearly that women were at the forefront of the looting. The number of women arrested in January, February,

NAIRN NATIVE KILLED BY DUBLIN REBELS

WHO CAME TO LOOT HIS SHOP.

A SURVIVOR OF LUSITANIA DISASTER.

Intimation has been received at Nairn that Mr Robert Anderson Mackenzie, grocer, youngest son of the late Mr John Mackenzie, sheriff officer, Nairn, was shot on 27th April by the rebels, who came to loot his shop in Cavendish Row, Dublin. In trying to resist them he was shot through the heart.

Mr Mackenzie was one of the survivors of the Lusitania disaster, and prior to taking up business in Dublin was in business in Manchester.

Article describing how a shopkeeper who had survived the sinking of the Lusitania *died during looting in the Rising,* Dundee Courier, *10 May 1916.*

March and April 1916 hovered just below the norm of 20 per cent of alleged lawbreakers in Dublin. In May, it jumped to 57 per cent, and in June fell back to 27 per cent. In the weeks after the Rising to the end of June, 633 people were charged with offences relating to looting.

Put another way, in February and March 1916, 343 Dublin people were charged with theft, but in May and June the comparable figure jumped to 873 – a 160 per cent increase – but presumably this is not the full picture.[28] The retreat of the police from the streets meant that a lot of crime went undetected and unreported, but the miscreants were back in action as the Rising ended on the eve of May Day and were scouring the city for goods to steal. 'Women accounted for 80 per cent of all those arrested for looting. In May 1916 married women (including widows) overtook British Army deserters and juveniles as the largest group of offenders in the city.'[29]

Bullet-pierced bedroom window in Northumberland Road, Dublin.

The occupations of those arrested for looting give us other insights into who was leading the rampage. Married women and widows comprised 51 per cent of those charged, while 'vagrants', mostly women, made up 14 per cent. 'Messengers', a job normally associated with boys, were also over-represented.

Within hours of the outbreak of the Rising, Corporation Buildings had become a killing zone. It was also where a number of looters emerged into North Earl Street, and for the rich pickings around Sackville Street. John Uzell lived in Corporation Buildings:

I was only eight years old when the trouble of 1916, the Rebellion, was on. Word had spread around that the IRA were after taking over the GPO and that there was lots of gunfire going on all over O'Connell Street. So I went out onto the street to have a look and I saw lots of people running down Talbot Street, carrying all sorts of things in their hands. They were after looting them from the shops in the streets. So I ran up towards O'Connell Street and on the way up I was told by someone not to go up any further as the British Army were shooting at people that were taking things out of the shop windows. I thought, Sure they won't shoot me, I am only a little boy, so up I went. I ran over to this confectioner's shop called Nobletts on O'Connell Street. There was shooting going on all around me. The British soldiers were hiding in the doorways firing at the IRA volunteers. I remember the shop window was blown in so I grabbed this wooden box from it and made a run for it. The bullets were flying all over the place but I did not care. Being only eight years old at the time, I didn't realise the danger of what I was doing. I ran down Talbot Street with the box in my hands and I ran all the way home with it. When I opened it there was nothing in it! To think, I nearly got shot for stealing nothing![30]

Workmen remove debris from buildings destroyed or damaged during the Easter Rising, on Dublin's Upper Sackville Street (O'Connell Street).

4. A World at War

THE BATTLES ON THE WESTERN FRONT WERE RAGING DURING
1916 – BUT AS THEIR OLDER RELATIVES SERVED IN THE GREAT WAR,
AT HOME ELEANOR WARBROOK, MARY KELLY AND PATRICK
RYAN WOULD DIE ON THE STREETS WHERE THEY LIVED.

In the years leading up to 1916, many in the Republican movement seized on the Great War as the distraction they needed to strike at the heart of the British Empire but, for many Dublin families, the war was not a distraction but a disaster. Several families were dreading bad news from the battlefields of Europe where their loved ones were fighting in British Army uniform. Bad news was coming for some – but from much closer to home. That week, they would lose a child to war on the Dublin streets where they lived and played.

For many Dubliners, there were two ways out of tenement life: the British Army or the British mainland. In late 1914, two of my great-uncles, Tom and Christopher 'Kit' Carroll, walked from their tenement room at 89 Church Street to the British Army recruiting office in Brunswick Street and, along with 53,000 others, joined the Royal Dublin Fusiliers.

September 1916, The Irish Brigade, some wearing captured German helmets, pictured after taking Guillemont, the Fricourt-Maricourt road.

In early 1915, they were shipped off to France. Uncle Tom survived the war and returned to Dublin with a bullet lodged in his shoulder. Kit was not so lucky: within weeks of landing in France he survived the notorious gas attack at Mousetrap Farm, near Ypres, only to die a year later in Bienvillers on the Somme, six days before the outbreak of the Easter Rising.

On 10 May 1916, the Carroll family placed a death notice for Kit in the *Evening Herald* – it was barely noticeable among those for the civilian dead of Easter week: 'Carroll, April 18th 1916, killed in action. Christopher Carroll, 89 Upper Church Street; deeply regretted by his sorrowing mother, father, sisters and brothers. R.I.P. Sacred Heart of Jesus, have mercy on his soul.' Interestingly, there was no mention of the war or the British Army. Christopher Carroll was one of 6,345 Dubliners killed in the First World War; more than 5,000 of whom were members of the Royal Dublin Fusiliers.[1]

Ten of the children killed in Easter week – Bridget Allen, Charles Darcy, Patrick 'Paddy' Fetherston, Sean Francis Foster, Neville Fryday, Mary Kelly, John Kirwan, Patrick Ryan, Eleanor Warbrook and Christopher Hickey – had close relatives involved in the Great War.

Private John Foster, the father of two-year-old Sean, the youngest victim, had already been killed in northern France when his son – with whom he had spent only a few months – was shot dead on Easter Monday afternoon.

Paddy Fetherston's uncle, Sergeant Joseph Gaynor, was a career army officer, a noted disciplinarian. Paddy's mother, Annie, was still mourning her twelve-year-old son when Joseph, her only brother, was killed in Flanders on 2 August 1918.

Neville Fryday, aged sixteen, was on his way to France to fight in the khaki of his Canadian Army uniform. He had been born in Tipperary, then gone with his widowed mother to Canada. He had joined the army there before travelling with his unit to England en route to the battlefields of France. He had a few days' leave before he went to France and had sailed to Dublin for Easter 1916 to see his mother, who had recently returned to Ireland. He was shot outside Trinity College as he walked across the city.

A parade to encourage recruitment for the Royal Dublin Fusiliers at the outbreak of the First World War, c. *1914.*

Charles Darcy wore the uniform of Na Fianna and had a brother, James, who would be decorated for his war efforts for Britain. The father of John Kirwan – the boy with the toy elephant – was with the Royal Navy when his son was killed on Easter Monday.

For the Warbrook family in Fumbally Lane, 1916 had already been a traumatic year. On New Year's Day, word had arrived that their second son, seventeen-year-old John, 'Boy 1st class', who had joined the Royal Navy the previous year, had been killed before he even left for the high seas. An accidental explosion on HMS *Natal* in Cromarty, Scotland, on 30 December 1915 sank the ship, killing 390 sailors and up to thirty other people visiting the vessel that day. Just a 114 days later, John's younger sister Eleanor, aged fifteen, was killed outside her home on Fumbally Lane on the first afternoon of the Easter Rising.

Within a few months, a third Warbrook child had fallen victim to a world at war: Thomas, aged nineteen, had left his job at the nearby Jacob's biscuit factory to join the Canadian Army and was killed on the Western Front. So in 1916, Bridget and Thomas Warbrook lost their two oldest sons and their third youngest daughter to war.

Fumbally Lane, near St Patrick's Cathedral, where the Protestant Warbrook family worshipped in the heart of Dublin's Liberties, is one of the capital's most historic streets. James Joyce mentions it in *Ulysses*, remarking on the 'tanyard smells' – Fumbally Lane was at the heart of Dublin's brewing, distilling and tanning industries. The pungent, hoppy smells, mingled with the aroma of roasting barley and the stomach-turning stench of knackers' yards and abattoirs, all wafted through the area, adding piquancy to the 'normal' Dublin fragrances of animal and human waste. Guinness, Jameson, Roes, Powers, Watkins and Barmacks were not just household names in the

Some rebels lying in wait on a roof getting ready to fire during the Easter Rising in 1916.

Dublin of a century ago: for the people of Fumbally Lane and the Liberties, they provided vital employment. As recently as 2006, archaeologists discovered evidence of medieval tanning near Fumbally Lane, which today is a quirky, trendy part of the city and now the home of Dublin's first new distillery in more than a hundred years.

It was Fumbally Lane's strategic location and high buildings, in the warren of alleys around New Street, that sealed the fate of the Warbrook family. First, it was a key route for British reinforcements from Portobello Barracks to Dublin Castle and the GPO. Second, the high buildings provided superb vantage points for Rebel snipers.

By 1911, Eleanor Warbrook was living with her parents at 5 Malpas Terrace, the narrow lane that connects Malpas Street to Fumbally Lane, just off New Street. It was her father's second marriage, which, of course, was not unusual in Dublin at the time, with many people succumbing to illness in their twenties and thirties. Antibiotics, which would have cured some, were not available until after the Second World War.

Thomas Warbrook was originally from Rhode in County Offaly but subsequently moved to County Meath, where his family had worked on the Beauparc estate of the Lambert family. He married Margaret Walker in 1879, and they had three children before she died six years later. In 1886, he married Bridget Mangan, and they had eight children. Eleanor was born in April 1901 – the same year her sixteen-year-old half-brother William died; Thomas was then forty-five.

In 1901, the expanding Warbrook family were living at 11 Wards Hill in the Liberties, a house once occupied by Irish Citizen Army leader Michael Mallin. In the 1911 Census, the parents and six children, including two further arrivals, Mabel and Beatrice, occupied 5 Malpas Terrace, just 500 yards from their first address in the Liberties. James, the oldest, was twenty-eight, married, working as a warehouseman and living in Aughrim Street, while Georgina, aged twenty, was a live-in servant at 31 Brighton Road, Rathmines, for James Cameron Smail and his family. In 1911, their brother Thomas was working at the nearby Jacob's biscuit factory but, by 1916, he had emigrated to Canada. In 1915, like many other Irishmen, he had enlisted in the 14th Battalion of the Canadian Infantry (Quebec Regiment) and was killed in France on 6 September 1916.[2]

At some point after 1911, the family moved around the corner from Malpas Terrace to Fumbally Lane. We don't know why – perhaps with Thomas working as a horse and cart driver and iron merchant, his daughter Anne, employed as a 'veterinary chemist assistant', and two other children also in paid employment, they could afford their own house – but we do know that it made all the difference to the family.

In 1916, Malpas Terrace didn't feature in the fighting – but Fumbally Lane was the scene of a fierce battle between local residents and the Rebels. Indeed, a number of Rebels subsequently spoke about 'the battle of Fumbally Lane', even though the British forces never engaged with them there.

When Seosamh de Brún, a member of the 2nd Battalion Dublin Brigade Irish Volunteers left his home in Irishtown on Easter Monday morning, he didn't know if the insurrection – which had been postponed the previous day – would go ahead.

Easter Monday morning gave promise of an ideal holiday. Brilliant sunshine and warm dry weather invited one to the mountains or seaside. Turning over in my mind which I should choose, as I left the house I noticed at the corner of Seville Place a group of volunteers in uniform.

Seems like a company mobilisation, I thought. Going over, I asked was such the case; they replied they had orders to mobilise. I decided to go to Fairview Park and at Newcomen Bridge met Captain Weafer cycling towards the city. Hailing him, I enquired if the parade was general. 'Yes,' replied the Captain. 'Get over to Stephen's Green. The 2nd Battalion mobilises there at 11 o'clock.'

I will be late for this parade, I thought – for it wanted only a couple of minutes to the hour. I went back hotfoot to the house in Amiens Street, stripped myself hurriedly of my holiday attire and got into service rig. I took the precaution of taking extra accoutrement, for somehow I felt anything might happen though the actual rising was far from my thoughts. I jumped on a tram for the Pillar, another to St Stephen's Green. I got there at 11.20. A large number of volunteers had assembled, others were arriving, the mobilisation I perceived had only begun.[3]

Seosamh de Brún, in his well-written account of his part in the Rising, describes the scene in St Stephen's Green and the beginning of the rebellion:

About twelve o'clock Commandants Hunter, MacDonagh and other officers were moving briskly about; suddenly we got the order to fall in and quick march.

We right turned into Cuffe Street and, in somewhat loose military order, proceeded to Kevin Street. Alongside those I marched was Sam Ellis on a hackney car, his arms around a heavy-looking box which I surmised was ammunition. When we came to Jacob's biscuit factory part of the troops commanded by Thomas MacDonagh took possession of the building; the large section in which I marched were to cross Kevin Street past the police barracks to New Street, down Fumbally Lane where we took possession of Barmacks buildings which we put immediately into a state of defence. Extra ammunition was distributed. On the top floor where the windows commanded the approach to Blackpitts, we were paraded by Commandant Thomas Hunter who in short characteristic address said: 'Men, the Irish Republic has been proclaimed in Dublin today; we are in action. The headquarters of the Irish Republican Army is at the General Post Office which has been taken possession of by Republican troops. We are fighting to establish the Irish Republic. I trust every man here will give loyal and obedient service and will acquit himself as a gallant soldier in the cause of Irish independence.' We were standing to attention. We relaxed, a loud cheer rang through the building, some saluted, others raised their guns; one, a recruit evidently, called for spiritual ministration, thinking he was going to be sent at once to his maker. An order was issued, windows were smashed, glass crashed, rifles were thrust out in search of appropriate positions; the realisation we were in action was swiftly upon us.

The people of the neighbourhood gathered with lively curiosity. They seemed at a loss to know whether we were in action or merely on manoeuvres; as the day wore on they began to realise the seriousness of their position especially when a tall Volunteer not quite seasoned to arms during a false alarm that the British were approaching let his Howth gun fall to the ground; a charge was released with a report that made his comrades as well as a number of the people jump with shock. It was the first shot, although an accidental one, fired by our lot.

One chap declared that it nearly took the tip of his ear off. After this the people kept a respectful distance, though numbers considered at the time to be British soldiers' dependants or sympathisers were definitely hostile. Several times they essayed to tear down the barricades; our men displayed great good temper. It was the first real lesson in actual discipline we learned. It was justified, as before the week was out those very people were madly enthusiastic in the cause of the Irish Republic.[4]

It's hard to underestimate the animosity that existed in some sections of society in Dublin towards the 'separation women' – the wives and mothers of those away fighting with the British Army: 'From 1914 a new figure on the Irish scene became an odious symbol of British rule, and a symbol overtook the prostitute in the public understanding of immorality.'[5] The wives of soldiers away at war were known pejoratively as 'ring-women' because they had to present a booklet, bound with a ring, at the Post Office to col-

Soldier's Separation Allowances: 'Increased Rates from 1 March, 1915.'

lect their vital weekly separation allowance.[6]

In the Warbrook family, two sons had joined the army, one of whom was already dead, and another son, John, was in the Royal Navy, until he was killed.

The figures for the number of Dublin families dependent on the allowance are unclear. In one survey conducted by Dublin Corporation of north-inner-city tenements, just under 4,000 heads of households were labourers, earning between seven and sixty shillings per week, but nearly 2,000 families indicated that their main source of income was the 'separation allowance' of between six and sixty shillings per week.[7]

Does this mean that, during the war, 50 per cent of Dublin's inner-city families were getting some form of war payment from the

British Army? Easter week coincided with the first anniversary of the attack on St-Julien where the Royal Dublin Fusiliers had suffered heavy casualties. One can only imagine the heightened family sensitivities during that week.

Throughout Easter Monday, the main difficulty the fifty Rebels faced in Fumbally Lane was from the local residents. Ominously, and unusually, there are three separate admissions by the Rebels that civilians were shot. In Bureau of Military

Women and children queuing outside the post office on Aungier Street to collect their separation allowance, which was paid to women whose husbands and sons were serving in the British Army, c. 1916.

History statements, Volunteers describe the hostile atmosphere in the area. According to Volunteer Thomas Pugh, the women were like 'French Revolution furies'.[8]

Volunteer Michael Walker recalled, 'The inhabitants of Blackpitts were very hostile, singing and dancing to English songs of a quasi-patriotic type – pelted stones at us and generally showed great opposition which eventually culminated in an attack on a Volunteer by a man who formed one of the crowd with the object of disarming the Volunteer. This man was shot and bayoneted, I believe fatally.'[9]

Volunteer Vincent Byrne – a fifteen-year-old from Errigal Road in Crumlin, who revealed that he had cried the previous day when the Rising was called off – was possibly describing the same incident when he wrote, 'Lots of soldiers' wives and I suspect imperialistic people – men and women – came around us. They jeered and shouted. One man in the crowd was very aggressive, he tried to grab the rifle off one of our party. Lieutenant Billy Byrne told him to keep off or he would be sorry. The man however made a grab at the rifle. I heard a shot ring out and saw him falling at the wall.'[10]

At Jacob's biscuit factory around the corner, one Volunteer, Martin Walton – who was only sixteen, mentioned the anger of the locals as they jeered, 'Get off and fight in France, you crowd of slackers.' He described one woman's face 'exploding' after she was shot by a Volunteer from the window of the biscuit factory as she raised a stick to hit another Volunteer at the door. It was the first blood he saw shed. This is undoubtedly Eleanor Warbrook, who died from gunshot wounds to her face.[11]

Volunteer John J. Murphy revealed, 'It was then between 3.30 and 4 o'clock. Hunter [the local Rebel commander] informed me that he was after having trouble at the junction of New Street/Kevin Street/Patrick Street, that some civilians had become very aggressive towards our men and that they had

Letter from Bridget Warbrook, Eleanor's mother, to the chief secretary's office, Dublin Castle enquiring about compensation for the death of her daughter, 23 February 1917.

attacked one of the Volunteers, and in order to save his life they had to shoot one of the civilians.'[12]

We can only surmise as to when Eleanor Warbrook was shot 'through the L. Jaw and Naso Pharynx' and killed,[13] but we can be fairly certain she died in the nearby Meath Hospital between noon and 8 p.m. as, by nightfall, all the Rebels had withdrawn to the Jacob's factory, having encountered hostility from locals. In his papers, Walter Hume Long, a British Unionist politician, who was chief secretary for Ireland, recorded, 'Civilians, all unarmed, Eleanor Warbrook, Fumbally Lane, shot on the street.'[14]

As we can see from the many Rebel witness statements, there are references to hostility, jeering, abuse and bottle and missile

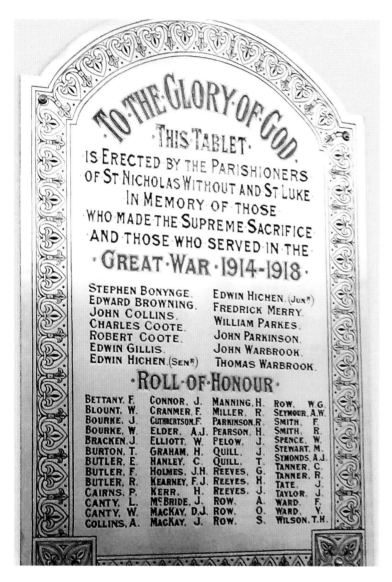

To the Glory of God. This Tablet is erected by the parishioners of St Nicholas Without and St Luke in memory of those who made the supreme sacrifice and those who served in the Great War 1914–1918.

Stephen Bonynge. Edward Browning. John Collins. Charles Coote. Robert Coote. Edwin Gillis. Edwin Hichen (Senr). Edwin Hichen (Junr). Fredrick Merry. William Parkes. John Parkinson. John Warbrook. Thomas Warbrook.

Roll of Honour

Bettany, F. Blount, W. Bourne, J. Bourke, W. Bracken, J. Burton, T. Butler, E. Butler, F. Butler, R. Cairns, P. Canty, L. Canty, W. Collins, A. Connor, J. Cranmer, F. Cuthbertson, F. Elder, A.J. Elliott, W. Graham, H. Hanley, C. Holmes, J.H. Kearney, F.J. Kerr, H. McBride, J. Mackay, D.J. Mackay, J. Manning, H. Miller, R. Parkinson, R. Pearson, H. Pelow, J. Quill, J. Quill, T. Reeves, G. Reeves, H. Reeves, J. Row, A. Row, O. Row, S. Row, W.G. Seymour, A.W. Smith, F. Smith, R. Spence, W. Stewart, M. Symonds, A.J. Tanner, C. Tanner, R. Tate, J. Taylor, J. Ward, F. Ward, V. Wilson, T.H.

Memorial plaque in Donore Avenue church listing among the dead John and Thomas Warbrook, Eleanor Warbrook's brothers.

throwing from the locals – but no engagement with the British!

Rebels reported that: 'The residents of Fumbally Lane even followed the retreating Volunteers to Jacob's, knocking off their hats and kicking them – and then tried to attack the Jacob's garrison by attempting to smash down the gate and attempting to burn it down with a sack doused in paraffin.'[15]

The *Irish Independent* reported: 'As far as could be ascertained on Easter Monday night the total number of dead and seriously wounded in the various city hospitals were dead 21, wounded 36.' Listed among the dead was 'Ella Warbrook, 7 Fumbally Lane (Jervis Street Hospital)'.[16]

The parents of Eleanor Warbrook claimed £130 compensation for the killing of their daughter.[17] On 23 February 1917, Eleanor's mother wrote from 'Fumbally Lane, off New Street' to the chief secretary's office in Dublin Castle:

Sir,

I take the liberty of enquiring if any further steps are necessary on my part with respect to my claim for compensation consequent on the death by shooting on Monday 24th April of my daughter Eleanor Warbrook.

A form was sent last Nov., which I duly filled up and returned to the Chief Secretary's Office but have not since had any communication.

I am Sir, your most obedient Servant,

Bridget Warbrook.

They were awarded fifty pounds (jointly) by the Rebellion (Victims) Committee.

Tragedy struck the family again in 1927 when Georgina Warbrook, Eleanor's sister, died by suicide in Fumbally Lane. A newspaper article reported: 'A verdict of suicide while insane was returned at an inquest in the Meath Hospital concerning the death of Georgina Frances Warbrook (37) Fumballys Lane, New Street. Thomas Warbrook, father of the deceased, said she had been rather strange in the manner for the past three weeks. On going to her bedroom at 2.40 p.m. on Tuesday, the witness found her lying on her back in the bed under the clothes. There was blood on her hand. Garda England deposed to finding an open razor in deceased's right hand when he was called to the scene.' A doctor gave evidence that Georgina had cut her throat.[18]

Thomas, Eleanor's father, died in February 1929 aged seventy-three, from bronchitis and heart failure. He had outlived five of his children: William, Thomas, John, Eleanor and Georgina. His wife Bridget subsequently remarried and died in 1950. She is buried under her new married name, McCormack, in Dublin's Mount Jerome Cemetery with her daughters, except Eleanor, who is buried in an unmarked grave there.

The bodies of Thomas and John Warbrook were never recovered. John's name is inscribed on the naval memorial in Plymouth, while Thomas' appears on the Vimy Memorial in the Pas-de-Calais, France. John and Thomas Warbrook are also remembered on a plaque and on the wall of St Catherine's Protestant church in Donore Avenue, Dublin.

Margaret Naylor lay in an unmarked grave for ninety-six years, until the detective work of her grandson, Frank McNamee, led to its discovery on Thursday, 14 June 2012. He contacted me with her story.[19]

Margaret Naylor was not a child when she was shot – but the effect of her death on her children, Margaret, Kitty and Tessie, was catastrophic. They were orphaned in Easter week 1916. Their father, Private John Naylor of the Royal Dublin Fusiliers, was killed on Saturday, 29 April, in France, the same day that his wife was caught in crossfire on Ringsend Drawbridge (now Victoria Bridge). He had been one of the 538 Irish soldiers killed in a gas attach at Hulluch, in Flanders. Accounts of what happened on what was effectively the last day of the Rising vary: some say Margaret's three young children were with her when she was hit as she went out for some bread; others say her sister, Mary Bridget Liscombe, accompanied her. All agree, though, that the situation was so dangerous that Margaret lay on the bridge for five hours. A priest who attended her believed she was dead but when she was eventually carried by two men on a makeshift stretcher to St Vincent's Hospital in St Stephen's Green, it was discovered she was still alive – but she died two days later on Monday, 1 May, a week after the Rising had begun.

The extended Naylor family truly were victims of a world at war. Almost exactly a year earlier, John Naylor's brother, Lance Corporal James Naylor, aged twenty-three, married and living at East James Place off Baggot Street, was killed in Flanders. He is buried in the British Military Cemetery in Boulogne, Pas-de-Calais. Days before the end of the war, and a week after the sinking of the RMS *Leinster* in the Irish Sea by a German torpedo, another brother, Private William Naylor of the Royal Dublin Fusiliers, was killed in Flanders. He is buried in Ypres Reservoir Cemetery in Belgium.

The tragedy of the Naylor family was not to end there. Despite losing their father and two uncles in the Great War, the Naylor orphans were treated abysmally by Britain, the country for which so many of their close relatives had died. There followed a most egregious series of letters from the government's Rebellion (Victims) Committee when the orphans and the woman who was rearing them, Margaret's widowed sister Mary Bridget Liscombe, sought financial help. The government had 'awarded' nineteen shillings a week, made up of seven shillings for the oldest child and six shillings for the two younger children, adding, 'The allowance for each child ceases when she attains the age of 16 years.'[20] The committee also granted a once-off payment of £10 on 'compassionate grounds'!

Corrigan solicitors wrote to Dublin Castle on behalf of the Naylor orphans on 5 September 1917, pleading for help:

But for the death of Mrs Naylor she would also be in receipt of an allowance on the death of her husband, and as her children would be living with her they would receive benefit of this allowance. As a result of her death this has been lost. In addition to the loss of their mother the children have become orphans and they certainly should be made some compensation for this. Further if

Private John Naylor (left) and his wife and family. Naylor, of the Royal Dublin Fusiliers, was 'gassed in action' on 29 April 1916. Tragically, his wife was killed during the Rising on the very same day, leaving their three children orphaned, Evening Herald, 13 June 1916.

the father had not been killed a very substantial sum would have been paid to him for the death of his wife . . . The amount which is now being paid by the War Office is hardly adequate to keep them in food and clothing and it would be utterly impossible out of same to put by any sum however small for their future needs and benefit.[21]

Another pleading letter on behalf of the Naylor orphans the following month elicited this reply, written in the margins, from the government: 'I acknowledge and state that the facts of this case have been placed before the Treasury whose decision is final and that he regrets to be unable to reopen the case with their Lordships.'[22]

In March 1918, Alfie Byrne, MP for Dublin Harbour, raised this outrage in the House of Commons, but the minister for pensions, John Hodge, rejected the plea.[23]

Margaret Naylor died not knowing that her husband had become another casualty of the Great War, and her sister was left to rear six children, her own and Margaret's, aged between one and eleven.

Margaret was taken from the hospital on Wednesday, 3 May, to Grangegorman Military Cemetery in Blackhorse Avenue.

Restrictions on the number of mourners meant that the story and the burial place were lost to family members for nearly a century.

It wasn't easy for Bridget Liscombe to raise the three Naylor children as well as her own boys. Eventually Tessie and Kitty married and settled down, but Margaret led a difficult life. In the late 1920s she was committed to Grangegorman mental asylum after she had tried to stab her stepfather; she remained in institutions until 1957 and died in 1987. For a number of years she worked in Holles Street Hospital, a short distance from where her mother had been killed seventy-one years previously. Neither she nor her sisters knew where either parent was buried.

In 2012, the McNamee family, using information they took from a torn undertaker's receipt, finally found Margaret Naylor's grave and erected a headstone in the Grangegorman Military Cemetery, just outside the walls of the Phoenix Park on Blackhorse Avenue. Margaret lies with some of the 116 British soldiers killed during the Easter Rising; her husband is interred in Loos Cemetery in France.

Two children of soldiers serving in the British Army were killed in Easter week. We have the stark information on their death certificates but little else. Twelve-year-old Mary Kelly died on Sunday, 30 April in Lombard Street in the centre of Dublin, from a 'gunshot wound'. Her body was 'taken in charge' by Annie Cullen of 128.1 Townsend Street, a mother of three living in a busy tenement house – perhaps she was a relation. The certificate also tells us that Mary was the 'child of Pte. Driver Kelly A.S.C.' (the Army Service Corps). The record in Deans Grange Cemetery, where Mary is buried, tells us his name was Joseph, but little else.[24]

We have more detail about another child of a soldier who was killed in Easter week: Patrick Ryan, aged thirteen, from 2 Sitric Place in Dublin's Stoneybatter – just around the corner

Advertisement for the play Mrs Mulligan Again! *starring Jimmy O'Dea and Harry O'Donovan assisted by Patrick Ryan's sister, Connie,* Irish Independent, *7 December 1932.*

from where Sean Foster, the first child victim of the Rising, lived and died.

In the 1911 Census, Patrick was one of a family of five; two of his siblings predeceased him, and he had two sisters, Frances and Mary, one older, the other younger.

His father, James Ryan, originally from Kildare, and his wife Frances married in 1900 when they were in their early twenties. James found a job at Guinness as a drayman and, like many in the brewery, joined the British Army when the war broke out. Patrick's older sister, Mary, was born a year after their parents' marriage. Patrick died in Richmond Hospital, near Church Street, on Wednesday, 26 April from a 'gunshot wound to the abdomen [and] shock'.[25] His family believe he was shot in O'Connell Street. He was buried in Glasnevin Cemetery the following Tuesday, 2 May, alongside his grandmother and aunt.[26]

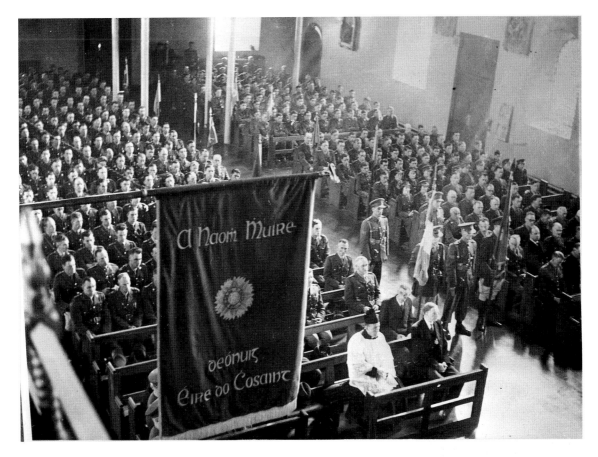

Glass plate negative showing Eamon de Valera sitting in the front row along with the congregation at Arbour Hill church during the Arbour Hill 1916 Ceremony, c. 1925. A flag party is present in front of the altar.

His grandmother, Jane Clarke, had died a year earlier from bronchitis, while tuberculosis had killed his aunt, Kathleen Clarke, in 1911; both were from Eustace Street in the Temple Bar area.

After Patrick's untimely death, his family applied to the Rebellion (Victims) Committee asking for a hundred pounds in compensation, stating that Patrick's father was in the Irish Guards Regiment of the British Army; the government awarded Frances Ryan twenty-five pounds.

James Ryan eventually returned to work at Guinness, and died at the age of forty-two, almost ten years after his son, on 30 January 1926. The family moved back into the city centre, where Frances, her two daughters and son, Michael, lived on St Stephen's Green. Frances 'Connie' Ryan, their eldest daughter, became a well-known dance troupe teacher. She trained Maureen Potter among others and was heavily involved in Jimmy O'Dea's theatrical productions. Her brothers, Michael and James – born after the 1911 census – were also involved in the theatrical variety scene in Dublin, which thrived from the 1930s to the 1950s.[27]

Patrick's mother, Frances, loved the theatrical world and was a regular in the Green Room bar in Poolbeg Street run by one of her sons. This was a well-known and highly regarded after-hours venue for the acting fraternity throughout the 1940s and early 1950s. Her family remember her as a 'stern, hard woman', who had suffered a lot during her life. She died in the early 1950s.

The neat, terraced house that Patrick Ryan lived in still stands on Sitric Place, just over the wall from where the signatories of the Easter Rebellion are buried in Arbour Hill.

The Great War lasted from 28 July 1914 until 11 November 1918, a total of four years, three months and two weeks. The Easter Rising lasted less than a week. But in that week in April 1916, a small area of Dublin had been, for children, the most dangerous war zone in the world.

Elvery's, Hotel Metropole and Post Office, Sackville Street, 18 May 1916.

The entrance to Trinity College being guarded by military during the Rising.

5. 'We Suffer in Their Coming and Their Going'[1]

REMARKABLE MOTHERS WERE AT THE HEART OF IRELAND IN 1916. THREE OF THEM SAW THEIR CHILDREN — NEVILLE FRYDAY, CHRISTINA CAFFREY AND BRIDGET ALLEN — DIE DURING EASTER WEEK.

Mother o' God, Mother o' God, have pity on us all! Blessed Virgin, where were you when me darlin' son was riddled with bullets, when me darlin' son was riddled with bullets? Sacred Heart o' Jesus, take away our hearts o' stone and give us hearts of flesh! Take away this murdherin' hate an' give us Thine own eternal love!

From *Juno and the Paycock* by Sean O'Casey

If Annie Fetherston of Long Lane was an example of a remarkable woman, battling against poverty in difficult times, what do we make of Elizabeth Ann Preston Wayland Kinnear, mother of thirteen, a horse trainer, who died in Toronto on Easter Monday 1942, twenty-six years after her sixteen-year-old son was shot outside Trinity College Dublin wearing the uniform of the Canadian Army on the first afternoon of the Easter Rising?

In 1946, the following notice appeared in the *Irish Independent*:

> Fryday. In loving remembrance of the best father and mother this earth could give, the late William Fryday, Tipperary, and Mrs Elizabeth Anne Preston Kinnear, who died in Toronto, Canada, Easter Monday 1942. To see her children and Tipperary the land that bred and fed us all, she crossed the Pacific twice and the Atlantic eleven times. With Christ, which is far better. Also in proud and loving remembrance of our brother Neville Fryday, aged 16 years, killed in the 1916 Rebellion. Neville gave his young life for the freedom that we all enjoy today – Mrs Meta Richardson.[2]

Elizabeth Anne Preston Wayland was born on 6 August 1864, to Palliser Wayland and Martha Rebecca Smithwick Manning. She married a farmer, William Jack Fryday, who was fifteen years her senior, in Ballintemple, County Tipperary, a week after Easter in April 1884, and gave birth to thirteen children before her husband was killed in a farm accident in April 1905. Elizabeth Fryday was widowed four months before Sarah Bristow was married. Nothing connected the two women until Easter week 1916.

If Dublin was notorious for its slum dwellings, Kavanagh's Court, near North King Street, was among the worst of the worst. Joseph Caffrey, one of six surviving children to the twelve born to his mother Margaret, and Sarah Bristow, his future wife, were neighbours in Kavanagh's Court. The buildings looked as if they were about to collapse, and the muddy, dank walkways were strewn with compacted horse and pig manure, sewage and other rubbish. It is little wonder that the street had disappeared by 1911 when the census was taken.

Kavanagh's Court, off Bow Street, off North King Street, c.1913.

In the 1901 Census, Sarah, like many other women in the city centre, was described as a 'dealer', which meant she sold fruit, vegetables or second-hand clothes from the side of the street. Then eighteen, she was living with her widowed mother, Lizzie, and three siblings, Christina, George and Sharlett, in a tenement at 11.3 Stirrup Lane. Six families – twenty-three people in all – shared six rooms.

In 1905, when she was twenty-one, Sarah Bristow married Joseph Caffrey, a labourer in a lime yard, at St Paul's Church on nearby Arran Quay.

By 1911, the Caffreys were living just around the corner from Annie Fetherston at 143 North King Street. Conditions were hardly any better. Seven families lived in the house, which was above a shop in the busy trading street; the twenty-eight tenants shared one outside toilet and tap.[3]

By the time Christina was born on 24 December 1913, the Caffreys were renting a room in 56 Church Street, with nine other families; twenty-three tenants lived above another shop on one of the busiest tenement streets in Dublin. Sarah was anxious to move to a home in the new Corporation Street complex, built by the city council in 1906 to replace the notorious tenements of the area. It was in the heart of the decaying Monto red-light district, and the corporation decided to change the name of Montgomery Street – 'Monto' – where it was situated:

> We believe the great improvement effected in the street by the Corporation, together with the name change, will have the desirable effect of obliterating its evil reputation. We therefore request and pray that it may be called Corporation Street, as the great change for the better has been effected by the Corporation.[4]

In 1900, Dublin's greatest concentration of tenement dwellings had been in the area between Montgomery Street and Gloucester Street, lower-bounded by Mabbot Street (which became Corporation Street) with the site of the future Corporation Buildings in the middle.[5]

But the four-storey blocks of 'flats' were not much better than the buildings they replaced. There were ninety-five 'halls', each with four rooms, a family in each room, which measured fourteen by eighteen feet. Tenants described them in horrifying terms:

We had a large family and there was no electricity or gas in the room. The rooms were so small, that you could only fit one bed in them. My sisters slept in the bed with my mother and father. My brothers and me had to sleep on the floor. We had a blanket to cover us and on top of that we had old coats to keep us warm. The fire was packed up with coal or anything that might burn at the end of the night to keep the heat in the room. There was just one oil lamp and when it was put out during the night if you had to get up to go to the toilet, which was in that one little room, it would be so dark that you would be standing on one another's head and legs. Cooking was on an open fire. There was no bathroom.[6]

By now, Sarah Caffrey had left dealing and become a charwoman, who cleaned for the middle-class community that bordered the artisans' dwellings of Stoneybatter. She went to houses in Aughrim Street, Rathdown Road, Manor Street, Prussia Street and Botanic Road – five days, five houses – at a rate of 'one shilling and sixpence, plus board and extras per day'.[7] The Gilligan, Ennis, Connor, Hunt and Moore households benefited from Sarah's daily toil. Eileen Gilligan's family in Prussia Street were fond of Sarah. Eileen's younger sister was the mother of Maureen O'Carroll, who became one of the Republic's first female TDs. The comedian Brendan O'Carroll is her son. Matthew Ennis was a cattle trader, living in a house with eleven other people on Prussia Street, while Peter Connor ran a butcher's at 5 Manor Street; he and his family lived above the shop.

Neville Nicholas Fryday was the tenth child born to Elizabeth Anne Preston in Ballyduff, near Thurles, on 3 September 1899. Elizabeth gave birth to three more children before tragedy struck. The family moved to a farm at nearby Mornmount, Dundrum, in County Tipperary, but after Neville's father died in 1905, he and his brother Edward were 'boarded out' with his 'St Leger' relatives. In the meantime, two of their older brothers, James and Frank, had been boarded out as apprentices to a Wayland relative, a photographer, in Cork city. In 1905, they left for Canada, their mother followed them in 1909.

In 1911, Elizabeth came back to Ireland for Neville and returned to Canada with him. They arrived from Liverpool on SS *Lake Manitoba* on 5 July 1912. Neville and his brother William enlisted in the Canadian Army, 75th Battalion, Central Ontario Regiment, on 19 July 1915, following their brother Harry, who had signed up a year previously. Like so many others, Neville lied about his age, saying he was twenty-one.

Following training in Niagara, Neville and William were despatched

Elizabeth Anne Preston Wayland Fryday, (1864–1942), mother of Private Neville Nicholas Fryday.

from Halifax, Nova Scotia, to Liverpool on the *Empress of Britain*, arriving on 9 April 1916. There were 20,000 Irishmen in the Canadian Army during the Great War and the two young men ended up at a British Army barracks in Brompton, Kent. There was no sign of them going to the front, so Neville was granted leave for Easter in early April and went to Dublin with William to visit their beloved mother, who had returned from Canada. She was then living at 6 St Malachy's Road, Glasnevin, with her brother Palliser Wayland, a railway clerk.

Neville and William had relatives in Terenure and Shankill, and Neville was travelling from one side of the city to the other wearing his Canadian Army uniform on Easter Monday afternoon when, at around 2.30 p.m., he was shot outside Trinity College.

By early afternoon, fighting had broken out at the GPO, Dublin Castle and the nearby Mendicity Institute in Usher's Island, which was opposite another battle site, the Four Courts and Church Street. Still within a three-mile radius of the GPO, battles were raging in the South Dublin Union in James's Street, on nearby Portobello Bridge, in Fumbally Lane and farther down the canal at Boland's Mills and Mount Street.

The journey that Neville Fryday made from Glasnevin towards the south side of the city effectively brought him into 'Snipers Alley': British forces in Trinity College took aim to the left at the Rebels in Dame Street outside City Hall and Dublin Castle and to the right to Sackville Street, with the Rebels returning fire. Arthur Hamilton Norway, secretary to the Irish General Post Office, wrote:

> Shortly after breakfast the next morning the police rang me
> up, by direction of the under-secretary, asking me to go to the

Castle. I asked by what route. 'By Dame Street,' was the answer. 'That is quite safe today.' I was surprised but to Dame Street I went and was just turning on to it, opposite Trinity College, when a storm of bullets swept down the street, evidently from Rebel rifles, and was answered by sharp, successive volleys from Trinity College.[8]

Neville Fryday was shot in the abdomen and lungs and rushed to Mercers Hospital where he died from his injuries six days later. His mother's cousin, Dr Robert Shaw Wayland, worked at the temporary hospital in Harcourt Street during the Rising. There has been some debate as to whether Neville was actually on leave when he was visiting his mother. While every soldier despatched from Canada to the UK in April 1914 was technically on active service, there is little doubt that Neville's presence in Dublin had nothing to do with the Rising. The first British troops to be 'rushed' to Dublin did not arrive until Wednesday morning, two days after the Rising had started.

Neville's family believe he was accidentally killed while on leave. The *Toronto Star* of 8 May reported that he died 'while on duty in Dublin, Ireland', and asked, 'Were the Toronto troops which left the city about six weeks ago rushed across to Ireland to assist in the quelling of the rebellion in Dublin?'

However, an article in the same newspaper four days later was headlined: 'Private Fryday was home on leave – was not serving with Toronto Battalion in Ireland when shot.' It went on to detail how he was on leave visiting his mother in Dublin.

Neville's mother Elizabeth could not afford to repatriate his body to Canada so he was buried in Mount Jerome Cemetery, in a marked grave, at the instruction of his sister Metta (who was also interred there in April 1985). Elizabeth subsequently returned to

Canada where, in 1932, she married Thomas Albert Kinnear in Ontario. Shortly afterwards they returned to the Kinnears' home in County Down, Northern Ireland but, after he died in 1936, she returned to Canada to live with one of her surviving sons, and died in Toronto on Easter Monday, 6 April 1942.

Some of Neville's siblings made lives for themselves in Canada. He had six brothers and six sisters. One sister, Ruth Downton, survived until 1998 when she died aged 103.

In 1901 dressmaker, Mary Allen, mother of another child victim Bridget Allen, was living with her husband Michael, a porter from Meath, just across the Liffey from North King Street. They had a three-bedroomed home of their own at 4 Chaworth Terrace on Hanbury Lane in the heart of the Liberties. The house was big enough to allow them to take in five boarders – three butchers and two post-office clerks.

Pte. N. N. Fryday   Pte. Wm. Fryday

Pte. H. Fryday   Piper J. Wayland

Neville and his brother William Fryday were both home on leave from the Canadian Army to visit their mother in Dublin on Easter Monday, 1916. Neville's brother, Henry, and his first cousin, Piper J. Wayland, were also enlisted. Neville's three relatives survived the war.

At the beginning of the twentieth century, life looked good for the hard-working Allen family. They had three young children –

Matthew, aged five, Edward, four, and Bridget, eight months, as well as the boarders, but Mary Allen was organised and diligent.

Within two years, disaster had struck. Michael died at his home from tuberculosis, aged just thirty-one, on 20 January 1903. There was no such thing as social welfare and, according to family members, 'Things went downhill from there.'[9]

In the 1908 voters register, Mary Allen is living at 25 Hanbury Lane off Meath Street in the south inner city.[10] But, by 1911, she and her ever-depleting family had moved again to a tenement room in 128 Thomas Street. It was closer to the Liffey – and poverty. Not only was her husband dead, but her oldest son, Matthew, now aged fifteen, was in the St Vincent de Paul Orphanage in Glasnevin.[11]

Foley Street flats. Corporation Buildings, where Christina Caffrey was shot and killed in her mother's arms.

With no widow's pension, Mary and her two children eked out a living; Bridget had a job at the Dublin Salt Works.

By two o'clock on Tuesday of Easter week – just over twenty-four hours after the start of the Rising – Sarah Caffrey, then aged thirty-two, had not only been shot but had also joined the ranks of grieving mothers.

Christina Caffrey was born on Christmas Eve 1913 at 56 Church Street, in the middle of the greatest strike Dublin had ever seen. Her father, Joseph, the lime-yard labourer, was more than likely on strike but at least Sarah's job as a charwoman was not affected by the 'great lockout'. The Dublin of Christmas 1913 was a bleak, hungry, unsettled city, with many families on the brink of starvation. The 'great lockout' was crumbling, the workers beaten by hunger, weather and ruthless employers. The poor had little to celebrate. No doubt little Christina's birth brought some joy to the Caffreys that Christmas – but it didn't last very long: less than twenty-eight months later, she would be dead.

From the newspaper reports of the time, at least seven people were killed in or around Corporation Buildings.[12] On the second day of the Rising, two-year-old Christina Caffrey was killed in 'the precincts of her home, at 27B Corporation Buildings at around two o'clock while standing outside her own door'.[13] Sarah was holding her baby daughter in her arms outside their home, near Amiens Street railway station, when a stray bullet 'struck me first, glided off my hand and entered my child's back'.[14] Sarah Caffrey, bleeding from her hand wound, carrying her seriously injured daughter, rushed to the hospital she knew best, the North Dublin Union near where she worked in Grangegorman, but Christina died.

Sarah Caffrey subsequently applied to the Rebellion (Victims) Committee for loss of earnings: she was no longer able to work as a 'charwoman for the four families in Prussia Street area'.

I discovered a bizarre and cruel series of letters in the National Archives about this tragic case. The committee replied to an initial communication from the Chief Secretary's office noting that:

> *It would be difficult to defend in the case of an infant of this age (2 years) the grant of any sum beyond funeral and incidental expenses and a solatium, say, not exceeding £5. They have again accordingly considered their recommendation but in view of the very sad nature of the case – the child having been shot in its mother's arms while the mother was endeavouring to call one of her other children which had wandered into the street on the second day of the outbreak – the committee feel that they must adhere to their recommendation of a compassionate grant of £25 to the mother.*
>
> *I am Sir,*
> *Your obedient servant,*
> *Hugh C. Love*
> *The Rebellion Victims Compensation Committee*

A letter from the Chief Secretary to the Treasury in Whitehall, London, of 24 April 1917 noted that the Rebellion (Victims) Committee had recommended a grant of twenty-five pounds:

> *. . . but His Excellency proposes to deal with the case by payment of a grant of £5 together with funeral and incidental expenses, when ascertained within a limit of £10.*
>
> *In the circumstances My Lords concur in this proposal, although the award under the Government scheme would not exceed £10 in all.*

Recommendation made by the Committee at their
Meeting of 29th January, 1917.

     Class of case –   Dependent of deceased,

     Name of deceased –   **CAFFREY, Miss Christina (aged 2 years).**

     Ascertained average
     weekly earnings of deceased –   ———

     Compensation claimed –   **£20.**

     There was no misconduct or default in this case.

     Solicitor for Applicant – **None.**

     Dependent –   ———

    Applicant – Mother.

Recommendation made by the Rebellion Committee with regard to Christina Caffrey's mother's claim for £20 compensation. In the end, she was granted the sum of £25 sterling, 29 January 1917.

An investigation was carried out by the police and the matter took another cruel turn. A letter written by a detective sergeant of the Dublin police to the Under-Secretary in Dublin Castle in reference to Sarah Caffrey stated:

I beg to report that I have made enquiries and as far as I ascertain there were no funeral expenses incurred in this case. The coffin was supplied by the North Dublin Union and the father and another man carried the remains to Glasnevin on 4th May 1916.[15]

This story is not uncommon: civilians were regularly treated badly by the authorities if they dared to seek compensation for their injuries or the deaths of spouses or children. Sarah Caffrey

127

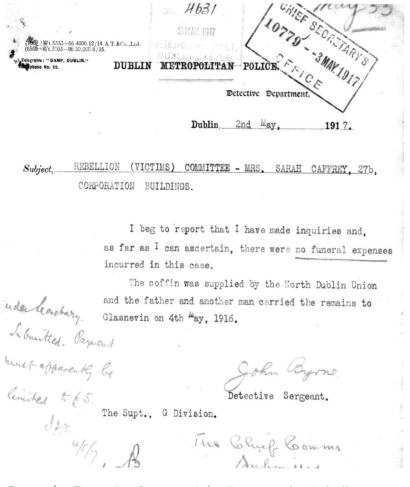

Report by Detective Sergeant John Byrne to the Rebellion (Victims) Committee regarding the cost of Christina Caffrey's funeral, 2 May 1917.

lost her child and her livelihood to a stray bullet. Five pounds for the life of a baby daughter and the livelihood of her mother says much about the treatment of civilians in life and death in the aftermath of the Easter Rising.

Christina was buried in an unmarked grave in the St Paul's section of Glasnevin Cemetery on Thursday, 4 May 1916. She lies with many other children and civilians under the walkway to the Republican Monument. At twenty-eight months, she was the youngest child to die in the Rising. Sarah also applied for forty pounds compensation for 'loss of earnings' as a charwoman because of her hand injury – the outcome is unknown.

Christina's parents continued to live in Corporation Buildings at least until 1934, when Joseph died of tuberculosis. Eventually, Sarah moved to nearby Liberty House and died on 15 March 1969, fifty-three years after her daughter. Joseph and

Sarah are also buried in Glasnevin Cemetery, but not with their baby daughter Christina.

By Easter 1916, the decline of the Allen family had halted. Mary was busy as a dressmaker, her daughter, Bridget, was at the Dublin Salt Works, her son, Matthew, had left the orphanage for the British Army and was on the Western Front – presumably sending money home to his widowed mother – while her second son, Edward, was working as a clerk in the civil service.

Close to Dublin's Four Courts, Arran Quay, in the 1911 Census, was a row of terraced tenement houses. At number 27, seven families were housed in five rooms – a total of thirty-seven people. It was here, on Thursday, 27 April 1916, that Bridget was shot and killed, with her mother close by. A doctor who lived next door was quickly on the scene but Bridget, aged sixteen, was pronounced dead immediately.

A grandniece of Bridget Allen tells me, 'The story I was told was that a bullet came through a window and she died as a result of her injuries.'[16]

On the first anniversary of Bridget's death, her family inserted a memorial notice in the *Evening Herald*:

Allen, in sad and loving memory of Bridie Allen, shot at her residence, 27 Arran Quay April 27th 1916, aged 16, RIP. Masses offered in St Paul's, Arran Quay, and St Audeon's, High Street.

Time cannot alter love so dear and true,
The year brings back our grief for you.

Inserted by her sorrowing mother and brother.

Destruction at the Four Courts during the Easter Rising.

In the compensation claim it was noted: 'Mrs Allen's daughter (Bridie aged 16) was shot during the rebellion. Dr Garland of 26, Arran Quay attended. She was employed by the Dublin Salt Company at 6/- [six shillings] a week. Stated to have been shot by Sinn Féiners 27th April.

'Compensation claimed, £150 – £50 awarded.'[17]

Mary Allen's oldest son, Matthew, was killed two years later in March 1918, while fighting on the Western Front in France. The same month, eight years later, Mary's only surviving child, Edward, succumbed to tuberculosis in the Harold's Cross Hospice. He was twenty-nine. Mary moved in with her daughter-in-law, and they ran a grocery at 62–63 Patrick Street, which remained in the family until the early 1980s. Up to the day she died, Mary kept a strand of her daughter's hair in a biscuit tin in her bedroom.

The unscathed O'Connell monument amid the ruins of O'Connell Street after fighting during the Easter Rising.

6. 'Oh, Please Don't Kill Father'

TRAGEDY STRUCK MANY FAMILIES MORE THAN ONCE IN EASTER WEEK: THE DEATHS OF GEORGE PERCY SAINSBURY; CHRISTOPHER HICKEY; WILLIAM O'NEILL; JAMES GIBNEY; MARY ANNE BRUNSWICK; PATRICK KELLY; EUGENE LYNCH; 'MALE' O'TOOLE; CHILD AND INFANT UNIDENTIFIED.

Given that about 500 people died in the Rising, the majority of whom were civilians, it is no surprise to learn that some families grieved for more than one member killed that week. As we know, many Dublin families endured casualties in both the Easter Rising and the Great War, but others suffered more than one tragedy at home during and beyond Easter week.

By 1911, Eva Neilan, originally from Kilteevan in County Roscommon, the wife of Dr John Neilan, had buried her husband and four of her twelve children. Three of her sons were in the British Army, two as doctors, while her second oldest son, Lieutenant Gerald Neilan, was a career officer.

By 1916, Eva was living at Mount Harold Terrace in Rathmines with three of her adult children; two sons, Gerald and Anthony, were also in Dublin, both in uniform, both bearing arms on Easter Monday – on opposite sides.

Gerald Neilan was at the head of a contingent of Royal Dublin Fusiliers, who, as the Rising began, marched in formation – led by their commander with his sword outstretched – from the Royal Barracks (now Collins Barracks, the National Museum) on Dublin's north quays, towards the city. The Mendicity Institute, a workhouse, had been taken over by the Rebels, and as the British soldiers neared Bridgefoot Street, the Rebels opened fire. Gerald Neilan was shot dead. Meanwhile, his younger brother, Anthony, a member of the Irish Volunteers, was less than half a mile away across the river in Church Street on the barricades. Rebel leader Ned Daly was about to lead an attack on British soldiers advancing up the other side of the Liffey quays.

Gerald was interred in the family plot at Glasnevin while, after the Rising, Anthony was interned in Knutsford Detention Barracks in Cheshire. Eventually, he returned to Ireland, where he died in 1944 aged forty-nine. He is buried with his brother.

In 1916, the Sainsbury family were leading a quiet, middle-class life at 57 Haroldville Terrace on the South Circular Road. Arthur Draper Sainsbury was born in Melbourne, Australia, in 1867, his English father and Irish mother having emigrated from Bath. After the father's early death, the family moved back to Liverpool and later the two children, William and Arthur, went to live in their mother's home country, where they set up a legal practice in Dawson Street, later moving the business to Sackville Street. Arthur worked as the firm's managing clerk, while William was a solicitor. By the end of Easter week 1916, however, as a result of the fighting Arthur Sainsbury had lost his youngest son, George, his older boy Arthur was seriously injured, and his workplace was destroyed. A year later he, too, would be dead.[1]

A neighbour five doors away told of how nine-year-old George Percy Sainsbury lost his life on day four of the Rising, Thursday, 27 April: 'My uncle Tom Maguire lived in Rialto at the time and told me of a Protestant boy neighbour who was killed in Easter week. When the British Army were advancing through Rialto, he stuck his head out a window and was shot dead.'[2]

In May 1917, the family applied to the Rebellion (Victims) Committee for compensation as the elder brother Arthur's injuries were still causing him trouble: 'The wound is still discharging and is likely to continue for some months. The boy will, I anticipate, make a full recovery.'[3] The family was awarded fifty pounds, provided it was administered through 'trustees'.

George Percy Sainsbury was buried from Dolphin's Barn Methodist Church on Saturday, 20 May 1916, in the family plot in Mount Jerome. His father, Arthur, died from tuberculosis the following April, aged forty-five and is buried in the same unmarked grave.[4] Arthur Sainsbury Junior joined the Royal Flying Corps and emigrated to South Africa in 1922. He died of a brain injury as the result of an accidental fall in 1943 aged just forty-one.[5]

While the Sainsburys had a family connection with Australia, the Hickey family of North King Street were linked to Argentina by trade. Thomas Hickey opened a butcher's shop in Tralee, County Kerry, shortly before 1911, selling only 'frozen Argentinian beef'.[6] His somewhat exotic project failed and Thomas, with his wife, Teresa Kavanagh, and their only child, Christopher, moved their butcher's shop to Dublin. By the end of Easter week, two of the Hickeys would lie murdered in their home.

Thomas Hickey's family were well-known cattle dealers from Mullingar in County Westmeath – indeed, their thriving business

CIVILIANS REPORTED SHOT IN DUBLIN.

THIRTEEN DEAD.

Dublin, Sunday.

The following appears in the Sunday Independent:—

"Startling list—fourteen casualties in King Street shot in one morning.

"We publish below the names of fourteen civilian casualties, thirteen of whom are dead, in the King Street area. The addresses at which the bodies were found are also given. Representatives have obtained reliable evidence in each of these cases. In the circumstances under which the bodies were found, we do not deem it right or prudent that any matter should be published in reference to these cases until official investigation has been made into them.

"The victims were all shot on the morning of Saturday, April 29, 1916:—

"27 North King Street—Peter Lawless, James M'Cartney, Patrick Hoey, James Finnegan.

"168 North King Street—Christopher Hickey, Thomas Hickey, Peter Connolly.

"172 North King Street—Mr Hughes, Mr Walsh.

"177 North King Street—Patrick Bealan, James Healy.

"175 North King Street—George Ennis, Michael Noonan.

"7 North King Street—Joseph Hayes (wounded).

"It is known that none of the above victims was in any way associated with the volunteers or Sinn Fein rebels, and no trace of arms or ammunition were found at the residences mentioned."

The writer adds that Mr Asquith's attention has been called to these cases.

The North King Street massacre shocked the British public as well as the Irish and was reported in many British newspapers, for example, 'Civilians reported shot in Dublin', Dundee Courier, 15 May 1916.

in the town continued into the 1940s.[7] Teresa's family had a poultry shop on Main Street in Dalkey for more than forty years; her brother, Joseph, ran the business from 1911. Teresa and Thomas were married on 25 April 1899, and Christopher was born on 30 November that year at 5 Mary Street in central Dublin. His father owned a butcher's shop on the junction of North King Street and Beresford Street, where Christopher also later worked. They and thirteen other civilians were shot or bayoneted to death in the North King Street massacre on Saturday, 29 April 1916 by members of the South Staffordshire Regiment under the command of Lieutenant Colonel Henry Taylor.

Accounts of the North King Street massacre are horrific. As the Rising was collapsing on the morning of Friday, 28 April, troops from nearby Linenhall Street Barracks started at 10 a.m. to force their way along nearby North King Street to Church Street. It took them until 2 p.m. the next day to cover the 150 yards. The South Staffordshire Regiment had suffered heavy casualties in the Rising, with fourteen men killed and many more wounded. Christopher Hickey and his father were in the wrong place at the wrong time. Kate Kelly, a local woman who worked for the Hickeys, gave evidence about the murders to the inquest:

> I used to do the housework for the Hickeys and was in their house in Easter week. When the military came in on Friday evening after Mrs Hickey went across the street, Mr Hickey and Mr Connolly were sitting together in the street outside.
>
> Mr Connolly was a carrier and had come over about the moving of two mirrors from the Hickeys'. As the military rushed up about 6.45 on Friday night, Mr Hickey and Mr Connolly ran into the house for safety. Connolly, although he lived only a few doors away, was never able to get back home. Connolly

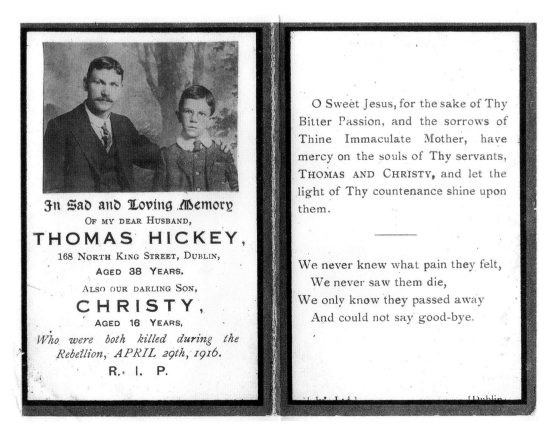

In Sad and Loving Memory
OF MY DEAR HUSBAND,
THOMAS HICKEY,
168 NORTH KING STREET, DUBLIN,
AGED 38 YEARS.
ALSO OUR DARLING SON,
CHRISTY,
AGED 16 YEARS,
Who were both killed during the Rebellion, APRIL 29th, 1916.
R. I. P.

O Sweet Jesus, for the sake of Thy Bitter Passion, and the sorrows of Thine Immaculate Mother, have mercy on the souls of Thy servants, THOMAS AND CHRISTY, and let the light of Thy countenance shine upon them.

———

We never knew what pain they felt,
We never saw them die,
We only know they passed away
And could not say good-bye.

Memoriam card for Thomas and Christopher Hickey.

remained in the house with us all Friday night and was killed with Mr Hickey and his son Christy the next morning.

Both Mrs Carroll and I heard poor Christy pleading for his father's life. 'Oh, please don't kill father.' The shots rang out and I shouted 'Oh my God' and, overcome with horror, I threw myself on my knees and began to pray.

Mrs Teresa Hickey also gave harrowing evidence about the deaths of her husband and son:

Next morning I was terribly anxious to get home and Mr Corcoran [a neighbour] at great risk went to the door and got an officer to pass me over the street. This was 10.30 on Saturday morning. There were five or six soldiers round our shop under cover and the firing was still going on. I said to one of the soldiers, 'I want to go into my home.' 'You can if you like,' he said, 'but there are a few dead bodies lying round over there, and you can cross them if you wish.' I was too terrified to venture and returned to Mr Corcoran until Sunday morning. On Sunday morning I saw people passing, returning from mass and from the technical school where they had been held by the military. I asked everyone I knew, 'Where is Mr Hickey?' I went about all day searching the hospitals, etc., until I was nearly worn out, little thinking that my husband and son were lying murdered in the house a few yards across the street.

About 5 p.m. on Sunday evening I again went round to our house at the corner of Beresford Street. Two soldiers were on guard outside. I said, 'This is my house. I left my husband and child here. I must go in.' He replied, 'No, you can't, you had better see an officer.'

I went round to the front hall door in King Street where I met

Mrs Carroll, the tenant in the next room. She said, in a solemn manner, 'I want to speak to you.' She then stopped and just said, 'Oh, poor Christy.' I knew then they were gone. I then rushed upstairs, the two soldiers following me and shouting: 'You can't be here, come on.'

When I rushed into the room, there I saw my poor angel, my darling. He was lying on the ground, his face darkened, and his two hands raised above his head as if in silent supplication. I kissed him and put his little cap under his head and settled his hands for death. Then I turned and in another place close by I saw poor Tom lying on the ground. 'Oh, Jesus,' I cried, 'not my husband too,' and not far off lay the corpse of poor Connolly. I reeled around and remember no more as the soldiers hustled me down the stairs and into the street. I was brought for examination to the Castle, and several times addressed the officers there asking them why they had killed my son, a young lad, not sixteen years of age.

Mrs Connolly knew nothing of what had happened to her husband until Sunday evening when 'I heard that he had been murdered by the military and I was brought over to the empty disused house this side of the Dunnes the butchers. The three bodies were lying in the back room of the first floor upstairs. My poor husband was greatly marked and had several gashes about the neck and head which appeared to be bayonet wounds.'[8]

A codicil to the story comes from a relative. A first cousin of Christopher was killed in France on the same day. Corporal Patrick J. Gahan, aged twenty-two, of the Royal Inniskilling Fusiliers, is buried at the Philosophe British Cemetery in Mazingarbe in France.

In the claim for compensation, Christopher's mother, Teresa, of 166 Church Street, sought recompense for 'husband and son

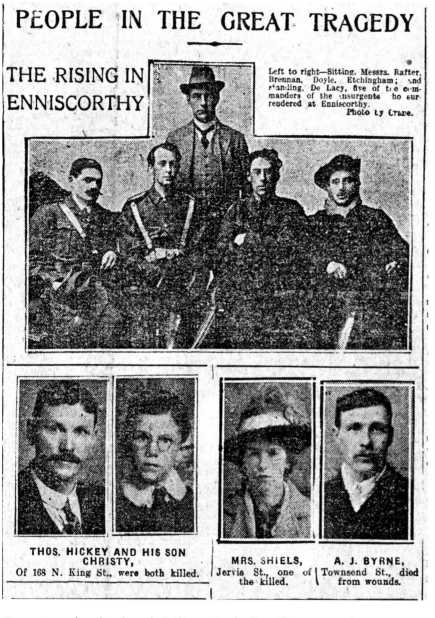

PEOPLE IN THE GREAT TRAGEDY

THE RISING IN ENNISCORTHY

Left to right—Sitting, Messrs. Rafter, Brennan, Doyle, Etchingham; and standing, De Lacy, five of the commanders of the insurgents who surrendered at Enniscorthy.

Photo by Crane.

THOS. HICKEY AND HIS SON CHRISTY,
Of 168 N. King St., were both killed.

MRS. SHIELS,
Jervis St., one of the killed.

A. J. BYRNE,
Townsend St., died from wounds.

Report on the deaths of civilians, including Thomas and Christopher Hickey, Evening Herald, *10 May 1916.*

(age 16) shot in house by military'.[9]

The British did not accept responsibility for the massacre – so they simply refused to even acknowledge the compensation claim.

The writer Monk Gibbon, son of a Protestant clergyman in Dublin, on leave from the British Army, reported for duty when the Rising started. Of the North King Street Massacre, he wrote:

Such deaths were pointless. They were like the action not so much of a 'frightened man' as of someone in whom the killing instinct had been roused or a desire for immediate vengeance. In the fighting in North King Street, five British officers were wounded, fourteen NCOs and men killed and twenty-eight wounded. General Maxwell, with masterly understatement, wrote later: 'Possibly some unfortunate incidents which we should regret now have occurred . . . It is even possible that under the horrors of this attack some of them "saw red"; that is the inevitable consequence of a rebellion of this kind. It was allowed to come into being among these people and could not be suppressed by kid-glove methods, when troops were so desperately opposed and attacked.' There was certainly nothing kid-glove about the shooting of the sixteen-year-old Christy Hicky [sic].[10]

Christopher's mother Teresa had been living at 18 Kevin Street, a tenement house in the shadow of St Patrick's Cathedral, but she died in Harold's Cross Hospice only four years later of the dreaded tuberculosis – she was forty-four. She was buried with her husband and son in Deans Grange Cemetery where, in 2015, a memorial plaque was finally placed on this tragic family's grave.

Documents released from the British Public Record office in 2001 refer specifically to the killings of Peter Connolly, a 'member of the Redmondite Irish national volunteers', and Thomas and Christopher Hickey. They were 'shot as rebels, taken red-handed'; the soldiers 'had orders not to take prisoners, which they took to mean that they were to shoot anyone whom they believed to be an active rebel'. A further caveat appears in the official report: 'Some of the persons were rightly shot; the others were not taking any active part, though the police evidence is clear the whole of the street was a nest of Sinn Féiners.'[11]

There is little doubt that the killings in North King Street amounted to nothing short of a massacre of unarmed civilians. The front page of the *Sunday Independent* on 14 May 1916 reported: 'Startling list . . . 14 casualties in King Street . . . shot in one morning'. It lists 'people shot on the morning of 29 April 1916, including Thomas Hickey, Christopher Hickey and Peter Connolly in 168 North King Street'. The report ended, 'It is known that none of the above victims was in any way associated with the Volunteers or Sinn Féin rebels and no traces of arms or ammunition were found in the residences mentioned.'[12]

Christopher Hickey's death certificate states that he died of a 'bayonet wound to the heart, no med. attendant'.

William O'Neill lived a few hundred yards from the Hickeys at 85 Church Street and was one of the six surviving children born to John and Alice O'Neill. Married when she was nineteen, Alice O'Neill had eleven children, including William but, by 1911, she had buried five and died herself of 'apoplexy' aged fifty-two in 1913.

Just around the corner from North King Street, William O'Neill became one of the last victims of the Rising when he was shot dead during the chaos on Saturday morning, four doors from where my grandmother was living at 89 Church Street. William was buried in Glasnevin Cemetery in early May 1916, in the same grave as his mother. Two of his siblings were also interred there: his sister, Elizabeth, who had died aged twenty in 1911 of 'endocarditis', and his sister, Margaret, who had died in 1910, aged eleven, of 'meningitis'.[13] The social and political history of Ireland from 1910 to 1916 in one grave.

In 1911, the O'Neills ran a boarding house at numbers 85

and 86 Church Street, with seven family members, including two grandchildren, and eleven boarders. William's surviving sister, Mrs Hughes, revealed at the time how William was killed:

> Another sorrow came over me at the same time, early on Saturday morning, my young brother William O'Neill a lad of 17 [his birth and death certificates confirm he was actually sixteen] was shot dead on Constitution Hill at the end of Coleraine Street, near the Temple. He was with another man who had gone over to look at the body of Beirnes lying on the ground in Coleraine Street as he thought it was his father who was killed.
>
> Both must have been shot by the soldiers in the window of Dunnes the butcher. This shop is in North King Street and is the only shop that looks up the street. It was full of soldiers at the time and there was no other position where armed men could fire on the spot where my brother and Mr Beirnes were killed. My brother was carried to Mrs Keller's close by and only lived about five minutes. The only words he muttered were 'Oh, Mother, Mother . . .'[14]

As if proof were needed that the area around Church Street was one of the most dangerous places in the city that week, James Gibney, who lived in a tenement house around the corner at 16 Henrietta Place, died as a result of the hostilities. He was five and a half, and is buried in Glasnevin Cemetery, where the daily ledger recorded that his death was caused by 'cannonading'. James Gibney's death certificate states that the cause of death was 'probably heart disease and shock, no medical attention, inquest unnecessary'. In other words, the child, who lived beside the Linenhall Army Barracks and had a pre-existing heart condition, died of shock during the fighting. The 1911 Census adds to the confusion around this young life: James Gibney is listed there as female but is correctly described as a 'son', though aged four months; his mother, Lillian, was twenty-six, living in a tenement on Jervis Street, and is named on the death certificate as Ellen. When so many could neither read nor write in this period the spelling of names tends to evolve over time on official forms!

By 1916, the family had moved from Jervis Street the few hundred yards north to Henrietta Place beside Henrietta Street, used as a typical tenement street in the TV production of James Plunkett's *Strumpet City*. The Gibneys seem to have been in luck: some of the houses had more than a hundred tenants with up to nineteen families living side by side. Number 16 had only nine families, with fifty-six tenants – other houses on the street had double this number.

During the course of my research, a number of other confusing cases came to my attention. Could the child whose body was recovered from the canal long after the Rising have jumped in to avoid the fighting in Easter week, as a later newspaper article suggested? He is named in the report as John Whately, and was buried on 6 May 1916 in Mount Jerome Cemetery.[15]

In May 2013, a few months after I began work on this project, I had a letter from Sean Brunswick, of Rathfarnham, Dublin, telling me the story of his aunt, Mary Anne Brunswick, who was fourteen when she was shot and killed outside her home on Wellington Street in Dublin:

Henrietta Buildings (Henrietta Place), c. 1913.

Her body was taken to the Mater Hospital and pronounced dead. It was then taken on a board to Glasnevin. However, with the Rising in the city nothing was normal, undertakers were not available and at Cross Guns Bridge, the British Army had a barricade and would not allow anyone pass beyond that point. The body on the board was taken by the army and buried in a mass grave on the left-hand side of Glasnevin opposite the main entrance.

Later that day my grandfather Patrick Stephenson was leaving his place of employment, Farrells the undertakers, at the junction of what is now Cathal Brugha Street and Marlborough Street, and he was shot dead, not knowing there was a curfew.[16]

In the 1911 Census, Mary Anne Brunswick, the third in a family of eight, was living at 58 Wellington Street; six families lived in the four-roomed house, twenty-seven souls in all. Her 1916 death certificate states that she lived at 57 Wellington Street, in a tenement house where the writer Sean O'Casey's family once lived. Only five minutes from Nelson's Pillar – off Dorset Street – 'old Wellier' was regarded as almost a village in itself, with many of O'Casey's characters based on people he had known there when he lived in the area.

Mary Anne was 'killed by gunfire' on Friday, 28 April, at 57 Wellington Street. She suffered a fractured skull and, according to her death certificate, 'laceration of the brain, shock'. One report says Mary Anne was simply going out of her door to the shops on Friday when she was shot in the head.

The local priest, Father O'Callaghan, happened on the scene:

> I was hurrying out on a sick call and when I came to the top of Wellington Street at the corner of Mountjoy Street, I saw a little girl of about twelve lying on the edge of the pavement, with the whole lower half of her face shot away. It was just as if she had had a surgical operation and although the sound of shooting was all around me, as I knelt there I was oblivious of danger so stunned was I at the tragic way the little girl had died. It was something I have never been able to forget.[17]

Mary Anne Brunswick was buried in an unmarked mass grave in Glasnevin Cemetery, with many other civilians.[18]

Her father, John Brunswick, a boiler-man, was present at her death, as was her elder brother, Sean, aged sixteen. As a direct result of his sister's killing, he joined the IRA. He fought in the War of Independence, and subsequently lost an eye in the siege of the Four Courts during the Civil War. Sean Brunswick married Anne Stephenson, who was also sixteen when she lost her father, Paddy, on 28 April 1916, from gunshot wounds. Paddy Stephenson, a coachman and father of nine, lived in a tenement at 76 Gloucester Street. He is listed in *The Irish Times* as a fatality of the Rising and is also buried in Glasnevin. Sean Brunswick's family tell me that he suffered from very bad health and died aged forty-seven in 1947.

Mary Anne's nephew, also called Sean, was a learned man, who researched his own family history after he retired from the New Ireland Assurance company. He worked hard to help me with this project, and died unexpectedly in January 2014 while he was still researching his family tree.

Another two children who were killed on that bloody Friday were Patrick Kelly and Eugene Lynch.

Patrick Kelly's father was originally from County Meath, and his mother, Mary, hailed from County Tipperary; they were married in 1902 and lived at 24 Buckingham Buildings, a sprawling corporation complex in Dublin's north inner city. Although Mary gave birth to five children, only three were still living with them in 1911 – Patrick, John and Mary.

Young Patrick died outside his home on Friday, 28 April from gunshot wounds to the neck, which fractured his lower jaw. He was rushed to the makeshift Dublin University Voluntary Aid Detachment Hospital set up in nearby Mountjoy Square East by women graduates and students of Trinity College Dublin.

His family, represented by the solicitor Edward McHugh of 43 Rutland Square, stated in their compensation claim that Patrick had average weekly earnings of three shillings and sixpence;

Order authorising the interment of Eugene Lynch in Golden Bridge Cemetery, 28 April 1916.

they claimed twenty-five pounds, with an extra twelve pounds for funeral expenses. The boy's wages helped the family, and it was said, 'There was no misconduct or default in this case.'

Patrick Kelly is buried near Batterstown, County Meath, in the townland of Rathregan; the overgrown cemetery contains the ruins of a church. His grave is situated in the southeast corner, where a stone survives: 'In loving memory of Patrick Kelly who was killed in the Insurrection 1916, aged 13 years, RIP'.

Goldenbridge Cemetery, in Inchicore, Dublin, is now closed but can be visited by arrangement; it was briefly in the news in 2014 when the grave of former Taoiseach William T. Cosgrave was vandalised. A burial record from Goldenbridge yielded the name of Eugene Lynch, aged eight years and nine months, who died 'from the effects of a bullet wound' on Friday, 28 April 1916 and was interred in Goldenbridge, across the road from his home at 4 Vincent Street, on Sunday morning, 30 April, at eleven o'clock.[19] His coffin was just under five feet long and just over a foot wide. Eugene was the child of Joseph, a clerk, and Annie Lynch (née McGrath). Both families were deeply involved in the life of Inchicore: most of Eugene's father's family worked in the nearby Inchicore railway works while his mother was one of only two surviving children born to local vintners Nicholas and Elizabeth McGrath. The interment cost two pounds.

Eugene Lynch, known to his family a 'Sam', was shot near Richmond Barracks in Inchicore and was carried to his grandmother's public house, McGraths, in nearby Vincent Street, where he died. The family believe he was shot by a British soldier, which, in turn, led his younger brother to join the Republican movement. His mother Annie was a well-educated, formidable woman, known locally as a 'queen bee' – she died in 1955 and is buried with her son.[20]

There were two unidentified children who died in the Rising. We know very little about 'Male' O'Toole, who died on Easter Monday. His death certificate refers to him as 'a schoolboy'. Many civilians were buried unidentified. The death cert states that 'Male' O'Toole's first name was unknown; he was brought in, already dead, to the Adelaide Hospital beside the Jacob's biscuit factory on Easter Monday. The fourteen-year-old had died from 'gunshot wounds to the chest and head'.[21]

In the course of making a TV documentary on this project another scenario was put forward as to the identity of this child. Taking the 'Male' O'Tooles from the 1911 Census and tracing their whereabouts after 1916, it was possible to eliminate all except one. The only O'Toole in the census fitting that age group was Christopher O'Toole, who was placed in the North Dublin Union in Grangegorman with his mother, a brother and a sister in 1906 – there was no mention of his father.

The workhouses of Dublin, the North Union and South Union, were the last refuge of the poor in the city. One hundred years ago, Dublin was the poorest city in Ireland and the UK; the workhouses were overcrowded to say the least, with children like Christopher existing in awful conditions. At any one time, there were 6,500 paupers in the workhouses of Dublin – in a year over 30,000 could pass through these institutions.

Christopher O'Toole's mother and sister left the workhouse – it seems his brother died there – but Christopher remained there until 1912, whereupon he was discharged. There is no trace of him after that.

After six years in care, how did ten-year-old Christopher fare back on the streets of Dublin and where he was in 1916? Was he one of the many Dublin children who survived by begging, street selling or petty thievery, effectively homeless, moving from tenement lobby to tenement lobby, with no parent or guardian? Was he nobody's child? Just as his bizarre death certificate indicates.

Could Christopher be the 'Male' O'Toole who lay unclaimed and unnamed in the Adelaide Hospital on Easter Monday afternoon? Would it be surprising that of the forty children

Dublin workhouse, 1895.

killed in Dublin that week, one of them would be from the group of barefoot waifs, orphans and ragged children who appear so often in photographs from that period? There is, I believe, a very strong possibility that the 'Male' O'Toole is in fact tragic Christopher.

Today, a hundred years after the Easter Rising, we still do not know the exact number of civilians who died – estimates vary between 250 and 300 – so it is not surprising that at least thirty civilian victims remain unidentified. Only two of the unknown dead recorded in the death registers were children.

In 1916, Dr Matthew J. Russell was the medical officer for

Dublin City, and he is the only connection we have with the two children he buried from the city morgue on or about 4 May 1916. The National Museum in Collins Barracks unearthed the death certificates, which refer to an 'infant' and a 'boy', unidentified, killed by 'gunfire'.[22]

In the 1911 Census, Matthew Russell is recorded as a thirty-five-year-old 'medical general practitioner', a single man originally from County Tipperary, living alone, save for his twenty-two-year-old servant Sarah Moloney, from Queen's County (now Laois). I originally believed that one of those two children might have been Lionel Sweny or John Kirwan, but the dates, locations and other details do not fit. I would dearly have loved to return those children's names to them.

Children of the Gardiner Street School in Dublin's north inner-city, 1923.

Nuns wearing traditional habits distribute bread to people queuing on a street, most likely in Dublin, c. 1920.

7. Bloody Friday

How the frantic search for food led to the deaths of
Joseph Murray, Bridget Stewart and Walter Scott.

The populace, without food or the money to buy it up to 28 April,
were on the brink of starvation; they had hitherto been kept indoors by
the firing, but were now coming out into the streets demanding food;
looting was going on and rioting was feared.
From the 'Interim Report of the Government
Committee appointed to deal with the Food supply to
Dublin and its environs', May 1916

One hundred years after the Great Irish Famine, the first 'stew house' was set up in Ballyfermot, the sprawling post-war suburb built by Dublin Corporation to house inner-city dwellers fleeing from collapsing tenements. When my parents left their one-room 'flat' in Dublin's Mountjoy Square in 1959, with three young children, for the rented Corporation house at 6 Claddagh Green, Ballyfermot, where my mother still lives, the 'stew house' was an essential part of the infrastructure of the massive estate, which soon housed nearly 40,000 people. They say poverty has a smell, which it does – dank, sharp, uric, smoky and stale – but poverty has something more powerful than that: a stigma.

Ballyfermot was seen as a step above poverty – you had made it out of the tenements, and the Ireland of the 1960s beckoned brighter, especially if you worked hard. Using the stew house had a touch of indolence about it – maybe you weren't trying hard enough to get a job. That was the perception, but not the truth. My father had gone to Canvey Island, near London, to help build a power station, while my mother budgeted brilliantly on his weekly wages which were posted home – and, no matter how tough it got, she would never let us near the public humiliation of the stew house. Yes, she used our granny's 'turf dockets' for free fuel – after all, everyone knew it was for her mother – though why we would trudge all the way from the bottom of the scheme to our house with three heavy bags of turf for our granny, who lived miles away in Kehoe Square, was beyond me!

My abiding memory is of our neighbour, Mrs Pender, heaving her overflowing pots of stew, potatoes, custard and sago onto the 78 bus, stacking them under the stairs for the journey from the stew house at the bottom of the 'scheme' to her home on Claddagh Road. As the bus lunged around the corner onto Claddagh Green, a teetering pot toppled over and thick, bright custard spread slowly across the open platform. By the time we reached our stop, the floor was a sea of yellow. The conductor surveyed his bus. 'Who left the pots of custard under the stairs?' he roared.

As the bus came to a standstill, the custard began to drip over the edge of the platform onto the road. Who would be first to walk through it? Of course it was Mrs Pender, a small, strong woman in her overcoat and headscarf. She left her food and her precious pots on the bus and walked away with her dignity. The shame of being so easily identified as a user of the stew house was too much to bear.

This was the new Ireland of the 1960s, approaching the fiftieth anniversary of the Easter Rising. In the city centre, from where Mrs Pender and my parents had come, fifty years earlier, there had been no such hesitation or embarrassment about taking whatever free food was available – after all, for the majority, it was a vital part of their existence. Poverty wasn't the exception, it was the rule.

A group of children from Dublin, c. 1913.

And you don't have to go back to the Famine to find a time the city gripped by chronic food shortages. The 'Dublin Lockout' of 1913 saw children and adults of the city on the brink of starvation. Then, food kitchens had been set up in Liberty Hall, stocked by eagerly awaited food ships from England, to feed the children of workers who were locked out of their jobs for refusing to leave their trade union. A desperate plan to get the children to England to save them from starvation was abandoned when the Church feared more for their souls than their stomachs.

The Dublin of 1916 was worse. The city's population endured the greatest shortage of food in Ireland since the Famine, with only a few 'food kitchens' and some religious orders offering assistance and 'penny dinners'. The war had sent the price of essentials, such as bread, coal, tea, milk, sugar and flour rocketing. In 1916, a number of city-centre schools had

While I was searching through the register in Dublin's Glasnevin Cemetery with the cemetery historian Shane MacThomáis for the period after Easter week 1916, I could not help noticing the number of children who were buried there: they were not casualties of the Rising but of the times: diphtheria, debility, meningitis, tuberculosis, pneumonia, smallpox, typhoid, whooping cough or croup.

I was baffled by one cause of death which came up repeatedly: 'lying over'. Shane explained that this happened tragically when a very young child was sharing a bed with adults and suffocated when an adult rolled over in their sleep.

begun to provide midday meals – some convents supplied breakfast to the children of the poor – but no schools were open in Easter week, and the convents were severely hampered by the battles raging outside. There can be little doubt that some of the children who were killed during Easter week were out frantically looking for food. As one of the Rebel leaders later recorded, 'Some of our first activities were to regulate the hundreds of people who came clamouring for bread to Monks' bakery in North King Street in the early part of the week.'[1]

The relatives of at least four of the forty children killed in Easter week – Walter Scott, Joseph Murray, Bridget Stewart and John Henery McNamara – told me that the deaths were related to the frantic search for food: the children were all shot on the Friday. In many other cases, we do not know the exact movements of the children but perhaps – streetwise beyond their years – they too had been sent for food, darting through checkpoints, barricades and crossfire. With curfews from seven o'clock in the evening until five the next morning and 'passes' needed to get across the city, it was a dangerous business.

On the evening of Thursday, 27 April, the first urgent demands for food were received by telephone through the Dublin Metropolitan Police for several districts in the disturbed area ranging from Howth and Bray along the coasts to Kilmainham and Cabra.[2]

It is hard to overestimate the dependence of the working-class population of Dublin on bread as a staple of their diet, which it had been since the potato famine of 1845–52. Bakeries, such as Kennedy's, Boland's, Johnston Mooney and O'Brien, Downes', Monks', Rourke's, West City Bakery, Dublin Bread Company and the Dublin Industrial Co-operative Society, dominated the city – and were good employers. But they weren't beyond running a cartel to keep bread prices up, aided and abetted at times by the Guild of Bakers. Baking was a highly unionised activity and was regarded as a very good job, well paid with decent working hours in the Dublin of the early twentieth century.

The bakeries kept going during Easter week of 1916 as best they could while this city's population risked life and limb to get their hands on the critical – and in many cases only – element of their diet. 'The staff at Monks' bakery in our area worked continuously, baking bread, and we formed queues of people from the neighbourhood and rationed the bread as it was baked. We also carried a supply to the convent at North Brunswick Street.'[3] But bakers also suffered casualties during Easter week: by Thursday, Rebel leader Frank Shouldice recalled, 'It was dangerous now to expose yourself at windows and doors. One of the men who had worked all the week in Monks' bakery opened the shop door to see if it was safe to leave home for work. He was shot dead. We kept a sharp lookout and fired whenever a target offered.'[4]

Imperial Hotel, Sackville Street, 18 May 1916.

One might have thought that the main Boland's bakery and flour mills in Grand Canal Street, opposite Sir Patrick Dun's Hospital, would have been taken out of commission when it was occupied by Rebels led by Eamon de Valera, but, no: in spite of Dev's instruction, parts of the bakery kept working for a while at least.

Holles Street Hospital, like every other maternity hospital in 1916 Dublin, was within the area of the curfew but still managed to get bread:

> The Committee also expressed their obligations to Messrs Boland's Ltd for their generous supplies of bread not only for the intern patients but also for the sick and hungry attending the dispensaries . . . and to the Royal Irish Automobile Club . . . who made ambulances available to the hospital to transport patients and carry bread from Messrs Boland's Bakeries.[5]

Another Rebel leader, Joseph O'Connor, recalled, 'When we took over the bakery a batch of bread was being baked in the ovens. The bakers, realising the position, very courageously volunteered to remain until the bread was ready. They did so and withdrew the bread before leaving.'[6]

Dublin families were not just dependent on fresh bread: sacks of stale loaves were eagerly sought after. The bread might have been hard, but it was cheaper and could still be eaten if soaked in milk or water. On 1 May, the *Liverpool Daily Post* reported:

> Con Colbert, one of the executed Rebels, worked as a clerk in Kennedys bakers in Parnell Street.
>
> Jacob's biscuit factory was taken out of commission on Easter Monday when the Rebels, led by Thomas MacDonagh, captured it – but even they complained of hunger as the week wore on.

Women and children were waiting in Church Street at the back of the hotel for the distribution of bread. They were being regulated by the military and shots from the river struck a girl and a boy. The girl was hit on the temple and the boy had his leg smashed by what was apparently a soft-nosed bullet. A few moments later another bullet from the same quarter killed a woman instantaneously.[7]

The north Dublin suburbs had been cut off since the Wednesday of Easter week: people in Phibsborough were kept behind a cordon and, by Thursday, the food situation was truly desperate. Shops were besieged and the flour mills at Cross Guns Bridge were targeted. 'Men and women of all classes were seen carrying away parcels of flour, potatoes, bread and everything in the way of foodstuffs. Soon all the shops were cleared.'[8]

Everyone was hit by the shortage of food: 'There was quite a run on vegetables at Mr Begg's place in Cabra last week-end. Respectable citizens of standing could be seen carrying cabbages, cauliflowers and rhubarb with the humblest.'[9]

By Tuesday, some efforts were being made to feed the people – as reported in the *Irish Independent* on the following day:

Bovril advertisement dating from 1916.

BOVRIL FOR THE STARVING PEOPLE

The military having taken over the Bovril warehouse in Eustace Street, the Dublin representative of the firm, Mr J. Sheridan, has since distributed through the military thousands of pounds worth of Bovril and Virol among the poor.[10]

On Wednesday, the author James Stephens wrote:

> This morning there are no newspapers, no bread, no milk, no news – the sun is shining and the streets are lively but discreet. All people continue to talk to one another without distinction of class, but nobody knows what any person thinks. Guns do not sound as bad in the day as they do at night and no person can feel lonely when the sun shines.
>
> In many parts of the city hunger began to be troublesome. A girl told me that her family and another who had taken refuge with them had eaten nothing for three days. On this day her father managed to get two loaves of bread somewhere and he brought these home.

When, said the girl, my father came in with the bread the whole fourteen of us ran at him and in a minute we were all ashamed for the loaves were gone to the last crumb and we were all as hungry as we had been before he came in. The poor man, said she, did not even get a bit himself.[11]

Boland's Mills, under the nominal control of de Valera, proved a rich source for bags of flour on the first two days of the Rising. Many families in Dublin have stories of how they 'managed' during Easter week. This one is typical:

When the Rising started the English put roadblocks on all the bridges in Dublin, including those over the canals. My grandfather had a job as a labourer on a site in Rathmines so he could not get to work and could not earn badly needed wages. He was obliged to sit around the house doing nothing. After a couple of days' hanging around the house my grandmother rushed home and told him that there was flour being given out free in Boland's Mills and everyone was over there helping themselves. Needless to say, knowing my grandmother and her tongue, he headed across from Annesley Place in Ballybough to Boland's Mills on the south quays.

Sure enough when he got there, there were very many men like himself helping themselves to bags of flour (about eight stone each in weight). Being a big strong man he hoisted a bag on his back and headed across the Liffey. However, when he arrived at the old Butt Bridge he was met by a British Army barricade. A Tommy came out to inspect him with a rifle and a very large bayonet on the end of it.

'Where do you think you're going with that bag? I could shoot you for looting.' My grandfather nearly died of fright. He then told the Tommy that there were four hungry children and a wife at home and not a crust for them to eat.

The Tommy looked him up and down and lowered his rifle. 'Go on and get home with you, sure I have six of my own at home in Liverpool.'[12]

James Stephens was no stranger to tenement life and poverty. Born in Pimlico, in Dublin's Liberties, and orphaned at an early age, his 1912 classic *The Charwoman's Daughter* captured tenement life through the character of Mary Makebelieve, 'who lived with her mother in a small room at the very top of a big dingy house in a Dublin back street'. Descriptions prevail of poverty and dilapidation: mildewed wallpaper, creeping cockroaches, grimy soot-covered windows, and water that had to be carried from the 'very bottom of the five-storey house up hundreds and hundreds of stairs to her room'.

But everyone in Dublin that week – insurgents, British Army, civilians – was

Group of children on Aylward's Yard, Thomas Street, c. 1913.

looking for food, as recalled by the assistant matron in the South Dublin Union. In 1916, it housed 3,200 of the poor and elderly of Dublin.

> At that time both sides had to be fed. The military demanded food from the store keeper and he supplied it to them as well as to the Volunteers. The bakers were in all week, I think, because we had tons of bread and we were able to supply bread to various people who came and asked for it. We supplied a good deal of bread from our bakehouse to people who were badly off during that week.[13]

The bakers at the South Dublin Union were singled out for praise:

> Whilst it is invidious to mention names, we cannot refrain from mentioning the Master Baker and his two assistants Kyne and Kelly who attended here daily and with the assistance of the inmates kept the bakery running, with the result that we had plenty of bread not alone for our requirements but we were able to give to the poor and others who were unable to procure bread elsewhere for love or money.[14]

Breakfast for the children of the tenements – if you got any – was tea, bread, margarine, cocoa and, if very lucky, jam or porridge. There was no choice: you got what there was. For dinner, it was mostly stews and soups, made from cheap meat scraps or 'parings', offcuts of meat, which were very fatty. Mothers would buy sheep's and cows' heads, rabbits, fish heads and, with potatoes, onions, cabbage, carrots and other vegetables, make a pot of stew or soup sufficient to feed the family for a week. Also popular were pigs' feet and cheeks, herrings, winkles, cockles and eels. It was always the rule that the father and oldest son, particularly if they were employed, received the lion's share of whatever food was available. Mothers wanted to make sure their children were decently fed and often went without.[15]

Bread laced with sugar was a treat, in a wretched, miserable city, with barefoot children clothed in rags. But children were children and, of course, their mission in life was survival – and the Dublin of 1916 was slowly emerging from a time when a shocking 62 per cent of children died before they reached their tenth birthday.[16]

So, the children of the revolution depended on their ability to scavenge, forage, pilfer, trick, cajole, hide, cheat, steal, lie, outwit and, above all, beg to stay alive. Begging was rampant in the Dublin of a hundred years ago – but in Easter week, when money was not to be had, and even if you had it you could buy very little – the challenge increased. And food was at the top of the list of necessities.

The Dublin labourers derived most of their protein from bread; their carbohydrates from bread and sugar. Rural diets relied more heavily on potatoes and contained a decidedly higher milk and meat content. Dubliners differed from their English counterparts in consuming virtually no cheese or pulse vegetables. The dependence on shop bread and lack of pulses was partly attributable to cooking difficulties. Tenement houses were generally equipped only with open fires; coal was costly and many of the poor relied for their fuel on cinders rejected by the rich.[17]

Jameson Distillery, c.1910.

Joseph Murray, at fourteen, was typical of many boys of that era: he was small for his age, but fleet of foot and streetwise. Like so many, he did not have to wait until Easter 1916 to experience tragedy and grief. At least he lived in an exciting part of the city: Augustine Street nestled in the shadow of the twin pillars of the Dublin of 1916 – the Church and alcohol. John's Lane Distillery and the local church dominated Joseph Murray's tenement home throughout his short life. The Murrays lived in the 'golden triangle' of Dublin distilleries: John Powers in John's Lane, the George Roe Distillery farther up Thomas Street and W. Jameson's in Marrowbone Lane and Bow Lane.

Within forty-eight hours of the start of the Rising on Easter Monday, the food shortages were serious. With people living from hand to mouth, they bought food when money was available. There was no such thing as stocking up for the week. By Thursday, the military had decided to do something to help the civilians:

> . . . the first action taken therefore was to seize various provisions from two city wholesale warehouses and to distribute them out of Military waggons under strong guards, free, to the starving mobs in the Coombe area and Aungier Street and to the hospitals, asylums, etc., for payment. The military repeatedly had to send for reinforcements and with fixed bayonets to prevent the mobs rushing the waggons; they reported women with babies were fainting from hunger, lying in the streets and in danger of being trampled on and crushed.[18]

By Friday of Easter week, as the battles intensified, food shortages were catastrophic.

The Mendicity Institute on Usher's Island, between Thomas Street and the Liffey, near the Murrays' home on Augustine Street, was one of the main centres in Dublin that gave food to the poor. But the Rebels, led by twenty-four-year-old Sean Heuston and his trusted sidekick eighteen-year-old Sean McLoughlin, had captured it on Monday, so the free dinners were no longer available – from that source at least.

Relatives relate the story of Joseph Murray's family with sadness.[19] In 1916, times were tough for the Murrays: the mother, Jane, had died in 1913 from tuberculosis, aged fifty-three, leaving a daughter and four sons – the youngest was eight at the time. The father, John, was a casual labourer, which meant unsteady work at about a pound a week, if you were lucky. Like most tenement families, the Murrays' basic diet consisted of bread, cabbage, scraps of meat – pig or rabbit – sugar and tea.

The Liberties were the industrial heart of the city, benefiting from the vital watercourses of the Poddle. At one stage, Guinness in James's Street and Jacob's in Bishop Street between them employed 8,000 people! Tanneries employed over 5,000 people, while up to thirty breweries thrived, including Guinness – producing 3 million barrels of stout a year, the biggest such output in Europe.

At the centre of the city's brewing, distilling and tanning industries, the busy spine of Thomas Street drew thousands daily to its markets. In 1911, when Joseph was nine, the streets he lived on were bedecked with bunting and Union Jacks for the visit of King George V and Queen Mary, who processed up Thomas Street to the Iveagh Play Centre in Francis Street, near Joseph's home, which provided free breakfasts on Sundays for the poor children of the area. Local children, including those who attended Joseph's school, St Patrick's in John's Lane, were selected to sing and dance for the royal party. The historian Maurice Curtis wrote, 'As the Royal Carriage pulled off from the Myra Hall in Francis Street a woman was nearly killed when in the regal excitement she fell under the horses, only to be rescued by a member of the Dublin Metropolitan Police.'[20] He added, 'After the visit King George donated £1,000 to the poor people in the area, which included the Iveagh Play Centre itself. Within two years the centre recorded 4,000 children coming through its doors.'[21] The free hot food from the 'Bayno', as the Iveagh was known locally, was the stuff of legend for many years afterwards.

By 1914, a pound per week had become the common unskilled wage. Indeed, of the 28,079 heads of tenement households in Dublin city then, 40 per cent were earning less than a pound per week, doing whatever casual work they might have been lucky enough to get.[22]

The breakdown of weekly expenditure in a poor Dublin household a hundred years ago was simple: about 60 per cent went on food, 15 per cent on rent and 10 per cent on fuel, with only a pittance left for other incidentals such as school, clothes or the demon drink.[23]

By Friday of Easter week, people were desperate for food, and teenagers were regarded as smart enough to make it to the shops and back quickly, in a week of curfews, gun battles, checkpoints and urban warfare in a packed city. What boy of that age would not have welcomed an adventure on the dangerous streets around his home? There were two older boys in the Murray family: John, aged twenty-two, a labourer, and James, who was seventeen, but it would have been deemed just too dangerous to have them running around the streets.

On Friday, fourteen-year-old Joseph was despatched to Ryans grocery in nearby Bridge Street, close to the Brazen Head pub. According to his family, the curfew was in force – and Joseph was shot 'through the ear and out his mouth'.[24] He was carried back to his home, where he died. Joseph Murray was buried in the St Paul's section of Glasnevin Cemetery 'in a christening robe, made from his late mother's wedding dress'.[25]

There is a reference in the Dublin Fire Brigade Ambulance log for that week to an incident on Friday, 28 April in St Augustine Street: '12.40 Ambulance to St Augustine Street, phone from "A" station . . . did not attend'.[26] In 1918, John Murray,

Joseph's father, drowned in the River Liffey close to his home. He was fifty-eight.

It's a long walk from Pembroke Cottages in Ballsbridge on the banks of the Dodder to the Pigeon House power station in Ringsend, which had been supplying electricity to Dublin since 1903. On Friday, 28 April 1916, the journey was not just long, it was dangerous.

At that time, Charles Stewart from Ballsbridge was working there. Mary Connolly, aged twenty-two, was the eldest daughter of the Stewart family and had been told to bring food to her father. That day, she was minding her younger sister, Bridget, and took the eleven-year-old with her. The two sisters were not looking for food but making their way with food towards Ringsend along the banks of the Dodder when they were caught in a gun battle. Their journey had brought them into danger zones near Mount Street, Northumberland Road and Beggars Bush, and Bridget was hit in the chest by a bullet.[27] Immediately, Mary carried her youngest sister to the Royal City Hospital in Baggot Street, but it was too late: the child died from 'gunshot wound to chest, shock and haemorrhage'.[28]

The tragedy befell the Stewarts just two months after Mary had married John Connolly, on St Valentine's Day, 1916. She had recently left her job as a 'live-in nurse and domestic servant' to a widow, Muriel Harter, at 31 Raglan Road. The Harters lived close to the Stewarts, an example of the class divide in Dublin at the time. Muriel Harter had two daughters, Gwendolen and Doreen, and four servants, Annie Lennon, a cook, Eveleen Gilsenan, a governess, Annie Newett, a parlourmaid, and Mary

Stewart. Maybe four servants were needed in the three-storey, ten-bedroomed house: they also looked after a twenty-eight-year-old 'professor of piano', Mabel Lander.[29]

Nichol's undertakers arranged Bridget's burial, which took place on 3 May; she was placed in an unmarked grave in Deans Grange Cemetery. Mary Connolly subsequently approached the Rebellion (Victims) Committee for help. A letter to the Committee in May 1917, from George Lidwell, solicitors, of 33 Upper Ormond Quay reads:

Mrs Mary Connolly of 42 Dodder View, Ballsbridge, has asked us to forward you the enclosed claim for the death of her sister, Bridget Stewart, aged 10 [sic] years, who was shot in the Rebellion on 26 April last year while fetching her father his dinner at the Electric Power Station, Ringsend Road.

I do not know whether you will entertain the claim but I am assured that it was entirely through ignorance it was not sent in before. Her father is alive but now away working in a Munitions Factory and his authority will be obtained to pay my Client the expense she was put to.

Yours sincerely
Lidwell solrs.[30]

There is no record of how much the family received, but as Bridget was a 'dependant', it is unlikely – as with many other cases – that they were granted anything.

According to relatives, Mary Connolly, having witnessed her sister's killing, suffered dreadfully from the effects of the tragedy. She died six years later, aged just twenty-eight, of tuberculosis.

On the day that Bridget was buried, the front page of the

Dublin Evening Mail was dominated by a public notice: 'Food Supply Dublin City and County' – bread vans were being robbed of their contents at gunpoint and the government was keen to put an end to such lawless behaviour, brought on, of course, by desperation.

> Wholesale and retail Traders are advised that business can now resume its normal course. Goods trains will arrive . . . today with food stuffs. Vehicles collecting or delivering food stuffs or coal will be permitted by the military to pass sentries. All food supplies which have been and are being delivered at pre-disturbance rates to retailers by the Government Food Supply Committee ARE PROCURABLE BY CONSUMERS AT THESE RATES.

The notice ended ominously:

> Any necessary protection to retail and wholesale traders will be given by the military authorities. BY ORDER.[31]

The army even used 'armoured cars' to transport the food around the city. The vehicles had been built hastily for use against the Rebels but food distribution now took priority:

> Guinness's Brewery have made three splendid armoured cars by putting great long boilers six feet in diameter on to their large motor lorries. Holes are bored down the sides to let in the air and they are painted grey. The driver sits inside too. They each carry twenty-two men or a ton of food in absolute security.[32]

Food supplies in Dublin were getting back to normal – or were they? In fact, the 'disturbances' and the ongoing Great War meant

Soldier walking behind a Kennedy's Bakery cart during the Civil War, c. 1920.

that the shortages endured by the population when it came to food could only get worse and, by the end of 1916, the authorities had to set up soup kitchens to prevent mass starvation.

No matter your status or income in Dublin in Easter week 1916, you did not escape the food shortages. Ernest J. Jordison, a Norwegian, who ran 136 oil depots in Ireland, recalled the situation in Clontarf on the first night of the Rising: 'Many of the people remained up the whole night and were about early on Tuesday morning looking for bread and provision for their meals, but very little or practically none were to be had, especially bread.'[33]

In 1899, William Scott and Anna Magdalena Bryce were married in their homeland of Scotland. They lived near each other in the port villages of Balloch and Alexandria, not far from Glasgow.

Anna gave birth to their first child, named William after his father, in Scotland but, shortly afterwards, on 10 August 1900, William was appointed skipper of a 'bucket dredger' in Dublin port. The young family moved to Dublin where five more children were born, including Walter, on 13 February 1908.

By 1911, William was 'sub-foreman dredging master' in charge of the three dredging vessels operating to keep Dublin Port clear,[34] and the Scotts moved to their own five-roomed house in Irvine Crescent, East Wall, around the corner from Irish playwright and activist Sean O'Casey.

By 1916, the Scott family were thriving. William, in his mid-fifties, now held the prestigious job of 'dredging master for Dublin port', with the children at this time aged between sixteen and five. The Scotts were comfortable, but as a family member told me with some understatement, '1916 was a very difficult year for the Scott family.'[35]

Two weeks after Walter celebrated his eighth birthday, his father died – and almost exactly two months later, Walter and his mother would lie wounded near their home on the Friday of Easter week.

While William Scott was working on the quayside on 22 February 1916, a hawser broke and he was thrown into the Liffey between the dredger and the quay wall. He was rescued from the water but succumbed to pneumonia three days later.[36]

With six young children to care for, Anna, like so many others, went in search of bread on the Friday of Easter week, taking with her the second youngest child, Walter. The family told me that Anna and Walter were both hit by gunfire – the mother in the leg and Walter in the head. He was taken to Mercers Hospital by a Dublin Fire Brigade ambulance – where he lingered for over two months. We can only imagine the suffering of a child with a bullet wound to the head, in an era before antibiotics, sophisticated painkillers or neurological surgical procedures.

The logbook of the Dublin Fire Brigade gives another insight into what happened to Walter. It records that on Friday, 28 April at 1.48 p.m., an ambulance was summoned to North Wall and 'left male 12 in Mercers hospital, bullet wound in ankle'. Then at '2.38 ambulance returned, left one male aged about 8 in Mercers bullet in head'. This was undoubtedly Walter Scott.[37]

Walter's family maintain that the bullet that hit him was poisoned, but his death certificate states that the cause of death on 5 July 1916 was 'gunshot wound of head – meningitis certified'.[38]

Anna Scott applied to the Rebellion (Victims) Committee – but to little avail. She asked for a hundred pounds in compensation – but was given a 'compassionate grant' of twenty-five pounds, slashed to ten pounds in Dublin Castle by senior civil servant John Taylor.

Walter's older brother, William, subsequently joined the British Army and was sent to the Crimea 'to help white Russians escape'.[39] Anna Scott needed an income to support her family and became an agent for the Royal Liver Assurance company. She died of a brain haemorrhage at her home in East Wall in November 1939; she was sixty-three.

Nuns from the Sisters of Charity distributing bread after the Rising.

The Society of St Vincent de Paul was also trying to deal with the food crisis: 'On Friday the 28th it became evident that there was widespread destitution in the city owing to the scarcity of food in the shops and the total cessation of employment in the city.'[40] By 1 May, seven days after the Rising had exploded onto the streets of an unsuspecting city, the food situation had settled somewhat, with the help of the society. Two central food depots had been set up at the North Wall railway station, the Point Depot, and the National Shell factory in Parkgate Street, with the food then sent out to '33 distribution depots' in convents and similar institutions.[41]

The government subsequently revealed that: 'The sum of £9,412 12s 2d was appropriated for the relief of distress in connection with the Dublin rebellion. The payments consisted of the recoupment to the Dublin Guardians in respect of relief expenditure incurred by them, together with the cost of supplies distributed by the military authorities and the Dublin Food supply committee.'[42]

Tragically, as the food supply improved, forty Dublin families had one less child to feed – and would soon discover that any attempt to quantify their loss would be callously rebutted by the authorities. The fact that they had one less mouth to feed was deemed to reduce the family's costs.

Middle Abbey Street before the fall of the corner house, 17 May 1916.

Christopher Whelan, who worked at Eason, O'Connell Street, was killed by a stray bullet through the window of his home on North Great George's Street. He had turned up for work that morning only to have been sent home.

Boy selling newspapers at Harcourt Street station, c. 1904.

8. The Child Workers

LIKE MANY OF THEIR AGE, CHRISTOPHER WHELAN, BRIDGET MCKANE, MARY REDMOND AND JAMES KELLY WERE YOUNG WORKERS WHEN THEY WERE KILLED IN THE RISING.

Is it well that, while we range with science, glorying in the time,
City children soak and blacken soul and sense in city slime?
From 'Locksley Hall', Alfred Lord Tennyson

It is hardly surprising that, in the Dublin of 1916, with unemployment rife, nearly half of the children who were killed in the Rising were working. Any employment, part- or full-time, augmented a family's meagre income.

Christopher Whelan was, like many of his age, a messenger boy. He worked for Easons, darting around the city on his bicycle, with its parcel shelf under the handlebars. He would have met many of the telegraph boys on their bikes as they left the GPO to deliver urgent messages around the city. Nearly every shop, office, hotel or factory employed a young messenger, always a boy aged between fourteen, when they could leave school, and eighteen: they were often dismissed when the adult wage rate applied on their eighteenth birthday.

Patrick Ivers was one of the many newsboys in Dublin city centre; the bestselling newspapers were printed within yards of Sackville Street. Such was the demand for this type of job, light work suitable for malnourished children, that a licensing system was introduced. (Heavy labour, on building sites, for example, was better suited to strong rural boys. The heaviest work to which a scrawny city urchin could aspire was as 'helper' to carters, bakers, porters or butchers.)

From 1915 onwards, a young person needed a 'badge' to trade on the streets. Girls were not allowed sell newspapers, and children were restricted in where they could trade – the red-light district of the Monto, near Amiens Street station, was strictly off limits. Children could not work during school hours; from April to September each year, girls could work until 8 p.m., boys until nine. Breaches of these rules led to prosecution of the parents – indeed, at that time there were many more prosecutions of 'exploitative' parents than employers. Many Dubliners felt no shame in buying newspapers, matches or bootlaces from barefoot, hungry children in the city's streets. Girls sold matches, bootlaces and fruit, and took up work in factories

Charles Darcy, killed on Easter Monday 1916.

when they reached the age of fourteen, but had to leave when they got married – at least Jacob's, the biscuit maker, gave them a wedding cake on their departure!

Bridget McKane, aged fifteen, worked in a 'fancy box' factory with her sister. Bridget Allen worked in the famous Dublin Salt Works, run by the Altman family on Usher's Island, near her home.[1]

The families of many children killed in Easter week were heavily dependent on the income of their offspring. Mary Redmond, aged sixteen, was a bottle washer, Charles Darcy, at fifteen, a draper's assistant. Sean Healy, who was fourteen, helped in his father's plumbing business, while James Kelly, fifteen, was serving an apprenticeship in the nearby Broadstone railway works.

In various compensation claims, families alluded to the wages their deceased children brought into the household. The higher the wage, the higher the compensation, in theory, but the amount granted was so small that it hardly warranted the humiliation of applying for it.

There was an ongoing campaign, led by the National Society for the Prevention of Cruelty to Children, the Dublin Advisory Committee for Juvenile Employment and various newspapers, to limit children working, especially on the streets, and it was held by the authorities that:

> The social conditions which are responsible for the existence of street trading must be recognised as a blot upon our civilisation. The idle, vicious and drunken parents who utilise their children as wage-earning instruments, utterly regardless of the baneful effects on the life of the child in after years, are deserving of no leniency.[2]

Bridget McKane had been in the wrong place at the wrong time, as those responsible for her killing later admitted.[3] She had been born and died within yards of the GPO. If the McKane family had not moved, before 1916, the short distance to the other side of the GPO, Bridget would perhaps have become the accountant and poet she aspired to be.

Bridget McKane was an unusual little girl: at eleven, she was regarded as a 'studious child', and was interested in current affairs and poetry. By 1916, she was working with her older sister in a 'fancy box making factory', earning six shillings a week, and took a great interest in Irish men who were fighting on the Western Front.[4] It was in death, though, that Bridget achieved fame: she was the only child killed who is mentioned – and accurately named – by the Rebels who gave statements to the Bureau of Military History. Volunteer Joe Good of the Kimmage garrison writes of the retreat from the GPO on Friday night as the Rising was collapsing: 'We were not able to proceed, stopping past the White House in relative safety to the top of Moore Lane. Most of the doors in Moore Lane were shut and the Volunteers attempted to break in. In doing so, they fired through the lock of one door, killing a girl and wounding her father in the chest. The Volunteers were unaware of who were behind the door.'[5]

The McKane family – all eleven of them – lived at 10 Henry Place, just off Moore Street. The family had two of the four rooms in the house, occupied in total by seventeen tenants. There were four windows at the front.

In 1892, Thomas McKane, from County Monaghan, married Margaret Byrne, from County Carlow. Margaret gave birth to twelve children, of whom nine (seven girls and two boys) were alive in 1911

THE BOY WHO WAS SHOT DEAD
BEFORE THE RISING

It can be argued that the first child casualty of the Easter Rising was shot and killed on Friday, 28 January 1916. Herbert Lemass, a twenty-two-month-old baby, was accidentally shot and killed by his older brother Seán (aged sixteen), a member of the Irish Volunteers, as he cleaned his revolver.

The inquest into Hebert Lemass' death took place in Temple Street Hospital where the jury declared that 'something should to be done to prevent young boys getting the possession of arms'.

But bizarrely nothing was said or done it seems about the possession of the firearm that killed the baby.

Indeed when sixteen-year-old Seán Lemass joined the GPO contingent on Easter Tuesday and took up position on the roof, he was probably carrying the gun that accidentally killed his younger brother!

Seán Lemass was part of the retreating party from the GPO on Friday night and was in Moore Lane along with the leaders of the Rising when Bridget McKane was accidentally shot and killed.

Lemass' older brother Noel was savagely killed during the Civil War and was buried in the same grave as his brother Herbert in Glasnevin Cemetery.

Seán Lemass went on to become Taoiseach and along with Eamon de Valera presided over the state's fiftieth anniversary commemorations of the Rising in 1966.

– three died in infancy. The family shared their two rooms with a boarder, fifty-eight-year-old labourer Patrick O'Sullivan.[6] In the 1901 and 1911 censuses, Thomas described himself as a bricklayer and 'general foreman'.

Bridget was born on 8 June 1900, in a tenement house at 21 Marlborough Street, beside the Pro-Cathedral and close to the GPO. She kept a scrapbook, inscribing on the cover, 'You do not need to look through this book, for well you know the writer's name, Bridget McKane.' It was a scrapbook, filled with transcribed poems and cuttings from newspapers about the Great War and events in Ireland at the time. There are two memorable insertions, both newspaper cuttings. The first is a letter from a Private P. Curran of the 4th Royal Dublin Fusiliers in the form of a poem about bravery in the trenches, which ends:

> Let all the slackers stay at home,
> And hide behind Sinn Féin;
> Another name for coward
> Are what these two words mean.
> The fight we'll win without them,
> Sure as morn and night appear,
> And home will come in triumph,
> The Dublin Fusiliers.
> God save the King.

Private Curran was killed on 27 April 1915 – almost a year to the day before Bridget would die.

The second cutting is from July 1914: it shows a photograph of a ten-year-old Dublin boy in hospital, a victim of the shootings at Bachelors Walk after the Irish Volunteers illegally imported arms, in an incident that became known as the Howth gun-running.

The caption reads: 'Luke Kelly, a ten-year-old Dublin boy, photographed in hospital seemingly quite oblivious of his serious injuries. He is suffering from a bullet wound in the lung and is not expected to recover.' In fact, Luke, who had been shot while cycling across Carlisle Bridge (now O'Connell Bridge), survived and went on to rear a large family in Dublin's Sheriff Street, among them his son, Luke, the famous Dubliner from the band of the same name.

Bridget transcribed – in beautiful handwriting – many poems, such as Thomas Haynes Bayly's ballad, 'Oh! Steer My Bark to Erin's Isle':

A page from Bridget McKane's scrapbook, where in her careful handwriting she has transcribed the poem 'Oh! Steer My Bark to Erin's Isle'.

> *Oh! I have roamed in many lands,*
> *And many friends I've met*
> *Not one fair scene or kindly smile*
> *Can this fond heart forget.*[7]

All that fateful week, the McKanes were at the heart of the battle. On Thursday and Friday, the family huddled together in their tiny rooms, crouched under the beds, saying the rosary. They had witnessed death that week, including the shooting of a looter whose body was unceremoniously flung onto a barricade, but what followed was almost beyond belief. Five of the seven signatories

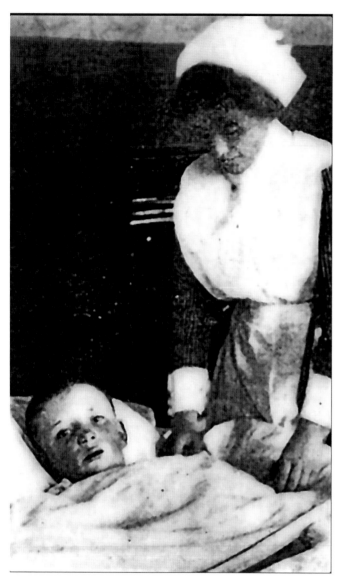

Luke Kelly was ten years of age when he was shot cycling over O'Connell Bridge. A cutting of the above was included in Bridget McKane's scrapbook. The caption to her cutting reads baldly: 'Luke Kelly, a ten-year-old Dublin boy, photographed in hospital seemingly quite oblivious of his serious injuries. He is suffering from a bullet wound in the lung and is not expected to recover'.

of the 1916 proclamation were in the McKanes' home as the Rising collapsed, with future leaders Michael Collins and Seán Lemass outside in the lane: 'Nearly all of the men were carried into the first house . . . James Connolly was carried up a narrow staircase. The staircase was so narrow that it was impossible to take him up the stairs until four strong men lifted him horizontally at extended arms' length over the banister rail.'[8] Thomas McKane claimed that Tom Clarke, who ran a newsagent's not 500 yards from Henry Place, and Sean McDermott 'sought refuge in his house'.[9] They were not the only ones.

Volunteer Sean McLoughlin in his description of the chaotic exodus says, 'Joseph Plunkett accompanied us.' He goes on to describe what happened after Bridget had been shot: 'Sean McDermott was consoling Bridget's mother Ellen McKane, with James Connolly laid out on a stretcher in the kitchen. Sitting by him was Miss Carney,

I believe Miss Grennan, Elizabeth O'Farrell, Sean McDermott, Tom Clarke, P.H. Pearse, Willie Pearse, Joseph Plunkett and several of our own wounded, including some British wounded.'[10] Michael Collins was outside the door, feverishly commandeering material for makeshift barricades.

In 1966, Elizabeth and Rosie McKane, who would have been eight and six when their sister was killed, were in the audience of a special *Late Late Show*. They said, 'Our house was the first house that Pádraig Pearse, James Connolly, Thomas MacDonagh and Count Plunkett came into.' They spoke about the shot that had wounded their father and killed their sister. They confirmed that 'James Connolly lay wounded on our floor, Sean McDermott was also there, as was Count Plunkett. Pádraig Pearse came over to my mother and tried to comfort her.'[11]

The sisters explained that their house adjoined Mr Cogan's grocery shop, which had been looted of all its produce – he was also their landlord. 'There was firing everywhere. My mother ran for a priest. When Father McInerney from Dominick Street arrived, he actually cried when he saw the wounded on the floor . . .'

The bullet that pierced Bridget's forehead, killing her, had already passed through her father's shoulder and right lung. Elizabeth and Rosie McKane recalled their 'mother getting to her feet, looking completely stunned – everything had happened so suddenly.'[12] Pádraig Pearse, on hearing what had happened to the child, said, 'My God, I'm sorry this happened. What can we do?'[13]

Margaret McKane, hysterical at the death of her daughter and the wounding of her husband, ran around into Moore Lane towards the British barricades, waving a white sheet over her head. 'Get back, for God's sake, or we'll fire!' shouted a Tommy.

'My husband! My husband!' yelled Mrs McKane. 'I must get a priest!'[14]

The mayhem continued on Saturday morning.

Sixteen-year-old Mary Redmond 'was shot while standing at her own hall door during Rebellion'.[15] The family applied to the Rebellion (Victims) Compensation Committee, the claim stating: 'Deceased helped her mother (who is a widow) to support deceased's grandfather, aged 84 years, and deceased's younger sister, aged 14 years.' A subsequent letter from the committee read: 'Miss Mary Redmond, deceased, helped to support her widowed mother, her grandfather and her younger sister. Her earning of 18/ – a week as a bottlewasher – must have represented a very considerable portion of the family income.'[16] Bottle washing was a common enough occupation for young women in Dublin of 1916. Pubs bottled their own beer, and massive factories like the nearby Williams and Woods food producers needed clean jars and bottles for the sauces and jams they produced.

Like many women in her position, Alice Redmond, Mary's mother, was a 'dealer':

> Dealing was predominantly the refuge of women. Many were widows, a situation all too common in a city where the adult male death rate, due mainly to tuberculosis and other diseases of poverty, was far in excess of the UK average. Others became charwomen or washerwomen.[17]

On 28 December 1916, the committee made a 'compassionate

grant of one hundred pounds sterling to deceased's mother Mrs Alicia [sic] Redmond, 8 Mary's Abbey' – but, as with most such recommendations, the amount was halved by the assistant under-secretary at the Irish Treasury, John Taylor. Taylor acted as if public funds were his own. In four cases where the families were awarded twenty-five pounds on the death of their child, Taylor reduced the amount to ten pounds.[18]

> Mary's Abbey, the busy street at the heart of the Dublin markets, had hit the headlines in early 1910 for a notorious murder and suicide, which had taken place in the tenement house next door to the Redmonds. On 9 January William and Catherine McKeown were found dead, with their throats cut. It was presumed that William, a wood-cutting machinist originally from Scotland, had murdered his wife, then cut his own throat with a newly sharpened knife.[19]

The photograph of Mary Redmond reproduced on p.198 shows a strong, confident girl, who appears older than her age. The daughter of a 'fowl dealer', she lived in a tenement house at 8 Mary's Abbey, at the heart of the markets area, with her four siblings, grandfather, mother and uncle.

Mary's relatives report that she was 'killed in Mary's Abbey as she tried to pull a drunk man into the hall of the building. She simply stepped out the door to pull him to safety during the curfew, as there was firing from Capel Street towards the Four Courts and Bridewell direction, and was hit by a bullet.'[20] Her death certificate states that she had been shot through the left lung and died with 'no medical attention'.[21]

The compensation award was made to Alice Redmond on 8 May 1917 – too late to pay for the first anniversary notice the family had inserted in the *Evening Herald*:

Redmond – first anniversary: in sad and loving memory of my dear daughter Mary Redmond, who was killed at her residence, 8 Mary's Abbey on Thursday, 27 April 1916, aged 16 years. On whose soul sweet Jesus have mercy. Queen of the most Holy Rosary intercede for her. Mass offered [this] Friday morning for the repose of her soul in St Michan's Church, Halston Street.

In health and strength she left her home,
Not knowing death was near,
But short and sudden was the call,
On one we loved so dear.
You are not forgotten, Mary dear,
Nor ever shall you be;
As long as life and memory lasts,
We will remember thee.

Inserted by her loving mother, brother, sisters and uncles.[22]

Mary Redmond was buried at 2 p.m. on 1 May in the main section of Glasnevin Cemetery. Outside the door where she was shot, a cross was carved into the kerb until it was removed to make way for the Luas tram system.[23]

Researching the short life of another worker, Christopher Whelan, I was struck by the similarities he had with Bridget McKane. Both lived within a very short distance of Sackville Street, with Christopher, like Bridget, a bookish, studious child. He was employed as a messenger boy in Easons bookshop on Sackville Street until it was burned to the ground in the Rising.

Christopher Whelan, fifteen, was shot dead in his bed while reading a book. His father, Laurence, ran the busy Post Hotel (later known as the European Hotel) in North Great George's Street – and the tragic death of his youngest son was the latest in a litany of tragedies to visit the family.

Twelve years earlier, Laurence's wife, Mary Bradshaw, had died at the age of thirty-seven of meningitis while giving birth to a daughter, also Mary. Within twelve months, the baby had caught diphtheria and died.[24]

Meningitis, diphtheria, measles, pneumonia, typhoid, cholera, whooping cough, rheumatoid arthritis, smallpox and tuberculosis were among the diseases that caused Dublin's mortality rates to soar in the early twentieth century. Chronic overcrowding, almost non-existent sanitation, filthy streets, back-lane slaughterhouses and piggeries supplied a fertile breeding ground for rats, other vermin and death. In 1906, of the city's 167 packed national schools, 146 had playgrounds – but only sixty-three had toilets.[25]

Although the Whelans would have been regarded as a middle-class family – and social class was then, as today, a key determinant of health – they would not have been immune from the many infectious diseases that struck down Dubliners. And in 1916, Dublin city centre was not a healthy place for anyone to live.

As well as running the hotel, Laurence Whelan was a 'letter carrier' based in the GPO. After his wife's death, he was left with three young children to rear, Christopher being the youngest. Christopher's two older sisters, Mary (May) and Annie, were sent to live with their mother's sister, Anne Bradshaw, a publican, in Cahir, County Tipperary. Christopher stayed with his father in Dublin. On 14 September 1905, Laurence married Mary

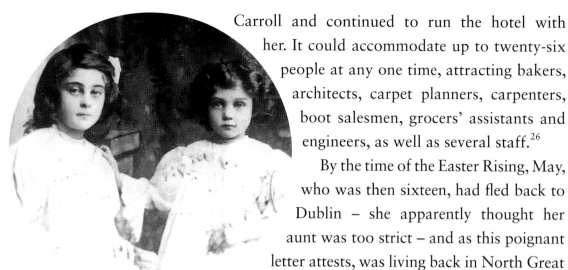

Christopher Whelan's two sisters, May, the letter writer (left), and Annie 'Cuckoo' (right).

Carroll and continued to run the hotel with her. It could accommodate up to twenty-six people at any one time, attracting bakers, architects, carpet planners, carpenters, boot salesmen, grocers' assistants and engineers, as well as several staff.[26]

By the time of the Easter Rising, May, who was then sixteen, had fled back to Dublin – she apparently thought her aunt was too strict – and as this poignant letter attests, was living back in North Great George's Street, a few hundred yards from Sackville Street, when the fighting broke out. She is writing to her aunt – Annie Cuckoo is the pet name for her younger sister, who was then thirteen.[27]

My Dear Aunt Annie

I received your letter on Thursday. Sorry to hear you were not well lately but the weather is very changeable. I know Cuckoo took good care of you when you were ill.

I got her letter alright at Easter. I hope the seed cake turned out satisfactory for her. Tell her to give my love to Sr Bonaventure and Sr Malachy.

Well now Aunt Annie about dear little Christy RIP, he got up to business on Friday morning 28th ult, father went out with him and on coming to Abbey Street they learned that Easons was burned to the ground, both returned home quickly as the bullets were flying through the city and all people warned to keep indoors.

He was tired he said, so mother said he should go to bed, he read a book for a while and then fell asleep, he had his right hand out over the clothes when a bullet went through his wrist he awoke crying mother bandaged up his little hand and father took him into his own room and laid him on the bed while doing so a bullet passed my father's chin and cut him slightly.

Christy RIP was not long in the other bed when eight bullets came through the window and each and all went through his little head poor child, he died a martyr. Well I never saw a face so radiant so joyful happy and peaceful he looked just like a saint and certain he is one. He stretched very much and looked about 10 years of age. When the shots were fired the military thought all in the house were killed but God only called one. An officer came into the room where Christy RIP lay dead and took my father heart broken and bleeding from the child he loved and lived for to prison and kept him there from Friday morning until Sunday.

You can think what sorrow father be in thinking about his little man RIP lying at home killed dead.

I was speaking to father on Saturday and he said that he got a great letter from you. Poor father is after going through plenty of troubles and sorrow and did anyone ever get such persecution? Father sent his love to Annie Cuckoo. I must now conclude with best love from all,

I remain Dear Aunt Annie, your loving niece,

May

Christopher was buried in the Bradshaw family plot in Glasnevin Cemetery. The grave, with twenty-six interments over a very long period, is a history of the capital in itself, with children who died from 'decline' and young adults from tuberculosis. The Bradshaws had bought the grave in 1886; the first burial was that of twenty-nine-year-old William Bradshaw, a draper's assistant, who died in June of that year from 'congestion of lungs'. Mary Whelan was buried there in April 1904, her baby daughter Mary joining her a year later. Christopher was buried with his mother and sister on 3 May 1916; the register simply states 'killed by gunfire' and gives his occupation as 'porter'; his slightly. Christy R.I.P. was not long in the other bed when eight bullets came through the window & each & all went through his little head poor child, he died a Martyr. Well I never saw a face so radiant & joyful happy & peaceful he looked just like a saint & certain he is one. He stretched very much & he looked just about 10 years of age. When the shots were fired the Military thought all in the house were killed but God

only called one. An officer came into the room where Christy R.I.P. lay dead & took my father heart broken and bleeding away from the child he loved & lived for to prison & kept him there from Friday morning until Sunday. You can think what sorrow father must be in thinking about his little man R.I.P. lying at home killed dead I was speaking to father on Saturday & he said that he got a letter from you. Poor father is after going through plenty of troubles & sorrow, did anyone ever get such persecution? I am glad that you won that case about the pony. Stick to the little ass as they are lucky, father sent his love to annie Cuckoo. I must now conclude with best love from all to all
I remain
Dear aunt Annie
Your loving neice
May

Excerpt from the letter (transcribed on pp 194-5) from Christopher Whelan's sister May to her aunt Annie, dated 14 May 1916, in which she describes her brother's death.

death certificate tells us he was a 'messenger'.

Laurence Whelan lived until 1957 when, aged ninety-one, he died in St Kevin's Hospital (formerly the South Dublin Union) of 'heart failure'; he was described as a 'retired postman'.[28]

May emigrated to the Britain two years after Christopher's death, where she married and had ten children; she died in the 1970s. Annie Cuckoo married late in life in Cahir, and had no children.

We know that James Kelly was another young worker killed on Tuesday, 25 April, by a gunshot wound to the head. His relatives tell me that he was killed at Blacquiere Bridge in Phibsborough – it is believed that he had gone to work as usual that morning in the nearby Broadstone railway yard where he was serving an apprenticeship.[29] Apparently his mother promptly burned his Na Fianna uniform – but that did not stop British soldiers raiding the house, leaving bullet marks that were visible in the cottage at 205 Phibsborough Road, opposite All Saints Church, until it was demolished in 1980.[30]

James was taken to the nearby Mater Hospital, where he died from a 'bullet wound in skull, laceration and compression of brain, shock' in St Aloysius's ward.[31] He was buried in Glasnevin Cemetery at one o'clock on Saturday, 29 April. His funeral would have been a lonely affair: the military had established checkpoints outside the cemetery and the numbers allowed to attend were kept to a minimum; often the sole mourner and makeshift coffin were searched for arms.

The *Evening Herald*, in a list of events associated with the Rising, simply reported that 'James Kelly a youth of Phibsborough, was fatally shot at Blacquiere Bridge on 25th April.' A few weeks later the paper published a photograph of James, showing a well-dressed, strong young boy.

> In an eye-witness account of fighting in that part of the city – Glasnevin, Cabra Bridge, Berkeley Road – John Higgins, from the west of Ireland, a young man 'in rather delicate health', visiting Dublin to see his doctor, wrote:
>
> *Through that gate huge covered motors, like Boer wagons on a trek, tore down the North Circular Road and Berkeley Road at nightfall, filled with soldiers, their bayonets glinting in the gloom. Short as was the fight it had tragedy to spare. The fatuous spectators, lingering too long and heedless of the rain, ran amok when the fusillade opened. Not all of them escaped.*
>
> *Knots of hysterical people helped with linked arms some limp victim to hospital, face and clothes running blood. A priest, materialising from nowhere, hastened with the viaticum from a dying girl to a man with his brains splashed over his trousers. Two boys with head wounds and dark clotted hair lay dead. An old man was shot – blind.*

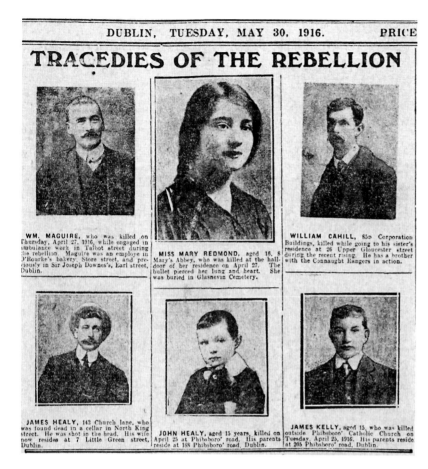

DUBLIN, TUESDAY, MAY 30, 1916.   PRICE

TRAGEDIES OF THE REBELLION

WM. MAGUIRE, who was killed on Thursday, April 27, 1916, while engaged in ambulance work in Talbot street during the rebellion. Maguire was an employe in O'Rourke's bakery, Store street, and previously in Sir Joseph Downes's, Earl street, Dublin.

MISS MARY REDMOND, aged 16, 8 Mary's Abbey, who was killed at the hall-door of her residence on April 27. The bullet pierced her lung and heart. She was buried in Glasnevin Cemetery.

WILLIAM CAHILL, 85D Corporation Buildings, killed while going to his sister's residence at 26 Upper Gloucester street during the recent rising. He has a brother with the Connaught Rangers in action.

JAMES HEALY, 143 Church lane, who was found dead in a cellar in North King street. He was shot in the head. His wife now resides at 7 Little Green street, Dublin.

JOHN HEALY, aged 15 years, killed on April 25 at Phibsboro' road. His parents reside at 188 Phibsboro' road, Dublin.

JAMES KELLY, aged 15, who was killed outside Phibsboro' Catholic Church on Tuesday, April 25, 1916. His parents reside at 205 Phibsboro' road, Dublin.

'Tragedies of the Rebellion', Evening Herald, *30 May 1916. Mary Redmond (aged 16), James Kelly and John (Sean) Healy (both aged 15) are pictured (top middle, bottom right and bottom middle respectively).*

A year later, the family inserted a memorial in the same paper: 'First Anniversary – In loving memory of our dear son James Kelly, 205 Phibsborough Road who was killed during the rebellion. Mass will be offered at St Joseph's, Berkeley Street on Monday for the repose of his soul. Inserted by his loving mother.'[32]

I found a further indication that James Kelly did not see action in the Rising among the papers of Walter Long Hume, a prominent British Unionist politician, who had a list of 'Civilians – all Unarmed, Killed' in the Rising. Listed among the dead is 'J. Kelly of 205 Phibsborough Road – would not join rebels.'[33] James's brother, Francis, had been involved, though, and, it was said, died a few years later of pleurisy as a result of regular sleeping out when he was on the run.

It is clear from my research on the children in employment who were killed in the Easter Rising that they were all bright, diligent, hard-working young people, making sacrifices for their families in poor circumstances. Yes, their prospects were grim but they were trying – and sometimes succeeding – to break free from the cycle of poverty that engulfed so many Dublin families under British rule in 1916.

Group portrait of Kathleen Clarke in mourning clothes and her sons, John, Tom and Emmet, taken in the aftermath of the execution of her husband Tom Clarke in 1916. This photograph was used in various publications, especially to raise money for the Irish Volunteers Dependents' Fund.

9. 'The Reply Is in the Negative'

AFTER THE DEATHS OF WILLIAM MULLEN, CHARLES KAVANAGH, PHILIP WALSH, JAMES FOX, CHARLES DARCY, SEAN HEALY, THEIR FAMILIES WERE TREATED ABYSMALLY WHEN THEY SOUGHT COMPENSATION.

Q. To ask the Under-Secretary of State for War, whether he is aware that there were 200 innocent persons, non-combatants, killed during the rising in Ireland; and if the Government intends to make any provision for their dependants.

A. Apart altogether from 116 sailors, soldiers and policemen killed on duty, it appears from cemetery records that 224 civilians were buried whose deaths were due to wounds received during the recent outbreak in Dublin, but there is no evidence to show whether these persons were innocent or not. The reply to the concluding part of the question is in the negative.[1]

The British government paid out more than £2.5 million in settling 830 claims for damage to property as a result of the Rising, but to those who claimed compensation for the death or injury of a loved one, it was considerably less generous.

The total paid in compensation to the families of the forty children aged sixteen and under who died in the Easter Rising came to just over eight hundred pounds. Twenty quid per life!

On 10 October 1916, the government finally relented from the position it had taken in June, as outlined in the House of Commons statement above, and set up a Rebellion (Victims) Committee to 'inquire and report with regard to applications for payment out of public funds to (a) persons who have suffered loss by reasons of personal injuries sustained by them without misconduct or default on their part in the recent rebellion and (b) dependants of deceased persons who without misconduct or default on their part were killed or injured in the recent rebellion'.[2]

The committee comprised Charles Orpen, president of the Incorporated Law Society of Ireland, Charles H. O'Connor, inspector, Local Government Board, and J.J. Taylor, principal clerk at the Chief Secretary's Office, Dublin Castle.

The families of twenty-two children killed during the Rising applied for compensation, and were awarded between zero and fifty pounds each. Little did those grieving families realise that, though their children had died in a battle that was not their own, another battle awaited: for compensation. Money cannot be compared to life, but the outcome for them would be humiliating.

The committee was based in a small office at 13 St Stephen's Green, at the junction with Dawson Street; H.C. Love was its secretary.

The Irish Volunteer Dependants' Fund had been founded in May 1916 to help those families who had suffered from their participation in the Rising, funded mainly from the USA, and Joe McGrath, later of the Irish Hospital Sweepstakes, was its first manager. Michael Collins took over in early 1917. It set out to help those who had fought in the Rising, and the dependants of those who had been killed. The children of the sixteen Rebels executed after the Rising were regarded as a priority and were looked after up to third-level education.

The Irish National Aid Association was a more broadly based fund, supporting the families of those imprisoned after the Rising. It had the active support of the Catholic Church at home and abroad, especially in America. In September 1916, the two organisations amalgamated – at the instigation of American supporters – as the Irish National Aid and Volunteer Dependants' Fund. As well as collecting and disbursing £134,520 in two years to families of the Rebels, the fund also built up a parish network of support and solidarity for the Rising.[3] Civilians who had been bereaved or injured in the Rising had to look elsewhere for help – and the plight of the majority was all but ignored.

Meanwhile, the businessmen of Dublin, led by William Martin Murphy, had set up the Dublin Fire and Property Losses Association to 'seek compensation for the terrible losses inflicted on them in Easter week'. It featured names such as Eason, Goodbody, Bewley, Dockrell, Jacob, Mitchell, Downes and Minch, all family-run companies dealing in a range of goods from books to bread, biscuits and grain. As far as business and property owners in Dublin were concerned, the Rebellion (Victims) Committee was highly successful because it settled many of their claims quickly – but for suffering individuals it was another story altogether. Perhaps this was what prompted those businessmen on 13 June, ten weeks after the Rising, to address a letter to the prime minister, H.H. Asquith, noting:

We desire to lay before the Government the hard case of persons guiltless of all complicity in the Dublin revolt and who have been injured and rendered either wholly or partially incapable of work and the support of their families . . . The Government has recognised the justice of claims for compensation by persons whose property has been destroyed, and we desire to point out that life lost is as deserving of compensation as property destroyed . . . We suggest that compensation should be awarded by the Government for loss of life or injury on the same terms as those on whom compensation would be awarded for death or injury under the provision of the Workmen's Compensation Act.[4]

Public opinion forced the British government to change its mind on the need for compensation: there was growing revulsion over what had happened in Easter week, not just with the execution of the leaders but with atrocities, such as the North King Street massacre.

Four hundred and fifty claims were made by civilians to 13 St Stephen's Green. The vast majority were rejected, while the seventy who won awards received only a fraction of the meagre amounts they had claimed, a total of £14,000, an average of two hundred pounds per family. Based on the Workmen's Compensation Act, as suggested in the businessmen's letter addressed to Asquith, it applied only to those earning less than £250 a year. Of all of the dead children whose families were compensated – primarily because they could prove their child had been working – there was little doubt that they had been killed without 'misconduct or default' on their part. The families of at least eighteen of the children killed did not apply for help. Either they did not know they could or they lacked the ability to claim compensation – or, indeed, they might have realised that only frustration, humiliation and refusal lay ahead.

Thomas McKane – father of Bridget McKane – applied to the Rebellion (Victims) Committee for seventy-five pounds. He was awarded twenty-five pounds to compensate him for the death of his innocent daughter. If he was disappointed by the miserly grant from the British government, he didn't fare much better when he sought recompense from the Irish state many years later. It did not matter that five of the seven men proudly proclaimed as the fathers of the nation were in his house on the night his daughter was killed and he was wounded.

On 3 November 1937, Thomas Mc-Kane applied to the Military Pensions Board:

TRAGEDIES OF THE REBELLION

BRIDGET M'KANE, aged 15, who was killed on April 28, 1916, at her parents' residence, 10 Henry place, Moore street, Dublin. Her father was severely wounded at the same time, and is at present in hospital.

MRS. ROSANNA HEFFERNAN, aged 55, shot on April 25 in a room of her own residence at 176 James's street, Dublin. She died at Steevens' Hospital on April 27, 1916.

MRS. FLYNN, aged 57, who was shot while sitting at the fire in her own residence at 47 Railway street, Dublin, on April 26. She is still a patient in Jervis street Hospital.

CHRISTOPHER WHELAN, aged 15, who was killed in his own residence at 30 North Great George's street, Dublin. His father was wounded in the mouth while carrying his son from one room to another His parents reside at above address.

'Tragedies of the Rebellion', Evening Herald, 15 June 1916, showing Bridget McKane (top left) and Christopher Whelan (bottom right) both aged 15.

When the volunteers took refuge in my house one of their guns accidentally went off the bullet passed through my right shoulder and right lung killing my daughter Brigid who was immediately behind me, I have been partly disabled since. Thomas Clarke and Sean Mac Diarmada who were in the house at the time promised to make full restitution when all was over.

If you have any doubts of the foregoing statement I would refer you to the Minister of Agriculture Dr Seamus Ryan TD who rendered first aid to me and who kindly appended his name to the application form.

Mise do chara, Thomas McKane[5]

In his statement to the Bureau of Military History, Joe Good corroborated what McKane had said of McDermott:

> The civilian who had been wounded was approached by McDermott when it was found that we were responsible for the death of his daughter and his wounding. I think it was McDermott who told him that if he thought there was any carelessness or recklessness in what had befallen him he, McDermott, would endeavour to bring the culprits before him.[6]

The McKane family in 1915. Standing: Mary, Alice and Bridget; Front row: Micheal, Elizabeth, Margaret, Harry, Nan, Thomas, Nellie and Rosie.

However, Thomas McKane did not receive the support he had been told to expect by one of the Volunteers who was there that fateful night: Dr Seamus Ryan, who, by 1937, was Minister for Agriculture in the first Fianna Fáil government, and had, as McKane pointed out, 'plugged the wound'.

The minister wrote to the Army Pensions Board: 'I believe he suffered from some slight wound but it was not serious. I had not known McKane previously and cannot therefore answer whether he was a member of any of the organisations referred to.'[7] Thomas McKane was put through the mill: he was subjected to a series of interviews, a medical examination, a report by the gardaí and enquiries as to whether 'Mr McKane's house [was] a place Volunteers could expect a hospitable reception'.[8] The medical examination, at St Bricin's Hospital, found that he was 'permanently incapacitated due to multiple gunshot wounds on right chest and shoulder'. Even so, it was determined that he was not entitled to a pension as he had not been a member of any of the organisations that had fought in the Rising. Eventually, he was awarded a 'gratuity' of £100 in September 1938.

Thomas McKane was working for the Dublin United Tramway Company, and still living in Henry Place, when he died suddenly at his home on 11 November 1941. His thirty-six-year-old son Michael died on the same day. Family I spoke to believe Michael had been injured in the North Strand bombings – when German aircraft brought the second world War to neutral Ireland – causing his death six months later, and that his father dropped dead when he heard the devastating news.

The coffins of Thomas and Michael were placed side by side in the Pro-Cathedral during the Requiem Mass, and they were buried together in Glasnevin Cemetery on Thursday, 13 November 1941.

Bridget McKane lies in an unmarked plot in the same cemetery.

We don't know why the family of William Mullen moved to the Moore Place near to the McKanes, but they were living with a relative when William suffered the same fate as his neighbour Bridget McKane: he was accidentally shot and killed on Friday, 28 April, as the Rebels retreated from the GPO.

In 1906, Richard Mullen, a bread-van driver, had married Elizabeth, and they had had two children: William, born in 1907, and his brother, James, born two years later. The family had left one of Dublin's most notorious tenement areas, Gloucester Street (now Sean McDermott Street). The numbers living there speak for themselves: there were eighty-four terraced three-storey tenement houses, in which 433 families rented rooms, with 1,864 people calling it home![9] Within the houses, there was a hierarchy of rents: depending on size, number of windows – one or two – and location at the front or back of the building; the rent varied between 1/9d and 3/6d a week.[10]

Maybe the Mullen family thought Moore Place, in the heart of the markets district, cramped around Moore Street and Coles Lane, was a better place to live. With its slaughterhouses, fishmongers, butchers, bakers, clothes-sellers, haberdashery shops, pig yards and second-hand furniture outlets on and off the streets, lanes and cutaways, it was simply the busiest, noisiest and, at that time, one of the most exciting parts of the city. The stench of horse dung, the slaughterhouses, rotting fish and fruit meant that it was also one of the smelliest parts of Dublin.

By now Richard Mullen was no longer driving a bread van but described himself as a 'handyman caretaker'. Perhaps the family had fallen on even harder times and had had to move in with Richard's brother, Joseph, in Moore Lane. Maybe being close to so many tradesmen, hawkers and small businesses gave Richard the opportunity of more casual work at short notice.

William's death certificate tells us bluntly that he died at his home, with his mother, from a 'gunshot wound to the thorax' on Friday of Easter week.[11]

Richard applied to the Rebellion (Victims) Committee for compensation of seventy-five pounds for the death of his son, but the family was only awarded twenty-five pounds – less than three pounds for every year of William's short life.

William Mullen (9) was buried in an unmarked grave in Glasnevin Cemetery on 3 May – the family did not register his death until seven months later.[12]

Denis Kavanagh, a general labourer originally from County Wexford, and Mary Kavanagh were married in 1886. By 1911, three of their older children had left home, and they lived with the younger three, Elizabeth, aged nineteen, Bridget, sixteen, and nine-year-old Charles, in a room in one of the many tenement houses on Great Britain Street (now Parnell Street). They shared the house with four other families – nineteen tenants in all. On 5 December 1911, Denis was summonsed for failing to keep his children at school.

By 1916, the family had moved to 4 North King Street, a 'tenement business house' with electric lighting. On the afternoon of Thursday, 27 April, Charles Kavanagh was shot in

At that time, more than twenty hospitals were located between the two canals – effectively the war zone for the seven days. As well as general hospitals – such as the Richmond (Brunswick Street), the Adelaide, the Meath, Mercers, Sir Patrick Dun's, St Vincent's, Jervis Street, the Mater, Dr Steevens' and the Royal City of Dublin (Baggot Street) – there were three large military hospitals: King George V (St Bricin's), the Portobello and the Richmond (Inchicore), as well as specialist maternity hospitals – the Rotunda, Holles Street and the Coombe – two children's hospitals (Harcourt Street and Temple Street), and the specialist eye and ear hospital on Adelaide Road. All were within the curfew area – which made it very difficult for medical staff to attend.

During that week, temporary hospitals were set up in Dorset Street, Mountjoy Square, Trinity College, North Great George's Street, Dublin Castle and St Stephen's Green. And, of course, there were the massive medical complexes of Grangegorman (the North Dublin Union) and the South Dublin Union in James's Street.

In Easter week, a total of eleven gunshot casualties were admitted to Temple Street, and six beds were cleared on the first floor for child casualties.[13]

Upper Sackville Street and rushed, bleeding from the stomach, to nearby Temple Street Hospital. That week, doctors had great difficulty in getting to Temple Street but the Sisters of Charity record tells us that: 'Fortunately one of the doctors got in by one of the lanes to the hospital.'[14]

On Friday, a surgeon arrived to attend to him. The operation was complex and difficult: 'A single bullet could cause numerous holes and tears as it traversed the abdomen, each of which needed to be sutured with the attendant risk of contamination by faecal matter.'[15] That evening, Charles died. Even when casualties were in hospital, the nature of the wounds, and the damage inflicted by the type of guns used in 1916, especially the 'Howth Mausers', gave little chance of survival.

A bizarre sequence of events followed Charles's death: because no coffin was available, he was placed in an egg crate; the driver of the horse and cart who had arrived to take the crate to Glasnevin Cemetery was shot and killed; the priest who had administered the last rites to the driver then had to take the reins and deliver the body to the cemetery.[16]

In death, many of these children had no public mourning. Some were buried with no family present, most in unmarked graves. 'One man, apparently the father, carried under his arm a rough improvised coffin containing the remains of a child. The little procession crossed the Drumcondra district on their way to the cemetery, the parent changing the coffin from one arm to another as they made the journey. They were greeted everywhere with expressions of sympathy, which touched them frequently to tears, the father breaking down again and again on the route.'[17]

Denis Kavanagh applied for £350 compensation to the Rebellion (Victims) Committee, claiming that the 'deceased wages helped to support family' as Charles had brought in an average of '6 shillings a week' to the household.[18] The committee

Anniversary notice from the *Evening Herald*, April 1917.

Kavanagh – first anniversary: In sad and loving memory of Charles Kavanagh, 4 North King Street, accidentally shot in Upper O'Connell Street on 27 April 1916, deeply regretted by his loving father, mother, brothers and sisters. On whose soul Sweet Jesus have mercy. Eight o'clock Mass offered up for the repose of his soul in St Michan's, Halston Street, this morning.

Hackett's Court, c.1913.

offered him a 'compassionate grant of fifty pounds'. John Taylor was obviously in good spirits that day because he wrote: 'Pay £50 to father.'

The compensation claim made by the mother of Philip Walsh was not subjected to the red fountain pen flourish of John Taylor – but maybe it was because the committee's recommendation had been made three days after Christmas 1916, or that there was an acceptance that his mother, Ellen Walsh, was 'partially dependent on her 11-year-old son' – but the cutting hand of Taylor did not on this occasion halve the fifty pounds awarded.

Philip Walsh of Hackett's Court – the child of a bricklayer – died of gunshot wounds to the abdomen in Mercers Hospital on Wednesday 26 April, two days after the Rising began. He was buried in an unmarked grave in Glasnevin Cemetery.[19] His family were not living in Hackett's Court in the 1911 Census, but the tenement that they subsequently occupied there had six families sharing five rooms – thirty-one souls in all.

And Hackett's Court, as the photographs testify, could in no way be described as a step up in the world. The street itself, like so many in Dublin, disappeared shortly after the Rising, as it seems, did the Walsh family. No member of Philip's family has come forward since this project began in 2012.

In her claim for compensation after the death of her son James, aged fifteen, on Easter Tuesday, Teresa Kelly stated that he 'was killed whilst playing outside Phibsborough Chapel in the field'.[20] She didn't – couldn't – mention that James was a member of the Republican Boy Scouts, Na Fianna. If she had, the committee would have dismissed her claim out of hand as he would not have been regarded as without 'misconduct or default'. While it is accepted that James was indeed a member of Na Fianna, it is doubtful that he participated in the Rising.

Seven members of Na Fianna were killed in the Easter Rising: Brendan Donelan, Sean Healy, James Fox, James Kelly, Gerald Keogh, Sean Howard and Frederick Ryan, just three of whom – Healy, Fox and Kelly – were aged sixteen or under.

James Fox, of 3 Altinure Terrace, Cabra Park, was sixteen when he died in Mercers Hospital, a few hundred yards from where he had been shot as part of the St Stephen's Green garrison led

The writer James Stephens reports what he saw on Easter Monday evening as he walked past St Stephen's Green:

No one seemed able to estimate the number of men inside the Green . . . Among those were some who were only infants, one boy seemed about twelve years of age. He was strutting the centre of the road with a large revolver in his small fist. A motor car came by him containing three men and in the shortest of time he had the car lodged in the barricade, and dismissed the stupefied occupants with a wave of his armed hand.[21]

by Countess Markievicz and Michael Mallin on Easter Tuesday.

In the 1911 Census, his family can be found in Knockmark, Killeen, in County Meath. His father, Patrick J. Fox, was running the Spencer Arms Hotel in Drumree and had been married for fourteen years to Margaret, from Liverpool where their first child, Constance, was born. Margaret went on to give birth to four more children of whom three survived. James was their eldest son.

We don't know how the Fox family came down in the world or why they lost the hotel in Drumree but, according to his death certificate, James was living in Cabra Park at the time of his death. The events of Easter week would herald the total disintegration of the family.

In a RTÉ radio interview on the occasion of the fiftieth anniversary of the Rising, Frank Robbins, a founding member of the Irish Citizen Army, outlined how he first came to meet with young James:

At the doorway, I hear someone shouting, 'Robbins, Robbins.' On looking back, I saw old Pat Fox, formerly of Drumree, County Meath, living in Dublin for some years. From the early days, he was a great supporter of Parnell, and these were his words to me on that morning: 'I am too old to fight. Here is my son. I give him into your charge. Look after him. He wants to fight for Ireland. Look after him. He's all I have.' My parting words were, 'All right, Pat, I will look after him.' Young Fox was hardly eighteen years of age. He had no training of any kind. I saw little of him. When the fighting commenced, he was killed in Stephen's Green inside of twenty hours. I wondered what his father would have to say to me if we ever met again. We did meet again many months afterwards when he greeted me with tears in his eyes and a warm handclasp saying, 'My poor boy, my poor boy.' The only reply I could make was, 'Don't worry, Pat, he died bravely.' The old man brightened up very much with these few words of consolation.'

James Fox.

This was the full extent of what I could discover about James Fox until the release in October 2014 of the files from the Bureau of Military History, featuring the applications for pensions by those involved in the Rising and the War of Independence.

A bizarre story unfolded. The hundred-page file revealed a broken family, a desperate father and a callous State now being run by the

Scenes of the Easter Rising, as reported on the front page of the Sunday Herald, *30 April 1916. These photographs were 'the first to reach England of scenes in the heart of the Dublin rebels' stronghold'.*

so-called comrades of the late James Fox who, at sixteen, had become one of the youngest fighters in the Irish Rebel force but whose father's begging letters were rejected time and time again. There is plenty of evidence that the families of the signatories and others executed by firing squad were treated much better than those of other insurgents killed.

On 30 November 1923, by this time living in Drumcondra, Patrick Fox wrote to Joe McGrath, a comrade who was then on the recently established Pensions Board:

Dear Joe

I have been informed that the dependants of the men killed in action in Easter week 1916 are entitled to a gratuity. I venture to ask you to do your utmost for me in this matter. I have been going through bad times ever since and feel the loss of my good boy now. You doubtlessly know of my boy (Jim) and myself being out in the Easter 'scrap' and of his death in St Stephen's Green.

I am writing this note hoping you will do your best to see that I get a fair share of the gratuity which I feel you must know I am entitled to. Needless to tell you that for over 30 years prior to 1916 I gave my time and money to the cause and continued my bit up to the last unfortunate split. Since then I have remained neutral.

In your present position I feel you can do much for me. If at all convenient I would feel thankful for an early reply and if possible some advice as to proper procedure. Wishing you all the best of luck for old times' sake. I remain, yours sincerely,

Patrick J. Fox

PS Joe I am almost down and out just now.[22]

This searing, gracious, dignified letter was simply the opening salvo in a vicious, cold, humiliating correspondence. But it also raises the question as to why Pat Fox said he was 'out in the Easter "scrap"' when other witnesses give a different story.

On 4 April 1924, the director of military intelligence, Colonel M. Costello, wrote to the adjutant general:

I have the honour to inform you that Patrick J. Fox [he means James] was a member of the Volunteers prior to the 1916 rebellion but fought during Easter week with the Citizen Army. His father was a member of the Citizen Army and was out in Stephen's Green for a day or so but then went home. He was killed near the Dublin Fusiliers monument, Stephen's Green.

The applicant who is making the claim lives at the address given in Drumcondra and is out of work. The brother of the deceased who also lives there is employed as a builder's labourer. The mother and her two daughters are at present and have for some time past been living in Liverpool.

The family were at one time in possession of some means and owned a hotel in Dunshaughlin, Co. Meath, but prior to 1916 they came down in the world.

The statement that applicant was partially dependent on deceased would be more correct.[23]

This letter was passed to the Army Pensions Board in Molesworth Street – just a few hundred yards from the Dáil, where many of Fox's former comrades were now ensconced. The Army Pensions Board sought a police report on the Fox family, which was submitted by Sergeant Patrick Guinan of Bridewell garda station:

Applicant who is aged 56 years is unemployed for over 12 months past and has no means of living except the goodness of his son Thomas who is supporting and keeping him free for a considerable time past. Applicant's wife Mrs Margaret Fox is residing at 78 Lemon Street, Liverpool and is kept by her daughter Mary, an assistant in a provision shop, who earns about £2 per week. Applicant was partially dependent on deceased at the time of his death but had no private income. He was in regular employment and earned on average about £2 per week prior to his son's death. For the past few years he was only casually employed here and in Liverpool. He has no property. His son Thomas is a builder's labourer and earns on average £3 per week.

At this stage, it seems that the Army Pensions Board had decided that Patrick Fox was either a chancer or a liar. They wrote a long, detailed letter to the comptroller and auditor general, asking if Fox had any money from other sources. Then they wrote to Fox, asking him to come in for an interview. In that interview, Patrick Fox said that his son, Thomas, was 'under treatment' and his daughter in Liverpool could no longer work due to 'deafness'.

Five days later, they called him in again: 'He admitted that he received a small amount from time to time amounting to about £100 from a Mr O'Neill. He was not aware that the money had been advanced by the National Aid but understood it was collected by Mr O'Neill on his behalf. Mr Fox stated that deceased was employed as an assistant in the Maypole Dairy and was in receipt of 25/– p.w. which was wholly contributed to the upkeep of the home.'

On 18 June 1924, the Army Pensions Board rejected his claim as there was 'no dependency at date of death'.[24]

Patrick Fox pleaded again but, on 1 July, J.F. Horgan wrote to him, in tone and word uncannily like the rejection letters sent by the British state to victims of the Rising eight years previously: 'Reconsidered, but the Board does not see any way to recommending an award as there was no dependency whatever and the Board fails to see any special circumstances.'[25] In January 1925, Patrick Fox sought to reopen the case by writing to E.J. Duggan TD.

Sir,

Some time ago I applied to your Army gratuity or Pensions Board for allowance which I believe I am entitled to for the death of my son in 1916, but strange to say they have declined to acknowledge my claim . . . As TD for the Royal County where my father and mother's people belong to for generations, I will ask you to have my claim reconsidered. It is the first time in my life I ever asked for my services to the cause of Ireland and regret having to do so now, but circumstances compel me. As a matter of fact I have been out of work of the past 18 months. Hence I venture to write the request to have my case looked into.

I beg to remain,

P.J. Fox

Late of Spencer Arms – Drumree, County Meath.[26]

A long reply from the Army Pensions Board to Joe McGrath detailed their dealings with Patrick Fox, adding:

The only grounds on which the case might be reopened would be the grounds of special circumstances in as much as deceased took part in the Rising, but it is questionable whether claimant would be entitled to receive an award as presumably any contributions made by deceased towards the upkeep of the home were made to his mother who is not a claimant. If it is your wish however that the case should again be submitted please let me know and I will take the necessary steps in the matter.

Within a month the Army Pensions Board relented and gave Fox fifty pounds. They explained some of their reasons in a reply to Senator Oliver St John Gogarty – to whom Fox had also pleaded: 'In view of the possible slight dependency and the special circumstances that the boy was killed in Easter week a point was stretched and a gratuity of £50 was awarded. I am afraid with all sympathy to the father we cannot do any more. The father received about £100 from the National Aid Association.'[27]

In January 1926, Patrick Fox took up the cudgel again, this time in a detailed typed letter to the president of the Executive Council – effectively the Taoiseach, William Cosgrave (who had taken part in the Rising, serving under Éamonn Ceannt at the South Dublin Union, and was subsequently sentenced to death, later commuted to penal servitude for life and Cosgrave was interned at Frongoch, Wales).

Sir,

I beg to respectfully thank you for the past favours in the reference to my son's death in 1916 which the enclosed letter will bring to mind. Needless to say, Sir, the amount £50 awarded was for compensation for the loss of my good boy.

At the present moment my other son and only boy is walking about idle for the past twelve months. When I was going out with my boy in 1916 I little thought it would come to poverty if we escaped the bullet. I am told Mr Cosgrave that you have much influence with the Galena Signal Oil company and that if I wrote to you, you would possibly do something for my boy with the firm.

He is aged 22 years and a good refined honest boy not afraid of work and if he got any position in the firm I am sure he would give every satisfaction and improve himself. I should not trouble you but for the fact that we are really in a state of poverty. Poor Mr William Flanagan promised, if he had lived to do something for my boy. Hoping Sir, if not too much to ask, that you will do something for me in this matter.

There is no indication as to whether or not W.T Cosgrave did anything or even replied. But Fox did not leave it at that. In 1933, he took up his case again and wrote to another 1916 veteran, Frank Aiken, who was now the Minister for Defence. This handwritten letter asked about his right to a pension under the 1932 Pension Act just introduced:

With the execution of two years' work in Liverpool after 1916, I am practically idle ever since. Of course I have been offered jobs from the Free State gentlemen of the past 10 years but Mr Aiken, although poor down and out, I told them I had still a national soul to save. At present I am in very poor circumstances and I am not getting young.[28]

The Department of Defence wrote back to him seeking more information, which Patrick Fox supplied, adding, 'For over ten years I have been practically living on the generosity of good friends as I could not and would not accept a job from the Cosgrave people. If I am entitled under the pension act to an allowance and God knows I think I earned it, I will be glad to give you any further information you may require.'

On 4 May 1933, he wrote to Aiken again as he had 'heard from friends that owing to my having made a claim under the Cosgrave compensation act for the loss of my son (killed in action) that I will not be entitled to the pension which my many Republican friends always told me I should get. I have had a very hard time for the past 14 or 15 years owing of course to my national opinions. I gave practically my whole life to the movement.' He went on, 'I had to take money from a Government I despised, a sum which was totally inadequate', but 'such was the price of my good son who if alive today would be such an advantage to me . . . I gave my money, my home, my son and all that I had to the cause'.[29]

But all this pleading was to no avail.

On 26 June 1933, Aiken wrote back, through his secretary, informing Fox that he had already received fifty pounds for his 'slight dependency'.

But Fox hadn't finished. He wrote to the leader of the country, Eamon de Valera, who, after Fianna Fáil entered the Dáil for the first time in March 1932, had been elected president of the Executive Council on 29 September 1933. In the long handwritten letter, Fox suggests that: 'If either Jim Connolly, Michael Mallen [sic], Tom Clarke or Sean McDermott were alive today I would not be forgotten as they were indeed intimate friends of mine.'

On this occasion, he ended on a bitter note:

> . . . like many others who perhaps did more than their share I am to be cast aside while traitors and hirelings are living in luxury on the blood of Irish heroes.
> Faithfully
> P.J. Fox

The final act in this correspondence took place in October 1933 when Frank Aiken's office wrote to Fox, now living at 115 Parnell Street, referring to the letter he had sent to de Valera and reiterating that he had been awarded £50 for the 'slight dependence'. It concludes: 'Mr Aiken regrets very much that no further award can be made under the Army Pension Acts.'[30]

There is no other correspondence on the file.

James 'Seamus' Fox is buried under an impressive Celtic cross in Knockmark Cemetery, near where his family had a hotel in County Meath until they 'came down in the world'. His grave was refurbished in 1966. The resting place of his father, who was sixty-two when he finally gave up on the battle for a pension, is unknown.

The state file on the compensation claim for James Fox was finally closed in 1937, twenty-one years after his death, but the file on Charles Darcy, another boy who wore the uniform in 1916, was not finally signed off until fifty-six years after he had died outside Dublin Castle on the first day of the Easter Rising. Aged fifteen, Charles lived at 4 Murphy Cottages, Gloucester Diamond, Summerhill, in the centre of Dublin. He was a member of the Irish Citizen Army and was part of a unit holding the Henry and James clothiers store in Parliament Street, opposite Dublin Castle. He was shot dead on the roof of the store on the evening of Easter Monday and his body was brought into the Castle grounds the following day.

Matthew Connolly, who was on the roof of City Hall, stated, 'I could still see the men on the roof of Henry and James building – they were shouting down to pedestrians on the street, advising them to go home, but some people stood and stared in wonder. It was while thus engaged that one of our men, Charles Darcy, quite young and a particular friend of mine, came in the line of fire, received a fatal wound and I saw him fall back into the roof gutter.'[31]

Charles Darcy was born in 1901 to James Darcy, a labourer,

Charles D'Arcy's memorial card.

and his wife, Elizabeth, both from Wicklow. In the 1911 Census, the family are recorded as living at 4 Kane's Court, a two-roomed labourer's cottage off Gloucester Street, with their six surviving children (one had died): Thomas, James, Charles, Edith, Patrick and Agnes. The census also tells us that although James was thirty-five and his wife was thirty-four, they had an eighteen-year-old son, Thomas; it adds that they had been married for twenty-one years, which is surely incorrect.[32]

By 1916, the family were living in a similar dwelling at 4 Murphy Cottages, between City Quay and Great Brunswick Street (now Pearse Street). Charles had attended the Pro-Cathedral school on Lower Rutland Street from April 1912, when it opened, until May 1914 when, aged thirteen, he was no longer obliged to attend school.

A letter of reference from his schoolmaster, Mr A. Scully, describes him as obedient and respectful to his teacher, regular and punctual in attendance, attentive to his lessons and well conducted in every respect. He was also a member of the boys' sodality attached to the Pro-Cathedral on Marlborough Street and attended regularly to his religious duties. Having left school, he found work as an assistant at Pims department store in South Great George's Street. He earned ten shillings a week, all of which he gave to his mother. Around this time, he appears to have joined the Irish Citizen Army. When the Rising began, he reported for duty at Liberty Hall.

The details of Charles's death are contained in a letter from his mother to Lieutenant A. Rasdale of the Adjutant General's Office in 1923 when she claimed a military pension on her son's behalf: Charles was under the command of Captain Sean Connolly in the City Hall garrison and was allotted to a section under Sergeant E. Elmes to take possession of the Henry and James building as a support to City Hall itself.[33]

After the formation of the Irish Free State, the Military Service Pensions Act (1924) passed into law; any persons with proven service during the 1916 Rising and the War of Independence were to be awarded a certificate of service and were entitled to a military pension. In 1923, Elizabeth started the process of claiming a dependant's allowance because of her son's death. A number of supporting letters detailed Charles's involvement in the Rising.

Colonel M. Costello wrote: 'He was aged 15 and a half – his body was buried in Dublin Castle and was afterwards exhumed and buried in Glasnevin. Claimant's husband died in 1920 and claimant's children are two girls, aged 15 and 18, and a boy aged 9 years.'[34] He recommended the immediate payment of a pension.

Sergeant Thomas J. O'Neill, of Store Street garda station, wrote that Elizabeth had received an allowance of ten shillings a week from the National Aid and Volunteers Dependants' Fund. He added that although she was in delicate health she took in two 'nurse children at 7/6 per week to help supplement her income and the upkeep of her home as she is in very poor circumstance. She was never in any regular employment, neither was she at any time in receipt of any private income, and in my opinion she was partially dependent on the deceased at the time of his death.'[35]

In May 1924, Elizabeth received a letter confirming that she would be awarded one gratuity payment of £150 in recognition of Charles's service. In 1941, she received a 1916 medal on behalf of Charles, who would have been forty if he had survived. The medals were not generally awarded with inscriptions unless the recipient had been killed during the Rising: Charles's medal bore his name and a number. The medal, along with the various papers relating to Charles's service and claim, is now in the National Museum of Ireland.

In April 1971, Charles Darcy's first cousin asked if any of the family had ever applied for any medals or ribbons posthumously awarded to him. In 1972, Charles's name was inscribed in the 1916 Roll of Honour and another engraved medal was sent to John Seery.

Sean Healy has the unique distinction of being the only child killed in the Rising who is publicly remembered. There is a plaque in the pavement in Phibsborough near where he lived and was shot on Tuesday, 25 April 1916.

He was one of ten children, six boys and four girls, and the family lived at 188 Phibsborough Road with two other families. When the Rising began on Easter Monday, Thomas MacDonagh sent Sean home from the occupied Jacob's biscuit factory because he was too young to fight. But he was shot near his home and died in the nearby Mater Hospital. In her witness statement, a nun in St Aloysius's ward described 'his brain hanging out all over his forehead when he was brought in'.

Sean began training – at both plumbing and fighting – with his father who, along with two of his daughters, was very active in the Republican movement. The family believe that Thomas MacDonagh asked the boy to deliver a message, a warning about an ambush at the bridge in Phibsborough. Sean called into his family home on the way, then went back out and was shot by the British Army, who were based at the bridge – apparently someone had tried to blow it up. The hat he was wearing when he died is now in the museum at Collins Barracks. He was buried in Glasnevin Cemetery.

Sean's nephew tells me that: 'His name *as Gaeilge* was Sean Ó hEilidhe, but in the family he was called Jack.' He goes on: 'When he was 15 that Easter he promised my five-year-old ma – his youngest sister Chrissy – an Easter bonnet, not knowing the sequence of events that would leave my ma with this promised memory unfulfilled. As a member of the Fianna Éireann Boy Scouts, he of course was too young to bear arms but was en route delivering a message to the insurgents on the Circular Road, accompanied by one of his older sisters, Leney [Lena], when his head was ripped open with shrapnel at Doyle's Corner on Tuesday, to the awful shock of Leney. His older sisters Tess and Mary were on active service with Cumann na mBan on the south side. As I was called after Uncle Jack, I remember asking my granny – Sean's mother – if she would like me to die for Ireland. Her answer never left me as she said, 'It's easy to die for Ireland. What Ireland needs is people to live honestly for Ireland.'[36]

Sean Healy, the youngest casualty on the Republican side of the Rising at 15 years of age.

In 1924, Sean's father, Christopher Healy, who had served with the Hibernian Rifles during Easter week 1916, transferring to the Irish Volunteers in 1917, lodged a claim under the Army Pensions Act. In it, he outlined how his son had died and stated that he 'was partially dependent' on Sean, who contributed a pound per week to the household. He added that the family had received twenty pounds from the National Aid Association to help 'with the funeral of the deceased'. Healy submitted his application through Noyk and O'Reilly, solicitors, of 12 College Green.

In July 1924, the adjutant general wrote to the Army Pensions Board: 'He was a member of the Fianna, and being one of those who

Sean Healy in his Na Fianna Éireann uniform.

lost their lives during the Rising of 1916, he will be regarded as an Officer. He received the wounds which caused his death while on active service and they were not in any way due to negligence or misconduct on his part.'

Then the family received a visit from Inspector Richard O'Connell of the Bridewell garda station. He confirmed to the Pensions Board that Christopher Healy was a plumber and gas fitter, working from home, with weekly earnings of three pounds before his son's death; now aged fifty-nine, he was 'incapacitated from earning his livelihood by a rupture for which he has received medical attention'.

The inspector's full report gives us a glimpse of life in Dublin in the 1920s. All nine children, aged from thirty-two to twelve, were living at home. Mary, aged thirty-two, was employed as a general houseworker and contributed five of the ten shillings she earned each week to the household. Kathleen, aged thirty, earned about twenty-five shillings a week and gave a pound (or twenty shillings) to her mother. The oldest son, Christopher, aged twenty-six, had been unemployed for the previous two years; he had been a casual attendant in the Richmond Asylum, earning thirty-five shillings per week, of which he had given a pound to his mother. Teresa, twenty-eight, worked at Court Laundry, earning twenty-five shillings a week, of which she handed over ten shillings. Lena, aged twenty-four, was employed temporarily at the Tailteann tailoring company, earning twenty-five shillings a week, giving a pound to her mother. Elizabeth, aged twenty-two, and Bridie, fifteen, were unemployed. Joseph was a plumber's apprentice, earning eight shillings, of which he contributed six to the family. Cissie, the youngest, was still at school.

The inspector added that the deceased had been employed as a plumber's apprentice by his father and was 'in receipt of £1 per week, all of which he contributed to his mother for his support'. He concluded: 'The claimant appears to be in rather straitened circumstances. Owing to ill-health and trade depression he is practically unemployed, while the earnings of his family are scarcely adequate to support them. He is the tenant of the house of 188 Phibsboro Road for which he pays £1 per week rent. He has one room set, for which he receives 5/6d per week. If deceased was alive now he would be capable of managing the business of his father which is now almost at a standstill owing to the ill-health of claimant.'

On 10 October 1924, the family of Sean Healy were granted a gratuity of a hundred pounds.

That was all that appeared on the file until seventeen years later, when Sean's mother wrote to the Department of Defence asking if: 'I am entitled to a medal for my son Sean Healy killed in action Easter week 1916. Kindly let me know and oblige.'

What does it say that the mother of a 1916 hero had to wait twenty-five years before she was forced to ask if her dead boy was entitled to a medal?

Two young girls look on at the Easter Rising Memorial, Arbour Hill in Dublin, 1966.

Epilogue

I was really looking forward to the 1966 Easter Rising Commemorations: the fiftieth anniversary of the insurrection was set to be marked with a great display of pomp, ceremony, marching soldiers and lots of army trucks.

And, boy, did this ten-year-old love the array of trucks, armoured cars, tanks and second-hand British Army vehicles that the Irish Army paraded past the GPO every Easter Sunday. Once described as the most curious boy in the class by his favourite primary-school teacher, Mr Long, he even knew where the army secretly parked its massive tow-truck in case one of their behemoths broke down, which it invariably would!

For the previous four years, ever since my father had returned from working in England, he had brought my three brothers and me to the parade. He would point out the tall, imposing figure of President Eamon de Valera, now nearly blind, being guided from his Rolls-Royce Silver Wraith by his uniformed aide-de-

View of Nelson's pillar following the bombing in 1966.

camp through the guard of honour to the reviewing stand at the GPO.

But, in March 1966, Nelson's Pillar, opposite the GPO, had been blown up by renegade members of the IRA, their way of marking the fiftieth anniversary of the Rising. My father's reaction was swift and devastating: he would not be bringing us into the centre of Dublin on 10 April as he feared trouble would break out.

My father was born in 1926, the oldest of eight – six survived childhood – ten years after the Rising, in the same tenement house at 89 Church Street where his own mother had first seen the murky light of day twenty-three years previously. It was only three years before the fiftieth anniversary celebrations that my granny finally left the tenement to move to a Corporation house in St Eithne Road in Cabra – one of my aunts said it was like a hotel!

So, for me, the 1966 Rising commemorations were confined to watching *Insurrection*, the eight-part RTÉ black-and-white drama on our rented television set – provided we had enough money for the meter bolted to the back of the contraption – and listening to our Pilot wireless. We listened intently as RTÉ broadcast radio programmes about the event during their relatively restricted broadcast hours. The programmes, which went out from Radio Éireann's studios in the GPO, conveniently close to the major commemoration venues, were totally focused on the leaders of the rebellion, the state commemorations and little else. There was no reference to the civilian dead. This, after all, was 1966. Two years later Radio Éireann, the only radio station in the country, moved

A scene from RTÉ's drama series Insurrection, *an eight-part dramatised reconstruction of the events of Easter Week 1916, shown over eight consecutive nights to commemorate the 50th anniversary of the Rising. In this scene members of Cumann na mBan are attending to injured Volunteers inside the GPO. Wounded Volunteers are also in shot; a priest is tending to an injured man lying on the ground. RTÉ newsreader Pádraig Ó Gaora, who played Seán Mac Diarmada, is standing first left.*

The railway stations were all renamed after the Rebels who were executed in 1916. The front of every bus had wooden swords bolted to the radiator grille, representing the symbolic claidheamh soluis. They not only represented the fight for freedom but were also a reference to the newspaper of that name, edited by Pádraig Pearse from 1902 until 1909 – and lasted about two weeks – most were stolen by souvenir hunters.

from its daily schedule of closing down at 9 a.m. after an hour of music and news, then ninety minutes at lunchtime, with sponsored programmes, and resuming broadcasts to a breathless nation from five o'clock until midnight.

In some of those radio programmes children spoke. Many were interviewed as 20,000 pupils from 200 schools marched in strict formation past the GPO in teeming rain to a pageant in Croke Park on Sunday, 17 April, re-enacting the Rising. They spoke of their admiration for the leaders of 1916, but there was, of course, no reference to any of the child or civilian casualties. Patrick Kelly, who was proudly wearing two medals his grandfather had been awarded for fighting in the GPO in 1916, talked on the programme about the 'spirit of the men of 1916', oblivious to the fact that another Patrick Kelly, aged twelve, had been a victim of the Rising.[1]

In *Insurrection*, there is reference to looting but little mention of civilian casualties, although it includes a scene in which a child is shot. This is clearly the action of Captain J.C. Bowen Colthurst, who killed, among others, seventeen-year-old J.J. Coade outside Portobello Barracks. But at least a 'child fatality' was featured, even if only to highlight the brutality of some British soldiers. At a court-martial, Colthurst was found 'guilty but insane' and sent to Broadmoor Criminal Lunatic Asylum in July 1916; he was released in February 1918.

My knowledge of the 1916 Rising until recently included the main historical facts, the events of 1966 and a few scraps of stories Nana Duffy told me reticently about Church Street during the 'Troubles'. But while I've been working on this project, images of 1916 have exploded into life – and death. In my mind's eye, I can see Paddy Fetherston excitedly careering down

A Dublin bus on its way to Clontarf, 3 April 1966. The company's nod to the 50th anniversary of the Rising is the sword and the anniversary years displayed on the front of the bus.

towards the commotion in the sunshine, the sparks flying off the steel wheels of his boxcar on the cobblestones as he and his pals gloried in the mayhem that had broken out in the heart of his city, his playground.

I can see studious Bridget McKane in her cottage just off Moore Street, carefully clipping by candlelight from a discarded newspaper a photograph of ten-year-old Luke Kelly, who had been shot in crossfire two years earlier. The image stays with me of Katie Foster, the young widow, proudly placing her two little boys in their pram on that Easter Monday morning then

In an archived report on the state of public health prepared for Dublin Corporation in late 1916, a reference is made to the impact of the rebellion on the health of woman in particular.

The strain on the mother's nervous system owing to anxiety where fathers, brothers or sons are away at the war, I have known to be the cause of delicate nervous infants being born, and dying from convulsion. Also the terribly anxious times we have gone through at home during and after the rebellion have been the cause of a great many stillborn children, and of many who survived their births only for a short period of time.[2]

innocently walking into one of the first gun battles of the Rising. Within minutes, one child was dead.

There were deaths outside my grandmother's house in Church Street but she never spoke of them. I remember her telling me about the capture and subsequent execution in 1920 of eighteen-year-old Volunteer Kevin Barry just across from her home after an ambush at Monks' bakery. But she would not talk about 1916, and the two-week period in April when her elder brother was killed in France and many of her neighbours, including children, died violently in the Rising.

All of this reminds us that history is not a cold, clinical pursuit. We are of this world and are much closer to historical events than we imagine. The links between today and our past are not forged simply in history books: they are forged in flesh and blood connections between real people who are part of what we are and what, in turn, our children will be. So it is with my own family: my grieving granny, living as part of the British Empire, who saw bloodshed on her doorstep in 1916, and my three children, citizens of a proud, well-regarded, independent nation.

I hope my children will get a glimpse of how far we have come since 1916, and that even after the economic turmoil that has been the backdrop to nearly half their lives, they will recognise that the Irelands of 1916 and 2016 are worlds apart. As a nation, we are in a much better place than we were a hundred years ago, and there is no going back.

It can be argued that the children of Ireland got a new nation from the events that began on Easter Monday 1916. But forty of them were killed in the process. With this project, I have tried to reclaim their names and their stories, remember what befell them and find out what happened to their grieving families. They were the lost children of 1916. Perhaps now they will take their rightful place in Irish history, as the singer Declan O'Rourke wrote in this excerpt from the song he composed for this project:

> *But still missing from the pages are*
> *The Children of '16,*
>
> *Nor Pearse, nor Clarke,*
> *MacDonagh,*
> *Or the Connolly we know,*
> *Would rest were they remembered on*
> *A pedestal alone.*
>
> *Are they not the fathers of*
> *Our Nation, proud and free?*
> *And our sisters and our brothers, then,*
> *The Children of '16?*

The General Post Office from Abbey Street, headquarters of the provisional government, 17 May 1916.

Endnotes

The 1916 Rising: Day by Day
1. Thomas Coffey, *Agony at Easter*, Harrap, 1969, p. 9.
2. *ibid.*, p. 35.
3. 3 James Stephens, *The Insurrection in Dublin*, Maunsel, 1916, Chapter 2: 'Tuesday'.
4. *ibid.*, p. 110.
5. Keith Jeffrey (ed.), *The Sinn Féin Rebellion As They Saw It*, Irish Academic Press, 1999. From the diary of Mary Louisa Hamilton. The H and N refer to her husband Arthur Hamilton Norway, Secretary of the Post Office in Ireland, and their son Nevil, who subsequently achieved worldwide fame as the novelist Nevil Shute.
6. *Weekly Irish Times*, 29 April 1916.
7. Nevil Shute, quoted in O'Farrell, *1916*, p. 27

Prologue
1. Charles Dalton, *With the Dublin Brigade*, Mercier Press, 2014, p. 47.
2. Mary Daly, Dublin: *The Deposed Capital*, Cork University Press, 1984, p. 3.
3. John Cooke, *Housing Conditions of the Working Classes in the City of Dublin*, Her Majesty's Stationery Office (hereafter HMSO), 1914, p. 2.
4. Lionel Smith-Gordon and Cruise O'Brien, *Starvation in Dublin*, Wood Printing Works, 1917, p. 16.
5. George Bernard Shaw to Under-Secretary Nathan, quoted in Michael T. Foy and Brian Barton, *The Easter Rising*, The History Press, 1999, p. 271.
6. John Cooke, Honorary Treasurer, National Society for the Prevention of Cruelty to Children, to the Dublin Housing Inquiry, 1913.

1.   As I Strolled Out One Easter Morning
1. Online Historical Population Reports (www.histpop.org), Area, Houses and Population, Leinster, 1911.
2. *ibid.*, extrapolated figures.
3. Terence O'Neill, son of Joseph and first cousin of Sean Foster, to author, 2015.
4. Mary Dunne, great-grand-niece of Catherine Foster, to author, 2014–15.
5. *Evening Herald* archive, Gilbert Library, Dublin City Council.
6. Terence O'Neill, to author, 2015.
7. *Evening Herald*, 24 April 1966.
8. Commandant W.J. Brennan, Whitmore, *Dublin Burning*, Gill & Macmillan, 2013.
9. Census of Ireland, National Archives of Ireland (hereafter NAI), 1901, 1911.
10. *ibid.*

11. Mick O'Farrell, *1916*, Mercier Press, 2008 p. 142.
12. Cathy Clifford, grand-niece of Christopher Cathcart, to author, 2014–15.
13. A. Kinsella, *Medical Aspects of the Rising*, Old Dublin Society, 1996, p.138.
14. James Stephens, *The Insurrection in Dublin*, Chapter 1: 'Monday', Maunser & Co.
15. Rebellion (Victims) Committee, NAI.
16. Death certificate, James Jessop, General Register Office (hereafter GRO).
17. Ledger, presented by Charles J. McAuley, MB, FRCS, compiled 'by a very reliable person' who wishes to remain anonymous, Bureau of Military History (hereafter BMH).
18. Monsignor Michael Curran, BMH, witness statement 687, p. 64.
19. *Evening Herald*, 3 May 1916. The same report also includes: 'Paul Brennan, 9 months old, 37 Upper Abbey Street. The boy Paul Brennan was shot while in the arms of a man trying to take him to a place of safety. The man was killed by the same bullet that fatally wounded the child.' However, Paul Brennan's death certificate and the Glasnevin Cemetery Register both state that he died from 'convulsions'.
20. *Evening Herald*, 3 May 1916.
21. Glasnevin Cemetery Register, St Paul's section, GA 38: 'a Catholic who died from the effects of gunfire'.
22. Rebellion (Victims) Committee, NAI.
23. Marie Nolan, grand-niece of Michael, to author, 2015.
24. Brian Ó Conchubhair (ed.), *Dublin's Fighting Story*, Mercier Press, 2009, p. 101.
25. *Irish Independent*, 25 April 1966.
26. www.kildare.ie
27. *Evening Herald*, 24 April 1917.
28. Glasnevin Cemetery Register, St Paul's section, KA 37.5.
29. Rebellion (Victims) Committee, NAI.

2.   A Tale of Two Cities
1. Census of Ireland, 1911, NAI.
2. *ibid.*
3. Jacinta Prunty, *Dublin Slums 1800–1925*, Irish Academic Press, 1998, p. 46.
4. Norma Furlong and Ken Cooke, grandchildren of Frederick William Sweny, to author, 2014.
5. James Joyce, *Ulysses*, Sylvia Beach,1922, Chapter 2.
6. Rebellion (Victims) Committee, NAI.
7. BMH, witness statement 188, Sean O'Keeffe.
8. *Evening Herald*, 20 May 1916.
9. Ernest R. Jordison, manager and director British Petroleum, 1916, BMH, witness statement 1691, p. 4.
10. Elizabeth Keogh, niece of John Kirwan, and Lillian Nolan, grand-niece of John Kirwan, to author, 2015.
11. 'The cricket bat that died for Ireland', National Museum, Collins Barracks.
12. Richard Veale, grand-nephew of Margaret Veale, to author, 2014.
13. Aine O'Rahilly, BMH, witness statement 333, p.10.
14. Paul O'Brien, *Blood on the Streets*, Mercier Press, 2008.
15. Captain E. Gerrard, British Army, BMH, witness statement 348, p. 3.
16. L.G. Redmond-Howard, *Six Days of the Irish Republic*, Dodo Press, 2007, p. 32.
17. *ibid.*
18. Death certificate, John Kirwan, GRO.
19. Rebellion (Victims) Committee, NAI.
20. Lillian Nolan, grand-niece of John Kirwan, to author, 2015.
21. *The Irish Times*, Friday, 12 May 1916.
22. Vivian Hyde, grand-niece of Lionel Sweny, family correspondence.
23. Rebellion (Victims) Committee, NAI.
24. Death certificate, Christopher Andrews, GRO.

25. Glasnevin Cemetery Register, Dublin section, WG 14.5.
26. Rebellion (Victims) Committee, NAI.

3. 'The Sole Gorge of Their Lives'
1. *A Record of the Irish Rebellion of 1916*, Office of Irish Life, Dublin, 1916.
2. Brennan-Whitmore, *Dublin Burning*, p. 85.
3. *ibid.*
4. Census of Ireland, 1901, NAI.
5. Paddy Fetherston, grand-nephew of Paddy Fetherston, to author, 2014.
6. Marie Fetherston, grand-niece of Paddy Fetherston, to author, 2014.
7. James Stephens, *The Insurrection in Dublin*, Chapter 2: 'Tuesday'.
8. Sean O'Casey, Drums Under the Windows, Macmillan, 1945 p. 272.
9. St John G. Ervine, 'The Story of the Irish Rebellion', *The Century Magazine*, vol. 92, November 1916.
10. Sean T. O'Kelly, 'Easter Week Experiences', *Irish Press*, 6–9 August 1961.
11. Monsignor Michael Curran, BMH, witness statement 687, 1952, p. 52.
12. John Joly, *Reminiscences and Anticipations*, Fisher Unwin, London, 1920.
13. Barry Kennerk, *Moore Street: The Story of Dublin's Market District*, Mercier Press, 2013, p. 75.
14. Census of Ireland, 1911, NAI.
15. Kevin C. Kearns, *Dublin Tenement Life: An Oral History*, Gill & Macmillan, 1994, p. 28.
16. Death certificate, Patrick Fetherston, GRO.
17. Bulmer Hobson, *Ireland Yesterday and Tomorrow*, Anvil Books, 1968, p. 15.
18. *ibid.* pp. 75.
19. Census of Ireland, 1911, NAI.
20. Harold McNamara, *Tree of Life*, private memoir, p. 9.
21. *ibid.*
22. *Sunday Independent*, 7 May 1916, p. 6.
23. *A Record of the Irish Rebellion of 1916* (Irish Life), quoted in Mick O'Farrell, *1916*, p. 253.
24. Barbara Melbourne, grand-niece of John McNamara, to author, 2014.
25. Death certificate, John McNamara, GRO.
26. McNamara, *Tree of Life*.
27. Barbara Melbourne, to author, 2014.
28. Padraig Yeates, *Who Were Dublin's Looters in 1916?* Irish Labour History Society, 2014.
29. *ibid.*
30. Terry Fagan, *Monto*, North Inner City Folklore Project, 2000.

4. A World at War
1. Dublin casualties of the First World War, compiled from Commonwealth War Graves Commission.
2. Fred Baker, great-grand-nephew, and Daphne Whelan, great-grand-niece of Eleanor Warbrook, to author, 2014.
3. Seosamh de Brún, 'B' Company 2nd Battalion, Dublin Brigade Irish Volunteers, BMH, witness statement 312.
4. *ibid.*
5. Maria Luddy, *Prostitution and Irish Society*, Cambridge University Press, 2007, p.178.
6. *Going Strong*, RTÉ, 20 April 1981.
7. Padraig Yeates, *A City in Wartime*, Gill & Macmillan, 2011, p. 281.
8. Volunteer Thomas Pugh, BMH witness statement 397, p. 5.
9. Volunteer Michael Walker, BMH witness statement 139, p. 4.
10. Volunteer Vincent Byrne, BMH witness statement 423, p. 2.
11. Volunteer Martin Walton, TV interview with Kenneth Griffith, *Curious Journey*, 1973.
12. Volunteer John J. Murphy, BMH witness statement 204, p. 7.

13. Death certificate, Eleanor Warbrook, GRO. It also states she died in Meath Hospital.
14. The papers of Walter Hume Long, Wiltshire Council, 947/403/8. His papers also refer to the wounding of a child, Miss Carphin (aged eight), 4 Zion Terrace, Rathgar. She was shot from St Stephen's Green while walking with her father and mother past the Unitarian Church.
15. William J. Stapleton, BMH witness statement 822, pp. 4–6.
16. *Irish Independent*, 29 April 1916.
17. Eleanor Warbrook, letter on the Compensation Committee file, National Archives.
18. *Irish Independent*, 22 December 1927.
19. Frank McNamee, grandson of Margaret Naylor, to author, 2014.
20. Rebellion (Victims) Committee, NAI.
21. Rebellion (Victims) Committee, NAI.
22. *ibid.*, handwritten on original letter.
23. *Hansard*, HC Deb., 7 March 1918, vol. 103, cc 2138-9W2.
24. Deans Grange Cemetery Register, plot 9, A2 West.
25. Death certificate, Patrick Ryan, GRO, 6 May 1916.
26. Glasnevin Cemetery Register, St Paul's section, VF 54.
27. Catherine Creig, grand-niece of Patrick Ryan, to author, 2015.

5. 'We Suffer in Their Coming and Their Going'
1. P.H. Pearse, 'The Mother', in *The Collected Works of Pádraig H. Pearse*, Maunsel & Co., 1917.
2. *Irish Independent*, 24 April 1946.
3. Census of Ireland, 1911, NAI.
4. Donal Fallon, *Come Here To Me*, available at www.comeheretome.com.
5. Prunty, *Dublin Slums, 1800–1925*, p. 309.
6. Terry Fagan, *Dublin Tenements*, North Inner City Folklore Project, 2013.
7. Rebellion (Victims) Committee, NAI.
8. Keith Jeffrey (ed.), *The Sinn Féin Rebellion As They Saw It*, Irish Academic Press, 1999, p. 117.
9. Anne-Marie Fox, grand-niece of Bridget Allen, to author, 2014.
10. Voters register 1908, Dublin City Council, Gilbert Library.
11. Census of Ireland, 1911, NAI.
12. *The Irish Times Sinn Féin Rebellion Handbook*, Irish Times Publications, April 1917.
13. Rebellion (Victims) Committee, NAI.
14. *ibid.*
15. *ibid.*
16. Anne-Marie Fox, grand-niece of Bridget Allen, to author, 2014.
17. Rebellion (Victims) Committee, NAI.

6. 'Oh, Please Don't Kill Father'
1. Don and Peter Sainsbury, grand-nephews of George Percy Sainsbury, to author, 2014.
2. John Molloy, nephew of Tom Maguire, to author, 2014.
3. Rebellion (Victims) Committee, NAI.
4. Mount Jerome Cemetery, C 130, C3 South.
5. Peter Sainsbury, to author, 2015.
6. Mick O'Neill, *Tralee's Old Stock Reminisce*, self-published, 2001.
7. Joseph Hickey, nephew of Thomas Hickey, to author, 2015.
8. Coroner's report, *Freeman's Journal*, 16 May 1916.
9. Rebellion (Victims) Committee, NAI.
10. Monk Gibbon, *Inglorious Soldier*, Hutchinson, 1968, p. 53.
11. *The Irish Times*, 11 January 2001.
12. *Sunday Independent*, 14 May 1916, p. 1.

13. Glasnevin Cemetery Register, St Bridget's section, IH-146.
14. Sinn Féin, *A Fragment of 1916 History*, Sinn Féin Headquarters, 1916, p. 19.
15. Ray Bateson, to author, 2015. 'They died at Pearse's side.'
16. Sean Brunswick, nephew of Mary Brunswick, letter to author, May 2013.
17. Elizabeth Faye and Theo Mortimer, '"Old Wellier": The Story of a Dublin Street', *Dublin Historical Record*, vol. 52, no. 2, autumn 1999, p. 167.
18. Glasnevin Cemetery Register, St Paul's section, RA 38.
19. The late Shane MacThomáis brought Eugene Lynch to my attention when he was historian for the Glasnevin Trust.
20. Irene Lynch, niece of Eugene, to author, 2015.
21. Death certificate, 'Male' O'Toole, GRO.
22. Courtesy of Brenda Malone, senior researcher, National Museum of Ireland, Collins Barracks.

7. Bloody Friday
1. Frank Shouldice, BMH, witness statement 162, p. 5.
2. *Interim Report*, p. 2.
3. Frank Shouldice, BMH, witness statement 162, p. 5
4. Patrick J. Kelly, BMH, witness statement 781, p.12.
5. A. Kinsella, 'Medical Aspects of the 1916 Rising', paper read to the Old Dublin Society, 11 December 1996, p. 151.
6. Lieutenant Joseph O'Connor, 3rd Battalion, Dublin Brigade, BMH, witness statement 157, p. 27.
7. *Liverpool Daily Post*, 1 May 1916.
8. *Weekly Irish Times*, 29 April 1916.
9. *Evening Herald*, 2 May 1916.
10. *Irish Independent*, 26 April 1916.
11. Stephens, *The Insurrection In Dublin*, Chapter 3: 'Wednesday'.
12. Brendan Rooney, grandson, to author, 2015.
13. Annie Mannion, assistant matron, South Dublin Union, BMH, witness statement 295, p. 4.
14. Dublin Board of Assistance, Special Meeting, Wednesday, 3 May 1916, BMH, witness statement 622.
15. Kearns, *Dublin Tenement Life*, 1994, p. 33.
16. Prunty, *Dublin Slums, 1800–1925*, p. 46.
17. W.H. Thompson, *War and Food of the Dublin Labourer* (1916), quoted in Mary Daly, *Dublin: The Deposed Capital*, p. 269.
18. *Interim Report*, p. 3.
19. Celia Daly, grand-niece of Joseph Murray, to author, 2014.
20. Maurice Curtis, *The Liberties, A History*, The History Press, 2013, p. 81.
21. *ibid*.
22. *ibid*.
23. B. Seebohm Rowntree, *Poverty: A Study of Town Life*, Macmillan, 1901.
24. Death certificate, Joseph Murray, GRO.
25. Celia Daly, grand-niece of Joseph Murray, to author, 2014.
26. Dublin Fire Brigade Ambulance Log, 1916, Dublin City Libraries.
27. Deirdre Billane, grand-niece of Bridget Stewart, to author, 2014.
28. Death certificate, Bridget Stewart, GRO.
29. Census of Ireland 1911, NAI.
30. Rebellion (Victims) Committee, NAI.
31. *Dublin Evening Mail*, 3 May 1916.
32. Jeffrey (ed.), *The Sinn Féin Rebellion As They Saw It*, p. 57.
33. Ernest R. Jordison, BMH, witness statement 1691.
34. Dublin Port Archives, 1900–1910, Niall Dardis (retired archivist) to author.

35. Fr Michael Scott, grandnephew of Walter Scott, to author, 2014.
36. Andrew Ryan, grand-nephew of Walter Scott, to author, 2014.
37. Dublin Fire Brigade Ambulance Log.
38. Death certificate, Walter Scott, GRO.
39. Andrew Ryan, grandnephew of Walter Scott, to author, 2015.
40. Society of St Vincent de Paul, *Report on Relief of Special Distress, 29 April to 7 May 1916*, BMH, 234/1.
41. *ibid.*
42. *Irish Independent*, December 1916.

8. The Child Workers
1. Albert Liebes Altman ('Altman the Saltman'), who converted from Judaism to Catholicism, was a well-known Dublin councillor, upon whom many believe James Joyce's Leopold Bloom, in *Ulysses*, is based.
2. S. Shannon Millin, 'Child Life as a National Asset', *Journal of Statistical and Social Inquiry*, vol. XIII, 1917, pp. 301–16.
3. See for example BHM 388, p. 12, Joe Good, Kimmage Garrison.
4. McKane family memoir, supplied to author, April 2014.
5. Joseph Good, member of the Kimmage Garrison, Irish Volunteers, BMH, witness statement 388, p. 12.
6 Census of Ireland, 1911, NAI.
7. From 'Oh! Steer My Bark to Erin's Isle' by Thomas Haynes Bayly.
8. Joe Good, BMH, witness statement 388, p. 12.
9. BMH, Military Pensions Claim.
10. Sean O'Loughlin, BMH, witness statement 209, p. 23.
11. By Count Plunkett we assume they mean Joseph Plunkett and not his father; earlier they refer to Thomas MacDonagh being present – but he was in Jacob's biscuit factory at that time.
12. Max Caulfield, *The Easter Rebellion*, Gill & Macmillan, 1963, p. 261.
13. Thomas M. Coffey, *Agony at Easter*, Harrap, 1969, p. 228.
14. Caulfield, *The Easter Rebellion*, p. 264.
15. Rebellion (Victims) Committee, NAI.
16. *ibid.*
17. Daly, *Dublin*, p. 78.
18. Yeates, *A City in Wartime*, p. 167.
19. *The Irish Times*, 10 January 1911.
20. Padraig Tierney, great-grand-nephew, and Alison Rowan-Tierney, great-grand-niece, of the Mary Redmond, to author, 2015.
21. Death certificate, Mary Redmond, GRO.
22. *Evening Herald*, 27 April 1917.
23. Further information on Mary Redmond from local historian/folklorist Terry Crosbie, to author, 2015.
24. Glasnevin Cemetery Register, Garden, F 72.5.
25. Surgeon Colonel D. Edgar Flinn, *Official report on the special sanitary circumstances and administration of the city of Dublin with special reference to the causes of the high death rate*, HMSO, 1906, p. 47.
26. Census of Ireland 1911, NAI.
27. Sarah Kearney, grand-niece of Christopher Whelan, to author.
28. Glasnevin Cemetery Register, Garden, F 72.5.
29. Paul Brady, grand-nephew of James Kelly, to author.
30. *ibid.*
31. Death Certificate, James Kelly, GRO.

32. *Evening Herald*, 25 April 1917.
33. The papers of Walter Hume Long, Wiltshire Council, ref 947/403/8.

9. The Reply Is in the Negative
1. Alfie Byrne MP, Dublin Harbour, to Prime Minister, House of Commons, 26 June 1916, PQ 113, NAI.
2. *The Irish Times Sinn Féin Rebellion Handbook*.
3. Ann Matthews, *Renegades*, Mercier Press, 2010, p. 176.
4. 'Compensation for Loss of Life', Letters to the Editor, *The Irish Times*, 13 June 1916.
5. BMH, Military Service Pensions Collection, 1937, DP 9667/6.
6. Joe Good, BMH, witness statement 388, p. 14.
7. Letter from Minister for Agriculture James Ryan to Military Pensions Board, BMH, Military Service Pensions Collection.
8. Military Service Pensions Collection, BMH, SPG 1937/1/9.
9. Census of Ireland, 1911, NAI.
10. Joseph O'Brien, *Dear Dirty Dublin*, Joseph O'Brien, 1982, p. 139.
11. Death certificate, William Mullen, GRO.
12. Glasnevin Cemetery Register, St Paul's section, OA 37. 5.
13. A. Kinsella, *Military Aspects of the Rising*, Dublin Historical Society, December 1996.
14. Barry Kennerk, *Temple Street Hospital*, Mercier Press, 2014.
15. Kennerk, *Temple Street Hospital*.
16. *ibid.*
17. *Anglo-Celt* newspaper, 13 May 1916, p. 1.
18. Rebellion (Victims) Committee, NAI.
19. Glasnevin Cemetery Register, St Paul's section, PA 37.5.
20. Rebellion (Victims) Committee, NAI.
21. Stephens, *The Insurrection in Dublin*, Chapter 1: 'Monday'.
22. BMH Military Pensions Records, Letter from Patrick Fox to Joe McGrath, Minister for Industry and Commerce, departmental reference J.M. 755.
23. BMH Military Pensions Application, PB1/d/150, departmental reference A – 34083 – z. 7.
24. *ibid.*
25. *ibid.*
26. *ibid.*
27. *ibid.*
28. *ibid.*
29. *ibid.*
30. *ibid.*
31. Matthew Connolly, BMH, witness statement 1746.
32. Census of Ireland, 1911, NAI.
33. BMH Military Pensions Applications.
34. BMH Military Pensions Application, P14 1/D/204.
35. BMH Military Pensions Collection, 1/D/204 p. 17.
36. Jack Doherty, grand-nephew of Sean Healy, letter to author, 2014.

Epilogue
1. *Jubilee 1916*, with John Bowman, Niall Tóibín and Terry O'Sullivan, RTÉ Radio 1, 17 April 1966.
2. Sir Charles Cameron, *Report Upon the State of Public Health in the City of Dublin, 1916*, Dublin City Council Archives, p. 95.

Select Bibliography

Archives

Ambulance Log, April 1916, Dublin Corporation
   Fire Service, Dublin City Libraries

Dublin Casualties of World War I, compiled from
   Commonwealth War Graves Commission, www.cwgc.org

Bureau of Military History, Dublin, Department of Defence

Census of Ireland, 1901, 1911, National Archives of Ireland, Dublin
   (hereafter NAI) (with the kind permission of the director)

Chief Secretary's Office Registered Papers, NAI

Commonwealth War Graves Commission

Deans Grange Cemetery Register

Dr William Walsh Laity Papers, Dublin Diocesan Archives

General Register Office, Werburgh Street, Dublin

Glasnevin Trust, Glasnevin Cemetery and Museum

Guinness Archive, Dublin

House of Commons, Hansard, HC Deb 7 March 1918, vol. 103

Military Service Pension Records, Bureau of Military
   History, 1913–21, Department of Defence

National Museum of Ireland, Collins Barracks

National Society for the Prevention of Cruelty to Children,
   Annual Reports, 1911–24, National Library of Ireland

Nichols Undertakers Ltd, Lombard Street, Dublin 2

Online Historical Population Reports – Area, Houses and
  Population: Leinster, Ireland, 1911, University of Essex

Property Losses (Ireland) Committee, 1916, NAI

Rebellion (Victims) Committee, CSORP 1918/25183/25271, NAI

*Report of the Departmental Committee into the Housing
  Conditions of the Working Classes in the City of
  Dublin, 1914*, National Library of Ireland

Walter Hume Long Papers, Wiltshire Council

Newspapers

Daily Mirror (London)

Daily Express (London)

Dublin Evening Mail

Evening Herald

Evening Telegraph

Freeman's Journal

Irish Independent

The Irish Times

Liverpool Daily Post

Saturday Evening Herald

Books and Pamphlets

Bateson, Ray, *They Died by Pearse's Side*,
  Irish Graves Publications, 2010

Breathnach, Ciara and O'Halpin, Eunan, 'Registered "Unknown"
  Infant Fatalities in Ireland, 1916–1932: Gender and Power',
  Irish Historical Studies, vol. XXXVIII, no. 149, May 2012

Brennan-Whitmore, Commandant W.J., *Dublin Burning: The Easter
  Rising from Behind the Barricades*, Gill & Macmillan, 2013

Caulfield, Max, *The Easter Rebellion*, Frederick Muller, 1964

Coffey, Thomas M., *Agony at Easter*, George G. Harrap & Co., 1969

Collins, Lorcan and Kostick, Conor, *The Easter Rising: A*

Guide to Dublin in 1916, The O'Brien Press, 2000

Connell, Joseph E.A., *Dublin in Rebellion: A Directory, 1913–1923*, The Lilliput Press, 2009

Crowe, Caitriona (ed.), *Dublin 1911*, Royal Irish Academy, 2011

Cumann na mBan, *The Fianna Heroes of 1916* (pamphlet), Cumann na mBan, 1931

Curtis, Maurice, *The Liberties: A History*, The History Press, 2013

Dalton, Charles, *With the Dublin Brigade*, Mercier Press, 2014

Daly, Mary E., *Dublin, the Deposed Capital: A Social and Economic History, 1860–1914*, Cork University Press, 1984

Duffy, Joe, *Just Joe: My Autobiography*, Transworld, 2011

Fagan, Terry, *Monto: Madams, Murder and Black Coddle – The story of Dublin's notorious red-light district and the people who lived there*, North Inner City Folklore Project, 2000

—*Dublin Tenements: Memories of Life in Dublin's Notorious Tenements*, North Inner City Folklore Project, 2013

Foy, Michael T. and Barton, Brian, *The Easter Rising*, Sutton Publishing, 1999

Gibbon, Monk, *Inglorious Soldier*, Hutchinson, 1968

Hegarty, Shane and O'Toole, Fintan, *The Irish Times Book of the 1916 Rising*, Gill & Macmillan, 2006

Higgins, J.J., 'The Sinking of the RMS *Leinster* Recalled', *Postal Worker*, vol. 14, no. 11, November 1936

Higgins, Roisin, *Transforming 1916: Meaning, Memory and the Fiftieth Anniversary of the Easter Rising*, Cork University Press, 2012

Irwin, Wilmot, *Betrayal in Ireland: An Eyewitness Record of the Tragic and Terrible Years of Revolution and Civil War in Ireland, 1916–1924*, Northern Whig, 1966

Jeffery, Keith (ed.), *The Sinn Féin Rebellion As They Saw It*, by Mary Louisa and Arthur Hamilton Norway, Irish Academic Press, 1999

Joly, John, *Reminiscences and Anticipations*, T. Fisher Unwin, Ltd, 1920

Joyce, James, *Ulysses*, Sylvia Beach, 1922

Kearns, Kevin, *Dublin Tenement Life: An Oral*

History, Gill & Macmillan, 2006

—*Dublin Voices: An Oral Folk History*, Gill & Macmillan, 1988

Kennerk, Barry, *Moore Street: The Story of Dublin's Market District*, Mercier Press, 2012

—*Temple Street Children's Hospital: An Illustrated History*, New Island Books, 2014

Kinsella, Anthony, *Medical Aspects of the 1916 Rising*, Old Dublin Society, 1996

Lee, J.J., *Ireland, 1912–1985: Politics and Society*, Cambridge University Press, 1989

Luddy, Maria, *Prostitution and Irish Society*, Cambridge University Press, 2007

MacThomáis, Shane, *Dead Interesting: Stories from the Graveyards of Dublin*, Mercier Press, 2012

Mac Thormaid, Brendan Mary, *Deathless Glory*, Massey Brothers Ltd, 1966

McGarry, Fearghal, *The Rising. Ireland: Easter 1916*, Oxford University Press, 2010

McManus, Ruth, *Dublin, 1910–1940: Shaping the City and Suburbs*, Four Courts Press, 2002

Matthews, Ann, *Renegades: Irish Republican Women, 1900–1922*, Mercier Press, 2010

Murray, Christopher, *Sean O'Casey, Writer at Work: A Biography* Gill & Macmillan, 2005

O'Brien, Cruise and Smith-Gordon, Lionel, *Starvation in Dublin* (pamphet), Wood Printing Works, 1917

O'Brien, Joseph, *Dear, Dirty Dublin: A City in Distress, 1899–1916*, University of California Press, 1982

O'Brien, Paul, *Blood on the Streets: 1916 and the Battle for Mount Street Bridge*, Mercier Press, 2008

Ó Broin, Leon, *Dublin Castle and the 1916 Rising*, Helicon Limited, 1966

—*Juno and the Paycock*, Macmillan, 1928

—*The Plough and the Stars: A Tragedy in Four Acts*, Macmillan, 1930

—*Drums Under the Windows*, Macmillan,
  1945 (reprinted by Pan Books, 1973)
—*Inishfallen, Fare Thee Well*, Macmillan, 1949
  (reprinted by Pan Books, 1973)
Ó Conchubhair, Brian, *Dublin's Fighting Story*, Mercier Press, 2009
—*1916: What the People Saw*, Mercier Press, 2008
—*A Walk Through Rebel Dublin, 1916*, Mercier Press, 2009
O'Farrell, Mick, *The 1916 Diaries of an Irish Rebel
  and a British Soldier*, Mercier Press, 2014
O'Neill, Mick, *Old Stock Reminisce: An Oral History of Tralee and
  Its Surroundings* (edited by Timmy Griffin), self-published, 2001
Prunty, Jacinta, *Dublin Slums, 1800–1925: A Study in
  Urban Geography*, Irish Academic Press, 1998
Redmond-Howard, L.G., *Six Days of the
  Irish Republic*, Dodo Press, 2007
Sinn Féin, *A Fragment of 1916 History*,
  Sinn Féin Headquarters, 1916
Stephens, James, *The Insurrection in Dublin*, Maunsel
  & Co., 1916 (reprinted by Scepter Books, 1965)
Stokes, Roy, *Death in the Irish Sea: The Sinking of
  the RMS* Leinster, The Collins Press, 1998
Thom's Official Directory, Alex Thom & Co. Ltd, 1916
Townsend, Charles, *Easter 1916: The Irish Rebellion*, Allen Lane, 2005
Weekly Irish Times, *Sinn Féin Rebellion Handbook, Easter
  1916*, Weekly Irish Times, 1917 (reprinted as *1916
  Rebellion Handbook*, Mourne River Press, 1998)
Yeates, Padraig, *Lockout: Dublin, 1913*, Gill & Macmillan, 2001
—*A City in Wartime*, Gill & Macmillan, 2011
—*Who Were Dublin's Looters in 1916?*, Irish
  Labour History Society, 2014

Index

Abbey Street xii, 51, *179*
Adelaide Hospital 86, 149–50, 210
Aiken, Frank 221–22
Allen, Bridget xviii, 92, 123–24, 129–31, 183
Allen, Edward 123–24, 130–31
Allen, Mary 123–25, 129–31
Allen, Matthew 124, 130
Allen, Michael 124, 130
Altinure Terrace (Cabra) 213
Amiens Street xv, 125, 182
Andrews, Christopher xviii, 43–44, 45–46, 49, 57, 58, 59, 62–63, 65
Andrews, Maria 45–46, 63
Andrews, Patrick 45–46
Anglesea Market 77–*78*
Annesley Bridge xv
Army Pensions Board 207, 217, 219
Ashe, Thomas xx
Asquith, H.H. 203–4
Aughrim Street 96, 119
Augustine Street 167, 168, 170
Aungier Street 82, *101*

Baden-Powell, Robert 81
Ballintemple (Co Tipperary) 116
Ballyfermot 155–56
Barmacks buildings 98
Barry, Kevin 236
Bayly, Thomas Haynes 187

Beggars Bush 171
Beggars Bush Barracks xii, 53, 54, 56
Beresford Street 136
Bernard Shaw, George 11
Bishop Street *26*, 86
   see also Jacob's Biscuit Factory
Black, Major Charles Augustus John Albert RAMC 29
Blacquiere Bridge (Phibsborough) 196–97
Boland's bakery 160
Boland's Mills xxii, 41, 50, 54, 121, 163–64
Botanic Road 119
Bow Lane 167
Bradshaw, Anne 193
Bradshaw, William 195
Brazen Head pub 170
Brennan-Whitmore, W.J. 68
Bridewell 191, 217–18, 228
Bridge Street 170
Bridgefoot Street 134
British Army
   Irish soldiers 3, 17–18, 91–92
   pensions 3
   'separation' women 99–102
   wive's allowances 18, 38
   see also First World War
Broadstone railway works 183
Brunswick, Anne (née Stephenson) 147
Brunswick, John 146
Brunswick, Mary Ann xx, 144–47

Brunswick, Sean 144, 146–47
Brunswick, Sean (Nephew of
Mary Ann) 144, 147
Brunswick Street *see* Pearse Street
Buckingham Buildings 147
Bureau of Military History
53, 56, 101–2, 184, 215
Butt Bridge 163–64
Byrne, Alfie 108
Byrne, Lieutenant Billy 102
Byrne, Vincent 102

Cabra Park 214
Caffrey, Christina xiv, 39, 124, 125–29
Caffrey, Joseph 116–18, 125, 128–29
Caffrey, Sarah (née Bristow)
116–18, 119, 125–29
Cairo Café 82
Canes Court 77
Capel Street 191
Carlisle Bridge *see* O'Connell Bridge
Carroll, Agnes 1, 5, 8, 232, 236–37
Carroll, Christopher 'Kit' 1–3, 91–92
Carroll, Tom 3, 91–92
Cathal Brugha Street 145
Cathcart, Christopher xi,
16, 25, 28–29, 35–36
Cathcart, Julia 27, 28
Cathcart, Patrick 27, 35–36
Cathcart, Patrick (child) 35
Caulfield, Max, *The Easter Rebellion* 20
Ceannt, Éamonn xiii, 220
Chance, Lady Eileen 27
Chancery Lane (Bride Street) 9
Charlemont Street 25–26, 27, 29
Chaworth Terrace 123
children
   Easter Week mortality rates 11–12
   historical mortality rates 5
   living and playing conditions 10–11, 28
   working 182
Church Street xiv, 1, 8, 9, 11, 16–17,
   19, 21–22, 91, 110, 118, 139, 161
Claddagh Green (Ballyfermot) 155, 156
Clancy, Peadar 21

Clarke, Emmet *200*
Clarke, Jane 111
Clarke, John Daly *200*
Clarke, Kathleen 111, *200*
Clarke, Tom xxi, 188, 189, 205, 222
Clarke, Tom (Junior) *200*
Clonliffe Road 32
Coade, J.J. 234
Coady, Essie 29
Colbert, Con 161
Coleraine Street 143
Cole's Lane 77–78, 80, *167*, 208
Collins Barracks (Royal
Barracks) 134, 226–27
Collins, Michael xxi, 188, 189, 202–3
Colthurst, Captain J.C. Bowen 234–35
compensation claims *see* Rebellion
   (Victims) Committee
Connolly, James xv, xix, xxi,
   4, 74, 188–89, 222
Connolly, John 171
Connolly, Mary (née Stewart) 171–72
Connolly, Matthew 223
Connolly, Peter 137–38, 141
Connolly, Captain Sean 225
Connor, Peter 119
Constitution Hill 143
Cooke, Ken 60
Corporation Buildings 88–89,
   118–19, *124*, 128
Corporation Street (Mabbot Street) 118–19
Cosgrave, William T. 220–21
Costello, Colonel M. 217, 225
Cowley, Thomas 56
Cross Guns Bridge xvii, 145, 161
Cuffe Street 98
Cullen, Annie 109
Cumann na mBan 53, 227
Cumberland Street North 23, *25*, 28
Cumberland Street South 44, *45*
Curran, Monsignor Michael 32, 74–75
Curran, Private P. 186
Curtis, Maurice 169
Dalton, Charles 4
Daly, Ned xii, xxii, 134

Dame Street 121–22
Darcy, Charles xi, 92, 94, *182*, 183, 223–26
Darcy, Elizabeth *224–225*
Darcy, James 223–24
Davy's public house 27, 29
Dawson Street 134
de Brún, Seosamh 97–99
de Valera, Eamon 50, 54, *111*, 163, 185, 222, 231–32
Denmark Street 77
Dillon, Robert xxii
Dominick Street 68–69, 70, 77, 80, 189
Donelan, Brendan 213
Donore Avenue *104*, 106
Dorset Street 70, 146
    temporary hospital 210
Dowker's Lane 10
Downton, Ruth 123
Doyle, John 31
Doyle, Maria 47
Doyle, Mary 41
Doyle, Moses xi, 39, 41
Doyle, Patrick 41
Dr Steevens Hospital 210
Drumcondra 211
Drumree (Co Meath) 214
Dublin
    bakeries 159
    child mortality rates 5, 193
    public reaction to insurrection 83–84
    size and population in 1916 4–5, 6–7
    'stew houses' 155–56
    tenement conditions 5–7, 9–10, 45, 156, 165–66
    workhouses 150–*51*
Dublin Battalion Associated Volunteer Corps 55–56
Dublin Castle xii, 26–27, 40–41, *95*
    temporary hospital 210
Dublin Fire and Property Losses Association 203
Dublin Metropolitan Police (DMP) 67, 71, 169
Dublin Salt Works 125, 183
Dublin United Tramway Company 207
Duggan, E.J. 219

Easter Rising
    1966 commemorations 231–35
    food shortages xix–xx, 157–64
    looting 67–68, 71–77, 86–89
    surrender xxii, 13
    timeline xi–xxiii
Ellis, Sam 98
Elmes, Sergeant E. 225
Elvery's Elephant House 51–52, *113*
Emerald Street 32
Ennis, Matthew 119
Erne Place 60
Erne Street 50, 63–64
Errigal Road (Crumlin) 102
Ervine, St John Greer 73–74
Eustace Street 111, 162

Faddles's Alley *10*
Fahy, Peter *62*
Fairview Park 97
Father Mathew Hall (Church Street) 16–17, 21–22, 36
Fetherston, Annie (née Gaynor) 68–*71*, 80–81, 93, 115, 118
Fetherston, John 'Jack' 81
Fetherston, Patrick 69–70, 71, 81
Fetherston, Patrick 'Paddy' xi, *70*, 77, 80–81, 87, 92, 93, 235
First World War 3, 6, 17–19, 36–37, 49, 91–112, 121, 133, 173–174, 186
    Western Front 18–19, 94, 129–31
Foley Street *124*
Foster, John 17–18, 36, 39, 93
Foster, Katie (née O'Neill) 16–23, 36–39, 235–36
Foster, Patrick 18
Foster, Sean Francis xi, 1, 16, 19–23, 36–39, 92, 109–10, 235–36
Foster, Terence 'Ted' 1, 16–17, 36
Four Courts xii, 121, 129, 191
Fox, Alice 33
Fox, Edward 33
Fox, James xiv, 213–23
Fox, Margaret 214
Fox, Patrick J. 214–23
Fox, Thomas 217–18

Fox, William xiv, 16, 32–33
Francis Street 169
Frith, Constable William 71
Fryday, Edward 120
Fryday, Elizabeth Ann Preston
Wayland *120*–23
Fryday, Henry *123*
Fryday, Metta 122
Fryday, Neville Nicholas xi, xxii,
16, 92, 93, 116, 120–*23*
Fryday, William Jack 116
Fryday, William (Junior) 120–21, *123*
Fumbally Lane xiv, 94–99, 101, 121
Furlong, Norma 60

Gahan, Corporal Patrick J. 139
Gaiety Theatre 82
Gardiner Street 22, *153*
Gaynor, Sergeant Joseph 93
General Post Office (O'Connell Street)
x, xii–xiii, 24, 41, *113*, 121, 181, *238*
Gerrard, Captain E. 56
Gibbon, Monk 140–41
Gibney, James xxii, 143–44
Gibney, Lillian 144
Gilligan, Eileen 119
Gilsenan, Eveleen 171
Glasnevin Cemetery xvii, 33, 34,
128, *158*, 170, 197, 211
Gleeson, Father Francis *37*, 38
Gloucester Street *see* Sean
McDermott Street
Gogarty, Oliver St John 220
Goldenbridge Cemetery 148
Good, Joe 184, 206
GPO (O'Connell Street) 4
Grace, Section Commander
James 54–*55*, 56
Grafton Street 82
looting 84–85
Grangegorman Military Cemetery
(Blackhorse Avenue) 108–9
Grattan Court 45
Great Britain Street *see* Parnell Street
Great Denmark Street 79
Great Denmark Street School 71
Great War *see* First World War

Guinan, Sergeant Patrick 217–18

Hackett's Court *212*, 213
Haddington Road 49, *52*, 54, *55*, *56*
Halston Street 192
Halston Street School *70*, 71
Hammond Lane Foundry *57*
Hanbury Lane 123
Harcourt Street *180*, 210
Harter, Doreen 171
Harter, Gwendolen 171
Harter, Muriel 171
Healy, Christopher 227–28
Healy, John *198*
Healy, Sean xiv, 31, 183, 213, 226–29
Henrietta Place 144, *145*
Henrietta Street 9, 143
Henry Place xxi, 77, 79, 184, 188, 207
Henry Street 77–78, *79*, *167*
Heuston, Sean xvii, 168
Hickey, Christopher xxi, 92, 135–42
Hickey, Teresa (née Kavanagh)
135–36, 137–40
Hickey, Thomas 135–42
Higgins, John 197
Hobson, Bulmer 81
Hodge, John 108
Holles Street 160, 210
Holohan, Gary 20
Horgan, J.F. 218–19
Horseman's Row 77–78
hospitals, temporary 210
Howard, Sean 213
Hunter, Commandant
Thomas 98–99, 102–3

Irish Citizen Army 214, 223
Irish National Aid Association 203, 220
Irish National Aid and Volunteer
Dependants' Fund (INAAVDF) 203, *225*
Irish Volunteer Dependants' Fund 202–3
Irish Volunteers 134, 186–87, 227
Irvine Crescent (East Wall) 175
Ivers, Kate 29
Ivers, Kate (née Connell)
23, 24, 29–30, 34–35
Ivers, Michael 23, 24, 29, 35

Ivers, Patrick xx, 16, 23, 24, 28, 29–31, 34–35, 182

Jacob's Biscuit Factory *26*, 26–27, 41, 103, 149–50, 182–83, 226
James Street 169
Jervis Street Hospital 32, 80, 210
Jessop, James 31, 34
Jessop, Joseph 31, 34
John's Lane 169
John's Lane Distillery 167
Joly, John 76
Jordison, Ernest J. 174

Kane's Court (off Gloucester Street) 224
Kavanagh, Bridget 209
Kavanagh, Charles xviii, 209–12
Kavanagh, Denis 209
Kavanagh, Elizabeth 209
Kavanagh, Mary 209
Kavanagh's Court (North King Street) 116–*17*
Kehoe Square 156
Kelly, Francis 198
Kelly, James xiv, 31, 183, 196–*98*, 213
Kelly, Joseph 109
Kelly, Kate 137–38
Kelly, Luke 186–*87*, 235
Kelly, Mary xxii, 92, 109
Kelly, Patrick xx, 147–49, 234
Kelly, Teresa 213
Kelly's Row 23
Keogh, Gerald 213
Kevin Street 98, 141
Kings Inns 8
Kingsbridge (Heuston) railway station xv, 4
Kinnear, Elizabeth Ann Preston Wayland 115–16, *120–23*
Kinnear, Thomas Albert 123
Kirwan, Annie 44–45, 60, 63–65
Kirwan, John xi, 43–45, 48–49, 51–52, *57–58*, *59–60*, 65, 92, 94, 152
Kirwan, John (Senior) 44–45
Kirwan, Lily 51
Kirwan, Sadie *64*
Kirwan, Tommy *64*

Knockmark Cemetery (Co Meath) 223
Knowles, and Sons, fruiterers, Grafton Street 66, 82

Lahiff, Constable Michael 71
Lander, Mabel 172
Lemass, Herbert 185
Lemass, Noel 185
Lemass, Seán xxi, 185, 188
Lennon, Annie 171–72
Liberty Hall xvii
Liberty House 128
Liffey Street 75
Linenhall Street Barracks 136, 144
Liscombe, Mary Bridget 106, 107, 109
Lockout (1913) xvii, 125, 157
Lombard Street 50, 109
Long Lane 68–69, 70, 71, 80, 115
Long, Walter Hume 103
looting xiii, xv, 67–68, 71–77, 86–89
    Property Losses (Ireland) Committee 77
Love, H.C. 202
Lower Erne Street 50
Lower Rutland Street 224
Lynch, Anna Maria 'Niney' (née McGrath) 149
Lynch, Eugene xx, 147, 148, 149
Lynch, Joseph 149

Mabbot Street *see* Corporation Street
Mac Thomáis, Shane 158
McCormack, Bridget (née Mangan; Warbrook) 105
McDermott, Sean xxi, 188, 205–6, 222
MacDonagh, Thomas xxi, 26–27, 98, 161, 189, 226
McGrath, Elizabeth 149
McGrath, Joe 202, 216, 219
McGrath, Nicholas 149
McKane, Bridget xx, xxi–xxii, 183, 184–90, 192, *205–8*, 235
McKane, Elizabeth 189
McKane, Margaret (née Byrne) xxi–xxii, 185, 188–90
McKane, Michael *206*, 207–8
McKane, Rosie 189

McKane, Thomas 184–85, 188, 205–8
McKeown, Catherine 191
McKeown, William 191
McLoughlin, Sean 168, 188
McNamara, Henery 81–83, 86
McNamara, John Henery xx, 81–86, 158
McNamara, Lucy 81–*83*, 85–86
McNamee, Frank 106, 109
MacNeill, Eoin xi, 55
McSorley, Catherine 82
Maddock, Sir Simon 84
Maguire, Tom 135
Mallin, Michael 96, 213–14, 222
Malone, Lieutenant Michael 54–55, 56
Malpas Terrace 95, 96
Manor Place 36
Manor Street 119
Markievicz, Countess
Constance 81, 213–14
Marlborough Street 31, 33, 145, 186, 224
Marrowbone Lane xxii, 167
Martelares 82
Mary Street 136
Mary's Abbey 191, 192
Masons Market 77, 78
Mater Hospital 29–30, 197, 210, 226
Meath Hospital 103, 210
Meath Street 124
Mendicity Institute xvii, 41, 121, 134, 168
Mercers Hospital 122, 176,
210, 213, 213–14
Merrion Square 27
Military Pensions Board 205
Moloney, Sarah 152
Monks' Bakery (North King Street) 158
Montgomery 'Monto' Street 118, 182
Moore Lane 184, 185, 189–90
Moore Place 208
Moore Street (Riddell's Row)
xxi, 77–79, 184, 208
Mount Harold Terrace (Rathmines) 133
Mount Jerome Cemetery 84, 105, 122, 144
Mount Street xiv, 45, 46, 56, 121, 171
Mount Street Bridge 50, 54, 57, 58
Mountjoy Square 11, 155
temporary hospital 210

Mullen, Elizabeth 208
Mullen, James 208
Mullen, Joseph 209
Mullen, Richard 208, 209
Mullen, William xx, 208–9
Murphy Cottages (Summerhill) 223, 224
Murphy, John J. 102–3
Murphy, William Martin xvii, 203
Murray, James 170
Murray, Jane 168
Murray, John 168–69, 170–71
Murray, John (Junior) 170
Murray, Joseph xx, 158, 166–67, 168–71

Na Fianna 182, 213, 227
Naylor, Lance Corporal James 107
Naylor, Private John 106, *108*
Naylor, Kitty 106, 107–*8*, 109
Naylor, Margaret 106–9
Naylor, Margaret (Junior) 106, 107–*8*, 109
Naylor, Tessie 106, 107–*8*, 109
Naylor, Private William 107
Neil, James Crawford 75
Neilan, Anthony 133–34
Neilan, Eva 133–34
Neilan, Gerald 133–34
Neilan, Dr John 133–34
Nelson's Pillar (Sackville Street) xiii, 51, *232*
New Street 41, 98
Newcomen Bridge 97
Newett, Annie 171–72
Newmarket 6
Noblett's sweet shops xiii, 71–72, *72*, 82, 89
North Brunswick Street 19, 159
North Circular Road 4–5
North Cumberland Street 22
North Dublin Union 7, 150
North Earl Street xiv, 88
North Great George's Street 193, 194
temporary hospital 210
North King Street xix, 8, 23,
116–*17*, 123, 158, 209
massacre xxi, 136–42, 204
North Strand bombings 207–8
North Wall 176
Northumberland Road 53, 54, 56, 171

Northumberland Street *88*
Norway, Arthur Hamilton 121–22

O'Brien, Constable James xii, 71
O'Carroll, Brendan 119
O'Carroll, Maureen 119
O'Casey, Sean 15, 43, 72, 115, 146, 175
O'Connell Bridge (Carlisle Bridge) 187
O'Connell, Inspector Richard 228
O'Connell Street (Sackville Street) xi, xix,
    2, *14*, *40*, 51, *90*, 110, *113*, *132*, 194
    looting 74, 75, 84, 88–89
O'Connor, Charles H. 202
O'Connor, John 31–*32*
O'Connor, Joseph 160
O'Farrell, Elizabeth xxii, 189
O'Keeffe, Sean 50
O'Kelly, Sean T. 74
O'Leary, Martin *62*
O'Neill, Alice 142–43
O'Neill, Elizabeth 142
O'Neill, Reverend George 23
O'Neill, John 142–43
O'Neill, Joseph 18, 21–22
O'Neill, Margaret 142
O'Neill, Terence 19, 36–37
O'Neill, Terry 21
O'Neill, Sergeant Thomas J. 225
O'Neill, William xxi, 142–43
O'Rahilly, Aine 53–54, 55–56
O'Rourke, Declan 237
Orpen, Charles 202
O'Sullivan, Patrick 186
O'Toole, Christopher 149–50
O'Toole, 'Male' xi, 149–51

Parkgate Street xvii, 177
Parliament Street 40–41, 223
Parnell Street 77–78, 222
Parnell Street (Great Britain Street) 209
Patrick Street 131
Pearse, Pádraig xv, xxi–xxii, 13, 57–58, 189
Pearse Street (Brunswick Street)
    44, 48, 50, 91, 224
Pearse, Willie 189
Pembroke Cottages (Ballsbridge) 171

pensions, British Army 3
Pepper, Christine 22
Phibsborough 161, 226
Phibsborough Road 198
Pimlico 164
Playfair, George xii, 20
Playfair, Gerald 20
Pleasant Street 29
Plunkett, Joseph xxi, 188, 189
Portobello Army Barracks 26–27, 95, 234
Portobello Bridge 27, 28, 121
Prussia Street 119, 126
Pugh, Thomas 102
Purser, Sarah Henrietta 51

Raglan Road 171
Rasdale, Lieutenant A. 225
Rathdown Road 119
Rebellion (Victims) Committee 38,
    63, 85–86, 104–5, 111, 126–28,
    135, 172, 176, 201–3, 211–12
Redmond, Alice 190–92
Redmond, L.G. 58–59
Redmond, Mary xviii, 183, 190–92, *198*
Rialto 135
Richmond Barracks 149
Richmond Cottages (Summerhill) 33
Richmond Hospital 110, 210
Riddels Row *see* Moore Street
Ringsend Drawbridge *see* Victoria Bridge
Robbins, Frank 214–15
Royal Barracks *see* Collins Barracks
Royal City Hospital (Baggot
Street) 53, 171, 210
Royal College of Surgeons 41, 84
Russell, Dr Matthew J. 151–52
Ryan, Frances 110, 112
Ryan, Frederick 213
Ryan, James 110, 112
Ryan, Patrick xvi, 92, 109–12
Ryan, Dr Seamus 205, 207
Ryans grocery (Bridge Street) 170

Sackville Street *see* O'Connell Street
Sainsbury, Arthur 134, 135
Sainsbury, Arthur Draper 134–35

Sainsbury, George Percy xviii, 134–35
St Columba's Road (Drumcondra) 4
St Eithne Road (Cabra) 232
St Kevin's Hospital (South
Dublin Union) 196
St Lawrence's Hospital 19, 23
St Malachy's Road (Glasnevin) 121
St Stephen's Green 11, 41, 202, 204
    temporary hospital 210
St Vincent's Hospital (St
Stephen's Green) 106, 210
Sandwith Place 48–49, 64
Scherzinger, Abalone 56
Scott, Anna Magdalena (née Bryce) 175–76
Scott, Walter xx, xxii, 158, 175–76
Scott, William 175
Scott, William (Junior) 175, 176
Scully, Mr A. 224
Sean McDermott Street (Gloucester
    Street) 28, 30, 34, 118, 147, 208
Seery, John 226
separation women 99–102
Seville Place 97
Sheehy-Skeffington, Francis 73–74
Shelbourne Hotel 84
Sheriff Street 32, 187
Ship Street Great 39–40
Ship Street Little 39–40
Shouldice, Frank 159
Simpsons Lane 77, 78
Sir Patrick Dun's Hospital 58, 160, 210
Sitric Place 109–10, 112
Smail, James Cameron 96
South Dublin Union xxii,
    7, 41, 121, 165, 220
South Great George's Street 224
Stafford Street 31
Stephens, James 29, 50, 162–65, 214
Stephens Place 44, 46
Stephenson, Patrick 145, 147
Stewart, Bridget xx, 158, 171–72
Stewart, Charles 171
Stirrup Lane 117
Stoneybatter 16, 36, 109–10
Store Street 225

Summerhill (Gardiner Street) 5
Sweny, Frederick Lionel
    46–47, 58, 61–62, 63
Sweny, Lilian Caroline 61
Sweny, Sara Jane (née Owens) 47, 63
Sweny, Sophia Mary (née Johnson) 46–47
Sweny, William Lionel xvi, 44, 46–48,
    49, 57, 58, 59, 60–62, 65, 152
Sweny's shop 46, 48
Switzers 82
Synge Street 11
Synott, George 56

Talbot Street xiv, 89
Taylor, Lieutenant Colonel Henry 136
Taylor, John 38, 191, 202, 212
Temple Bar 111
Temple Street Hospital 185, 210
Tennyson, Alfred 181
Thomas Street 124, 164, 167, 168, 169
Townsend Street xiv, 109
Trinity College, temporary hospital 210

Uzell, John 88–89

Veale, John 54, 55, 63
Veale, Joseph 52–53
Veale, Margaret 'Madge' xvi, xxii,
    44, 49, 50, 52–57, 63, 65
Veale, Mary Johanna (née Kelly) 54, 55
Victoria Bridge (Ringsend Drawbridge) 106
Vincent Street 149

Walker, Michael 102
Walker, Patricia 75
Walsh, Ellen 212–13
Walsh, Philip xvi, 212–13
Walton, Martin 102
War of Independence 146–147, 215, 225
Warbrook, Bridget (née Mangan)
    94, 95–96, 103, 105
Warbrook, Eleanor xi, 92, 94, 95–97, 102–5
Warbrook, Georgina Frances 105
Warbrook, John 106
Warbrook, Margaret (née Walker) 96

Warbrook, Thomas 94, 95–96, 105
Warbrook, Thomas (Junior)
  94, 96, *104*, 105, 106
Wards Hill (Liberties) 96
Wayland, Palliser 121
Wayland, Piper J. *123*
Wayland, Dr Robert Shaw 122
Weirs 82
Wellington Street 144
Westland Row School (St Andrew's) 44
Whately, John 144
Whelan, Annie 'Cuckoo' 193–96

Whelan, Christopher xx, 181, 192–96, *205*
Whelan, Laurence 193–94, 196
Whelan, Mary 'May' 193–96
Whelan, Mary (née Bradshaw) 193, 195
Whelan, Mary (née Carroll) 193–94
Whitefriar Street 41
wives and widows, 'separation allowances' 3
Woolworths 82
workhouses, Dublin 150–*51*
Workmen's Compensation Act 204

York Street 11, 81, 82, 84

Acknowledgements

It was the Jack and Jill Children's Foundation that accidentally started this project in October 2012 when they asked me – and many better artists – to paint a large plastic egg to be displayed publicly the following Easter, to be then auctioned as a much-needed fundraiser.

A few botched attempts at landscapes and cracked eggs left me looking for an idea that might work – and it suddenly struck me: Easter in Ireland is associated with the 1916 Rising. The Jack and Jill Foundation looks after sick children. So I simply asked the question: does anyone know how many children – if any – died in the insurrection that led to our nationhood?

That was the beginning of a quest that has consumed me for the past three years – and still does.

Anna Mc Hugh of An Post contacted me early on after she saw my finished egg, commemorating children who had died during the Rising, on the *Late Late Show* and offered help. She and An Post had only one agenda: can we properly and correctly get the names and stories of the children who were killed? I am very grateful to both Anna and An Post for their continuing support.

When I met Hugh Comerford, who was working as a senior librarian in the Dublin City Public Libraries and Archive in

Pearse Street, he immediately understood the idea, and has been at hand almost daily with his forensic research skills and his encyclopaediac knowledge of the period.

The late Shane MacThomais of Glasnevin Trust was a great supporter and help from the get go; his tragic death in March 2014 was an inestimable loss – he was the first of a new slew of people's historians who have come of age. In May 2015, we lost another great Dubliner and dear friend of mine Peter Mooney, who was also unstinting in his support for the project.

Those 'people's historians' include Mick O'Farrell, Padraig Yeates, Lorcan Collins, Barry Kennerk, Ray Bateson, Ann Matthews, Diarmuid Ferriter, Conor Dodd, Paul O'Brien, Terry Fagan and Tom Burke, all of whom have been very helpful. Each in turn has written about the period with a fluency, accuracy and accessibility that I can only marvel at and strive to emulate. Writing a history book, as I now know, involves so much research, rigorous recording, annotation and proper attribution that it is truly a daunting task – my admiration for these historians has only increased.

The various research institutions I have used have also been very helpful. Declan O'Brien and the staff in the General Register Office; Brenda Malone and Lar Joyce in the National Museum, Collins Barracks; Gregory O'Connor, Aideen Ireland and the staff in the National Archives of Ireland; Margaret Hayes, Jane Alger, Dr Maire Kennedy and Tara Doyle of Dublin City Libraries and archives prove why these resources are so valuable. Pearl Quinn of our own photographic archive in RTÉ, Raziv Chatterjee of TV archives and Liam Heffernan and Sandra Byrne of RTÉ were, as always, generous and efficient.

Noel, Niamh, Tara and Catriona of Noel Kelly Management were with me from day one on the project and were as professional, energetic and competent as ever.

Heather Humphreys, Minister for Arts, Heritage and the Gaeltacht 2016 programme, and John Concannon have both been very helpful, publicly and privately.

The online resources of the National Archives and the Bureau of Military History are a goldmine – the staff who pioneered and run these treasure troves deserve much thanks.

Artist Brian McCarthy has been a great guide and teacher in the various artistic incarnations of the children and their stories – his new collection of paintings based on the Rising prove that he is a truly gifted and insightful painter. Another artist, songwriter Declan O'Rourke, wrote a beautiful song about the project and 'The Children of '16' is a powerful tribute to those forgotten young lives.

Another unexpected aspect of the project was the desire of the relatives of many of the children to have a public memorial service for these forgotten children. I was happy to organise this both in 2014 and 2015 and would like to thank the children of City Quay and Ringsend primary schools and their teachers, as well as all those who helped enormously: Fr Pearse Walsh, Fr Ivan Tonge, Canon Barbara Fryday, Fr Michael Scott, Donal Harrington, Des Kelly and Gerry Hoban. Minister Frances Fitzgerald in 2014 and President Michael D Higgins in 2015 delivered moving eulogies to the children at these services, the first time the deaths of the children of 1916 was formally acknowledged by the Irish state.

To those who have worked on *Liveline* over the past three years, led by Siobhan Hough, thank you for your daily toil and support. Roger Childs, Glen Killane and Adrian Lynch from RTÉ television have been behind the project from the start.

Dhruba Banarjee of Strike Films, author Julian Vignoles and Sebastian Hamilton, editor-in-chief of the *Irish Mail*, all read earlier drafts and were generous with their time and comments.

George McCullough of the Glasnevin Trust, Ian Whyte of Whyte's Auctioneers, Cormac Kennedy of Easons, Niall Dardis formerly of the Dublin Port Company, Laura Murtagh of Martello Media, Gus Nicholls of Nicholls undertakers and Stephen Mangan, Manager of An Post Print have all been very helpful.

To my own family, who had to get used to me confusingly and incessantly talking about 'my forty children', sincere thanks and love.

My children Sean, Ellen and Ronan and my wife June have made enormous sacrifices in the past three years, for which I am eternally grateful.

For a publisher to take on this history project was a massive leap of faith. To Ciara Considine of Hachette Ireland: thank you for your daily support, work and often times much needed encouragement to keep going on what turned into a mammoth undertaking. Thanks also to Hazel Orme and Aonghus Meaney who worked on the text – the mistakes herein, of which I hope there are few, are my own! – and Lucy Hogan who did picture research.

But, above all, I want to thank the relatives of the children who have come forward so far. They have endured my constant attempts to dig up any piece of information, no matter how small, on the children. I have sent many relatives on a wild goose chase into their attics in pursuit of any stored memorabilia that might throw some information on the children's short lives.

But there are still fifteen children of the forty in this project of those aged sixteen and under who died violently in Easter 1916 for whom no relatives have been found.

This is an ongoing project, any information you can add can be sent to me at joed1916@gmail.com or Freepost, P.O. Box 1916, Dublin 3.

Joe Duffy
July 2015

Permissions Acknowledgements

The author and publisher would like to thank the following for permission to use inside photographs in *Children of the Rising*:

Central Press/Getty images: 12
D.C. Thomson & Co. Ltd. Images created courtesy of the British Library Board: 76, 87, 136
The Dublin City Archives: 25, 45
The Evening Herald. Images courtesy of the National Library of Ireland: 59, 62, 72, 108, 140, 198, 205
The Glasnevin Trust: 148
Illustrated London News Ltd/Mary Evans Picture Library: 37
The Irish Capuchin Provincial Archives, Dublin: opp.p.1, 19, 93, 153, 167
The Irish Independent. Image courtesy of the National Library of Ireland: 110
The Irish Times. Image courtesy of the National Library of Ireland: 60
John Frost Newspapers/Mary Evans Picture Library: 2, 215
Joseph McGarrity Collection, Digital Library@Villanova University: 114
Local World Limited. Image created courtesy of The British Library Board: 162
Military Archives: 111
Mondadori Portfolio via Getty Images: 95
The National Archives of Ireland: 30, 34, 103, 127, 128
The National Library of Ireland: 88, 100, 151, 174, 180, 182, 200, 215, 227, 232
The National Museum of Ireland: 52, 73, 224
The National Transport Museum: 235
Popperfoto/Getty images: 92
Royal Irish Academy Library: x, 113, 160, 179, 238
Royal Mail Group Archive Ltd 1916, courtesy of the British Postal Museum & Archive: 101
The Royal Society of Antiquaries of Ireland: 5, 6, 8, 9, 10, 22, 42, 77, 78, 117, 145, 157, 164, 212
RTÉ Stills Library: 14, 40, 90, 124, 154, 233
Sean Sexton/Getty Images: 132
Spitalfields Nippers by Horace Warner: 79
Topical press Agency/Getty images: 26
Toronto Star: 123
Trinity Mirror: 66
Universal History Archive/UIG via Getty Images: 130
Whyte's and Private Collection, England: 51
Wilshire Collection. Image courtesy of the National Library of Ireland: 230

Family Album
The families of Paddy Fetherston, Sean Frances Foster; Neville Fryday, John Kirwan, Luke Kelly, Bridget McKane, John McNamara, John O'Connor, Lionel Sweny, Madge Veale and Eleanor Warbrook.

The author and publisher have endeavoured to contact all copyright holders. If any images used in this book have been reproduced without permission, we would like to rectify this in future editions and encourage owners of copyright not acknowledged to contact us at info@hbgi.ie.